PLEASE RETURN
UNSCATHED to:

John Atkinson
Apt. 113
Wesley Village I
191 S. High St
Painesville Ohio
44077

The Spiritual Quest
of a Scientific Mind

An engineer's search for
meaning beyond science

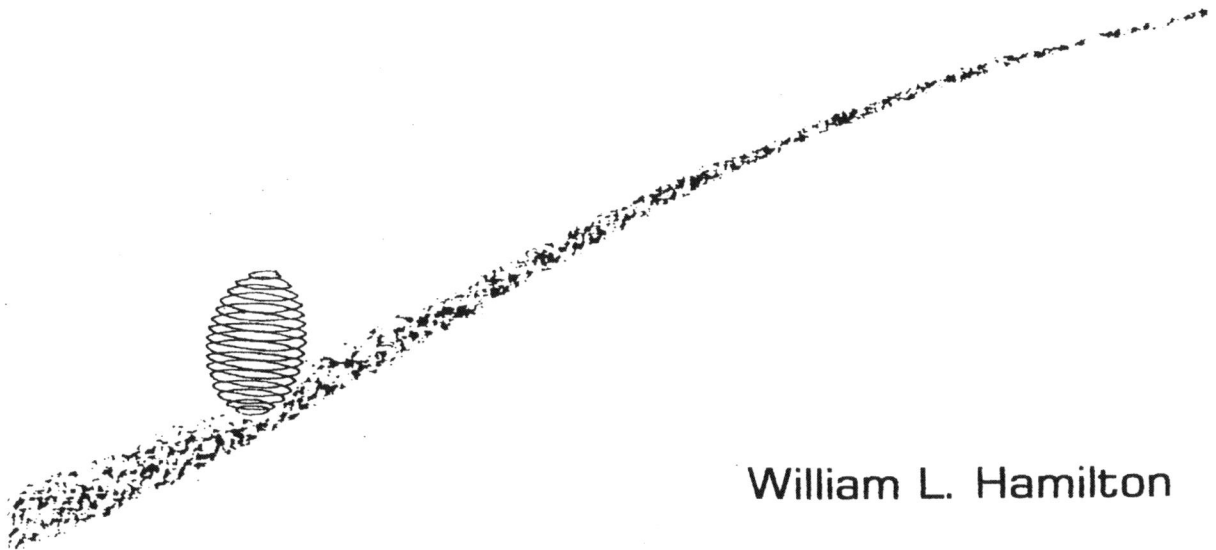

William L. Hamilton

The Spiritual Quest of a Scientific Mind

An engineer's search for
meaning beyond science

A Collection of Personal Essays

inner
power
books

Library of Congress Control Number 205912597
CreateSpace Independent Publishing Platform, North Charleston, SC
Printed by CreateSpace, an Amazon.com Company

Bible quotations are from the King James Version
Cover: "Keys", by author and John E. Atkinson
        See essay "Keys of the Kingdom"
Title Page: "Soul on the Spiritual Path" by author

ISBN - 13:978-1515174905

Table of Contents

Section 1 - First Look at Spirituality

Table of Contents

Section 2 - Beginnings of Wisdom

Table of Contents

Section 3 - The Higher Consciousness

Introduction

One of the most important things that you can do for yourself in this lifetime is to raise your spiritual consciousness — to some degree at least. So say the great sages of the past; so say the sages even of this day and age.

The reason is that it brings more satisfaction and contentment than anything else in life.

It is a process that Jesus came to teach, and others before and others after him. Although many people today do not understand it to be a process, that is the way that it is taught, and that is the way that it is usually learned. It is about gradually learning spiritual <u>fact</u> (in contrast to mere belief) and then growing in personal consciousness with it. In the end, it is what is usually called "a search for God" or "the pursuit of God". But don't let the big words and ideas scare you off. You can start in a simple way and go as far as you choose depending on your life situation.

Words cannot express the value of even a little bit of this effort, so I won't try. In the Book of Proverbs in the Old Testament, at 3:13 - 18 and repeated at 4:5-7, it describes the value of gaining this wisdom, but, true as it is, few want to believe it on first reading.

Spiritual consciousness is the ability to discern some of the invisible things in the world of the spirit. Many seekers first build an intellectual grasp which then gradually develops into a real experiential ability. It is the theme of this book.

As everyone knows, a basic part of religion and spiritual understanding is <u>morality</u>. And our churches of various denominations do a pretty good job of teaching the importance of our everyday practice of good morality; both for the obvious benefits of virtue in this life as well as those potential benefits believed to be waiting in an afterlife. A difficult wait for many.

However, the great <u>spiritual</u> teaching of Jesus, and others, is **much more than just morality**. Contrary to common belief, <u>this spiritual teaching applies mostly to this present life</u>, and only part of it is concerned about life after physical death. Sad to say, our churches are so busy with the morality part of the teaching that they seldom get to the big stuff. **But there is more ---** and most churches don't teach it because their congregations are not ready to accept the higher aspects of Jesus' teaching. Even so, there are always some individuals who hunger for a higher teaching, and may hear about it one way or another and then embark on a personal spiritual quest. This may last a lifetime to their own immense benefit and to those around them.

This book is about a mechanical engineer's spiritual search and is presented <u>primarily as a guide</u> as to <u>what might be possible</u> for others. My interest is the reality of the spirit. The scientifically-oriented mind of an engineer may well have a different perspective from others in approaching the world of spirituality. Perhaps it is more methodical, more thinking than feeling, at least in the beginning — but it is a solid approach!

The true teaching may not be easy to find at first. There are so many voices today, so many shallow ideas, so many simplistic interpretations of scripture that it may be puzzling. Once the true teaching is discerned (and there are ways to tell) and if followed, a person can become a new man or woman, as described in scripture. There is nothing new about the basic facts of the teaching or the results that are possible. The teaching is ancient.

What is new is the more effective way that it can be explained in this modern era.

There is so much more now in the physical world to compare it to, than there was 2000 years ago. Over the years, many have followed the teaching part of the way to their real benefit, and over the years some have followed it all of the way to become greater than they ever could have imagined.

The essays of this collection each express one or more aspects of spiritual fact. They start out on a simple level and progress to very high levels of spiritual truth. Together they form a 'meaty' book that is not meant to be read like a novel. Nor is it a complete how-to book, because that would take many volumes and there are already many hundreds of books on spiritual subjects available to you once you realize what the search is all about. And that is the purpose of this writing — to point out the reality of spiritual truths and where to find them. There are also teachers and there are courses in many formats for the rest of it.

Although it may not be for everybody, the so-called "spiritual search" is the most fascinating thing that a person can do. And once you start, you will have help in ways that you can't possibly imagine in the beginning.

As you will see, a personal approach to "truth" starts out as *wonder* — then advances to *belief* — and finally with some work, can become *solid fact*.

Nevertheless, people have been taught for years, perhaps centuries, that "it is all just belief until you get to heaven after your death on earth". Only then would great spiritual truth supposedly be revealed. Not true! It never had to be taught that way.

Spiritual truth is here and now. It is here for anyone who has a reverent desire to accept it.

WLH

2

The Search Begins

To learn about the world you can study science, or you can study religion or you can study some of each. I intuitively knew that science is factual, and was gratified to find out later that the basis of religion is factual also, to my considerable surprise, as I had been led to believe that it is all belief. Perhaps a different type of personality would experience the inverse — "know" intuitively at an early age that religion is real and then might have to struggle to learn that science is too. I know people like that and was surprised to find that they could see the world from such a totally different perspective from my own.

Even as a kid I was enthralled by science and technology. Being curious about how the "techno-things" of the Twentieth Century worked, I learned that there were scientific principles behind the operation of each. Later, with a degree in Mechanical Engineering,[1] I enjoyed using many of these principles of science as a creative engineer.

To our immense benefit, science dispelled the superstitions of the so-called 'dark ages' of Medieval times — well, at least some of them — and became the basis for the development of our incredible technologies. "Making progress" seemed to be the proper course for humanity. And technology was and is doing just that at an ever increasing pace.

Fortunately, in my younger years there didn't seem to be the disparaging view of sci-tech by some circles today that claim "it" is "ruining the planet". And I was completely unaware then of the disdain of science that some religious groups still exhibit today, while they enjoy without embarrassment the benefits and comforts that sci-tech has brought to daily life.

I reasoned that science could be a firm basis for a person's life. Many others followed the same idea. It was necessary, of course, to distinguish between proven science as opposed to that part of science that was still being investigated. The latter would not be "rock solid" until proven. However, there were already solid answers for many things so that the human race could advance on many levels. One of the essays here addresses the necessity of discerning the difference between facts that have been proven and those theories that are still in process.

I never had any interest in science fiction, popular then as now, because real science is more astounding than fiction — really.

1. The college was "Case School of Applied Science", a name that expressed exactly what I intended to do — apply principles of science for the benefit of people. An early faculty member, Albert A. Michelson, was the first American to win a Nobel prize in science, a significant role model for us students. Later, the college became "Case Institute of Technology", now part of Case Western Reserve University at Cleveland, Ohio.

Equally valuable to the splendid progress that science has made to date is the methodology by which scientific investigation is carried out. Most of the human race may not need to, or care to study a lot of science in detail. But it can be enlightening for anyone to know the basic steps of the process by which scientists work in order to properly interpret the daily news about science. More about that in a later essay.

In another aspect of my life, I attended a main-line church, man and boy, for some 30 years — took part in the activities, sang in the choir, thought that I understood what religion meant. But then at some point — like people have been doing for eons — I began to wonder about the "Big Questions" of life — the things that philosophers have puzzled about and argued about since the beginning of time.

Just by chance, I was chatting with an acquaintance, and was surprised by his depth of knowledge. He casually pointed out to me that the big questions may be in *philosophy*, but the big answers are in *religion*. Concise as his statement was, it seemed like real wisdom to me and I took note of it.

I had gone to church regularly but, by mid-life, had somehow missed these "big answers".

How could that be?

Not long after, like a miracle, a totally new chapter of life opened up.

Some great teachers appeared in my life (one had been an electrical engineer) and pointed out that there is much more to the universe than just science — in what is called the world of the spirit. They taught that there is spiritual truth, with real facts and true principles of a totally different nature in a totally different realm from my technical knowledge of the physical world. And they presented it with a degree of reality that I had never heard before. I slowly realized that there is more to religion than just belief — much more! And they began to demonstrate things that proved their words.

At first, the truths that they were trying to convey went harmlessly right over my head. Actually I didn't realize that I was missing anything. Furthermore, in the beginning I did not even realize that there is such a thing as an <u>authentic</u> teacher in this subject, and how rare they seem to be. And for a while, did not appreciate their depth or their dedication to their students. That came later.

In a year or two, with my intense enthusiasm, I found and then studied with several similar groups at the same time. This is not recommended because it can be confusing. A Yoga master in India spoke in this regard and said, "It is better to dig one deep well than several shallow ones". But in my case, over time, each group did give a perspective from a different context using different idioms that showed me that there is more than one way to teach about spiritual truth. More than one way to express the same great truth.

But one group that I joined was following a teaching that appealed to some, but I found it to be too convoluted, too vague for me. It involved several books and the "students" laughingly said that you could start anyplace with any of the books as there was no "starting place". So I slipped out of that and considered it to be just a harmless side trip along the way.

It took some years of experiences in this strange new spiritual side of life to be absolutely sure that I was on the right track and that the several groups were all teaching about the same thing.

Eventually, it became apparent that they were talking about (some aspect of) "The Ancient Wisdom". It is said that this body of knowledge has been taught to small groups for some thousands of years. Jesus came to teach it anew to a larger group in ancient Israel. He described His teaching as "a pearl of great price" that was well worth learning. In the centuries since, some have found it to be so.

As my studies matured, I wrote short essays of my experiences and insights. They were addressed to my three kids and sometimes an interested friend or two. So the informal format I used along the way was according to this intention. As the years have gone by, others have shown interest, not to follow my particular trail, incomplete as it is, but to realize that there is such a path. So there is no story here, just knowledge — divine knowledge, but no thrilling saga.

Here is the reason that I have compiled this book of my previously written essays:

In order to make this new type of knowledge real to me, it required the help of teachers who knew that it was real, and who could demonstrate it, to some degree at least. That could be said of teachers in almost any subject. But to my engineer's literal mind, firmly at home in the physical world of finite objects, it was especially necessary in this ethereal field that is so much less tangible, so much less familiar, especially in the depth that they were teaching.

Now after many years of study, my ongoing experiences have brought a solid reality to the spiritual aspects of my life — at least some of it — and to levels that I never dreamed of. The process has similarities to the study of a subject like chemistry. Like this: Because you have faith that there is something worthwhile to learn, you listen to lectures on the theory of the subject, at a beginner's level. Then you confirm in the lab what you have learned in theory. Result: you begin to prove that the lectures have some validity. With many repetitions you learn the subject, prove it by hands-on experience, and eventually you get it into your fingertips. Without the experience of the lab, you would just have 'book knowledge'. In a similar manner with spiritual teachings, the lab is the experiences that life gives you as you apply the principles.

And it is these on-going life experiences, underline: properly associated with the basic teaching, that can bring the reality to you.

To sum it up: Spiritual truth was real to my teachers.
                It was not just a traditional teaching or just a set of beliefs.

              And because it was real to them, they helped to make it real to me —
                at some level. Otherwise I would have just acquired some beliefs, unaware that there is actually a reality.

              My hope then is that these essays that are real to me might make spiritual
                truth real to you, to some degree, at least.

Should you become a serious scholar in this most important subject, you would validate important points as you go along by referring to other writings, to scripture, perhaps studying with an authentic teacher and always learning from your own experiences as you are led.

Once you start, an amazing amount of relevant literature opens up. I was surprised to find that it was there all along, but it had been oblivious to me.

And people may appear to you as guides at appropriate times. It is said that when a person is ready to learn, a spiritual teacher will appear. I believe it! I have seen it happen with several people. And the opposite is true, of course. Looking back, I realize that teachers came by, gave me hints, saw that I was not ready and went on their way. The loss was mine. Then I woke up!

(There is ample space throughout the book for you to write in your own notes, questions, doubts, rebuttals, etc. If you date your entries, you may realize your spiritual growth when you re-read at a later date.)

Some Early Religious Experiences

There should be no place for fear in the study of religion. Yet many sermons in many churches try to scare the members into a particular life style or particular beliefs or to fill them with terrifying events to come. Despite some apparent results, it just spoils a person's real heartfelt desire to pursue a real study. Study of this subject should be a delight.

And when I meet rabid atheists who rage at the mention of religion, I suspect that they have been badly treated at a young age by clergy. It should not be.

Fortunately my own early experience was innocuous, but somewhat disappointing for a little kid. Sometime before my fourth birthday, my father began to drive my younger brother and me to Sunday school at a neighborhood church.

In the Primary Department, we sang some silly songs; maybe the superintendent said a prayer — I don't remember. Then she asked those that had a birthday during the week to stand while we sang "Happy Birthday" as she lighted candles on a little birthday cake. After that, the group broke up into small classes to several nearby rooms for a Bible lesson.

Week after week went by as I patiently waited for my fourth birthday to arrive.

Finally, I got to stand up while the class sang the little song and the birthday candles blazed out, beckoning me. The kids broke up for their classes as usual, but this time, I went up to the teacher, announced my recent advance in age and asked for a piece of the cake. She looked at me like I was the dumbest moron on earth.

As my mouth watered in anticipation, she pulled the little cake out of a drawer. Alas, it was just a white enameled sauce pan with a few holes punched in the bottom for the candle holders.

This deep disappointment formed a solid concept in my little four year old mind concerning the meaning of religion. But it was decades until I found the words to describe it:

Religion is Ritual Without Reality

Fortunately, I suppose, the church was Presbyterian and, I would find out later, had very little ritual in its religious service.

Other weird things happened in this early "religious life". A few Sundays after the crushing birthday disappointment, the class lesson was about "the stoning of St. Steven". As the teacher related the event of biblical times, the little girls cried pitifully at the brutality of it, and the little boys said emphatically that "you are not supposed to throw stones." I was puzzled by it all; I could not imagine how the authorities would allow any body to be killed by that strange method. The teacher, a nice young woman with little biblical training, correctly surmised however that the story was not appropriate for our age.

So we turned to the Bible verse of the day. It came on a postage stamp-size card that each kid could take home and supposedly ponder and save. The verse was always written in the Old English of the King James Bible. As a kid, I never understood any of it.

Fortunately, I survived these religion-tarnishing experiences. But when I meet people who are "avowed atheists", often adamantly so, I often wonder what experiences they might have had in their formative years. I cringe when I see parents indoctrinating their little kids with theological concepts that baffle even grown-ups. Their little minds cannot help but misinterpret and then form distorted ideas as rock-hard memories to plague them as adults. If they ever want to advance in spiritual understanding, they may then have much to unlearn.

Despite the above, I attended this church regularly for some thirty years, played in the Sunday School orchestra, and was elected a deacon.

Then I began a more serious study.

Know Thyself

Know thy *real* self. This is the heart of all authentic religion, and the purpose of these essays.

According to ancient Greek writers, the admonition "KNOW THYSELF' was inscribed over the entrance to the Temple of Apollo long ago at Delphi in Greece. The ORACLE in the temple was believed to dispense great wisdom to the worthy. Kings and rulers came from afar for advice on weighty subjects. Even though there are archeological excavations in the area today, it is difficult to know whether this was actual fact or legend, but it does contain a lesson for us even today.

Down through the ages philosophers in many lands have postulated various meanings for these two simple words. However, in modern times in esoteric study groups, it has always meant that a person should delve deeply into his or her own inner self to realize their true divinity. Much more profound and valuable is this than a superficial study of personality or current events.

Ralph Waldo Emerson said that it means a person should become truly aware in his own life that God exists in every man. In his day, he had to be careful saying things like that, so he usually hid his wisdom in long carefully worded essays. And in ages before Emerson, you could be burned at the stake for saying the things that he said. Even today many people don't like these thoughts. It scares them, maybe because their (concept of) God would take offense. And some churches teach against the idea of the higher teaching as being the cause of the "fall of man", lest a person should "get himself puffed up when he is really a miserable sinner." [1] So, as you read this, please don't get puffed up!

I studied with several esoteric groups and each of these groups taught that the goal for each individual was to KNOW THYSELF — himself or herself. It was always made clear that it did not mean a superficial knowledge of one's personality or other worldly traits, important as these might be in the physical world. Rather it pertained to the deepest levels that have been attained by the spiritual greats who have lived among us and pointed the way to great truths. They are great words to keep in mind. And it is a great goal for one to contemplate.

St. Francis of Assisi gives us this conundrum with a clue of what to look for —

"What you are looking for is what is looking"

---

1. From the admonitions of a TV preacher.

A Chat in a Churchyard

A church was having a rummage sale in their parking lot. I stopped to look.

It was a long time ago and I don't remember where it was or the denomination of the church. But I was not acquainted with that denomination and so was somewhat curious about it.

A saleslady and I chatted over the merchandise a little bit. She seemed friendly and so I asked her about the beliefs of her church. She gradually saw that I was not antagonistic toward religion and so we traded our respective beliefs for almost one half hour. She seemed to enjoy telling about her religion.

Finally there was a pause, and then she made a remarkable observation.

She said, "You and I have almost identical religious beliefs, except that I attribute everything to Jesus and you attribute everything to God."

I began to formulate a response in my mind. I was going to say, "Jesus attributed everything to the Father. Why shouldn't I?" But it seemed like a put-down after she had been so open about her beliefs, so I said nothing, smiled and went on my way.

I often wonder if she ever reflected on what she had said — as I have.

Some churches, perhaps this was one of them, teach that <u>Jesus</u> created heaven and earth. Other churches leave that to God, while scientists usually leave creation to the laws of nature. There may be a misinterpretation of scripture here somewhere. When people read and interpret — and you do interpret anytime you read anything — it is always from the intellectual and spiritual level of the reader at that time. A person can "see it in a different light" as understanding grows. And this is especially true of religious scripture. And it applies to clergy too.

How Do I Know ....?

Believing is easy. We do it all the time.
Discerning <u>truth</u> is not so easy.   WLH [1]

In the Spiritual Quest, there is infinite
opportunity to delude one's self. [2]

When I first became interested in a serious study of religion and spiritual matters, there were many groups teaching mixtures of psychology, "depth psychology", traditional Christianity and Eastern religions.

There were "encounter groups" and "retreat organizations" that encouraged the individual in the ancient admonition to "Know Thyself". And there were many books on a great variety of religious subjects; there are even more books today.

And then there is the Holy Bible with its seemingly endless conflicting interpretations promoted by different church denominations. Said to be some 33,800 Christian denominations in the world, each having varying beliefs on the basic tenets of baptism, salvation, heaven and hell. [3]

Some of it seemed fresh and interesting to me. But, if I was going to get involved, the big questions in my mind were:

What part of it, if any, is really true?
How can one separate fact from belief, belief from fantasy?

On the other hand there were some people in these groups who were happy to just accept whatever was presented without question and then maybe sort it out later. I do it that way sometimes too. **If you prefer that direct path to learning, then you can skip my tedious method in this essay**. Maybe come back to it later. But in learning about this unfamiliar realm of spiritual knowledge, I felt, and still do sometimes, the need to validate new ideas with some sort of logical method that might make sense to my engineer's mind. **But if it seems too tedious**, skip to 'Final Note' page **19**.

---

1. See also later essay on "Sorting Knowledge — Especially one's Own"
2. A quotation from Emmet Fox, b 1886 - d 1951, a noted religious writer and lecturer in England and America during the 1930's.
3. One search on the Internet (March 2013) turned up 3,620,000 entries on the subject of "The Doctrine of the Fall of Man". Checking only a tiny sample, I can safely say that there is a great variety of conflicting opinion. Most people typically pick the interpretation that pleases them or that their church teaches. The "33,800 denominations" was taken from the 2001 edition of the "World Encyclopedia of Religion."

Many religious people, of course, stick with the conventional religion of their forefathers and don't trouble their minds in the slightest way about doing so. They are doing the right thing if their family religion still fits them. But I wanted more than that seemed to offer, although I was aware that following the "new" and non-traditional could lead to time-consuming dead ends or worse.

So I searched for ways to discern what is really true. Ways that would satisfy an engineer's methodical approach. Ways that would apply to the spectrum of things that interested me. But mainly, I wanted to know the reality that the **symbolisms** of religion were symbolizing — a reality that was often something hidden in a veiled form.

The ancients had already pondered this same problem. And so one of the five branches of classical philosophy is "epistemology" which deals with the nature of knowledge, its limits and validity. Without going into a lot of detail, let me say that this study proved to be rather useless in the practical need that I had at hand. Most of what I read was too scholarly and narrow — distantly theoretical. And it seemed as though the main ideas were developed before the age of science and "modern enlightenment".

So, over a period of years I gathered methods that would more nearly suit my purpose — that would help me to discern **"reality"** — sort the real from the false.

It should be noted that "proving what is true" does not necessarily guide a person in the right direction in his or her intellectual search or spiritual quest, at least in the beginning. It does, however, prove **after the fact** whether you are going in the right direction or not.

Without thinking about it, I used the engineer's intellectual, reasoning approach to the subject. I discovered later that there are other methods of determining truth that might have greater appeal to people of different personality and mind-set from that of the engineer. Even so, perhaps other "seekers" might adapt some of these methods to their own areas of interest. Briefly listed, they are as follows:

1. Human **reason**, even with all of its known limitations.

2. The **experimental** methods of science – **plus reason** – that have done so much to explain the physical world.

3. The methods of the "soft sciences"– **plus reason** – that compile **large numbers of experiments** where the variables can't all be controlled.

4. Direct **personal experience** – **plus reason** – which is especially suited to spiritual knowledge that may be obtained through direct impressions.

5. "Cross-symbolism **congruence**" – **plus reason**. This is my own term for a concept that helps to compare the scripture and writings of one religion to the scripture of another religion as a help to decipher a true meaning.

It may be apparent that these various methods do not have equal degrees of certainty. Nor will they ever be used to perfection, at least by me. But together, they add up to a level of certainty that is not approached by ordinary thinking. And their use has brought me much satisfaction. If additional methods are found to be applicable, they too will be adopted.

Now, lets look at these five methods in more detail:

Reason

"The ability to think logically, to understand, and to draw inferences. To analyze by reasoning."

Said to be mankind's greatest intellectual faculty – the pinnacle of man's evolution. (We may see later that there could be greater things.)

Understanding new things by reason requires at least two prerequisites:

a. A broad antecedent knowledge-base of facts that can be used as premises, often unconsciously, to confront the new circumstances.

b. A personal awareness of the known fallacies common to people's use of reason, and especially one's own tendency to unwittingly use one or more of these unsound methods.

In other words, it is just plain important to reason correctly.

Expanding on (a) above, it can be seen that building the knowledge base is going to take much living and much study to accumulate. So the use of reason, then, becomes a reiterative process over a period of a lifetime. As knowledge on a variety of subjects is accumulated – is proven to be true – a greater range of new items can then be reasoned upon with some degree of assurance. That is, you need to know certain things before you can learn or understand other things. Just as in grade school. And a person's ability to reason well should improve as his or her knowledge is accumulated.

Often times, I find that I must hold some questions in abeyance – to temporarily suspend my attempt to understand them – because I do not yet have enough basic knowledge to support any new understandings on a higher level. This, of course, requires patience. However, the impatient person, when confronted by "the new", usually just "fills in the gap" of understanding with whatever belief pops into his head that "seems right". And this is what keeps so may people's thinking in a kind of subliminal confusion. To avoid it, I set the question aside until additional understanding has been

13

built up to support a higher level of meaning. Scientists do this all the time, especially in the field of medicine.

Expanding on (b) above, let's look at some of the common fallacies in reasoning. Not necessarily the type of fallacies that may be knowingly used to win a debate, a court case or an argument. Rather the ones that might misguide our (my) thinking when we need to think critically.

1. Coming to a conclusion based on too few examples; in the extreme case, generalizing on one instance, even impetuously jumping to a conclusion. Psychologists say that generalizing on one instance is a basic survival mechanism. For example, if a pre-historic man encountered a dangerous animal or a poisonous plant, one encounter warned him that a similar encounter in the future could be just as dangerous. But in intellectual matters, our conclusions can easily go astray by unnecessary haste.

2. Rationalization – making the conclusion first. That is, bending the process to arrive at the conclusion that we emotionally want. Emotions can slyly confuse reason.   Typical political thinking! And, sad to say, some juries!

3. Denial of opposite facts.

4. Overlooking alternatives. "It's gotta' be this or that. What else could it be?" for example.

5. Making interpretations when we think we are making observations.

6. Who said it? Who gave us the basic data that we are reasoning from? If we admire, respect- say, parents, clergy, politicians, school teachers –   does that mean that the data   from them is accurate? Not necessarily! And so we must confirm as we go along.
   "My daddy tol' me" may not be a very good data base.

   The opposite may also occur.

   "Socrates was not good looking, but his friends knew that he was glorious within", Plato said.

   "And when He (Jesus) was come into his own country, he taught them in their synagogue, insomuch that they were astonished, and said, Whence hath this man this wisdom, and these mighty works? Is not this the carpenter's son?"Matthew 13:54 KJV

Truth is where you find it!

7. Majority opinion – popular opinion. On many things, the long accumulated wisdom of the the human race may be correct. But when we reach beyond the area of commonly held understandings, popular opinion may not be very firm ground. Many years ago, doctors, in recommending a treatment, would sometimes use the expression, "The best medical opinion is ......" Of course, that meant that the facts were not known. As a little kid, I fervently hoped that a doctor would never use that expression on me. I wanted only established facts in my treatments.

8. Using dualistic thinking where it need not apply. "This or that" thinking, although very common, does not apply to all questions.

My father worked for the railroad and traveled frequently by train. He sometimes said, "You either catch the train or you don't". Dualistic thinking is proper in that case. His job as "Engineer of Tests" involved physical testing of purchased mechanical goods such as boiler plate, rail, car wheels, locomotives, paint, etc. And his attitude in his work was, "The material either meets the specifications set down by the railroad or it doesn't." It was a perfect career for dualistic thinking, and he did it well. The railroad kept him on the job four years after retirement age.

But it is wrong when people say things like, "Every last word of the Bible is absolutely true or else none of it is true." Some years ago, there was a full-page "statement of belief" to that exact idea in newspapers across the country by a major church. I wish I had clipped it or at least remembered the denomination.

Why must they (we) see it in those simplistic terms — terms that often do not apply?

9. Untrue cause-and-effect relationship. Just because B occurs immediately after A, does not mean that A caused B. Scientists are always cautious about jumping to such a conclusion. Unfortunately most people are not. And superstitions are born.

There are other fallacies, of course. But these are common ones and that I have had, on occasion, to guard against myself.

Even though the faculty of reason may have these limitations of accuracy, it has the broadest range of usefulness. It can be applied, with some benefit at least, to all areas of human interest, and I consider it a necessary adjunct to my other four "methods of knowing" adding power, avoiding error.

Experimental Method of Science

The basic idea of science is to establish facts and discern principles, and is pretty much limited to the physical world. Scientists prove a theory or belief by means of experiment. It may often take many scientists and many experiments, sometimes over many years. And to the average person, the great benefit of knowing some basic science is that it replaces superstition with fact concerning the world that we live in so that we don't have to hold erroneous beliefs about things that are already well known, well understood and well proven — sometimes proven centuries ago.

Examples of erroneous beliefs are in the essay "Difficult to Change One's Beliefs in Section 2.

One of the problems that many people have with science is that they do not make a distinction between a) well established science that is in text books and b) the latest theories popping up in the news. Scientists normally publish new theories in obscure journals with the expectation that other scientists will dispute the findings, or add to them or do independent experiment to corroborate. But popular writers like to bring the more striking unproven theories to the immediate attention of the public. And the public often mistakes these vague new ideas to be the true findings of science. They do not understand that the part of science that is on the cutting edge is always subject to revision or even to be proven wrong. However, many theories are eventually found to be either correct or fallacious, and proven to be so.

To benefit from the solid feeling of understanding the physical world, to some degree at least, a person must be able to make the above distinction. And this requires some knowledge of basic, well-established science. Here is an example that illustrates the point:

> An incident that took place at a refresher course for older drivers (55-Alive by AARP). In connection with winter driving, the workbook mentioned that ice on the road is more slippery when the temperature is about 32 degrees F. The instructor was to explain why.

> Before it could be explained, one of the older men in the class jumped up and argued that this just couldn't be true. It made no sense to him. He said that "ice is ice and everybody knows that it is slippery." Then, he continued on, "it is just as slippery one place as another because ice is ice."

> He went on and on in this argument for about 15 minutes, repeating over and over that "ice is ice", while the instructor (who had laryngitis) tried to explain, that at 32 degrees, melting ice can have a film of water that makes the surface much more slippery.

> Finally I was ready to scream, "Engineers test these things; that's how they know. It is not a matter of opinion!" It would have done no good however — because the man just had no concept of how facts are determined.

Methods of the "Soft Sciences"

In many areas of investigation, the experiments cannot be as precisely controlled as in the hard sciences. However, by having large numbers of experiments, some understandings can be determined, but the results are usually in statistical form. A familiar example is, "Does cigaret smoking cause lung cancer?" The number of experiments (smokers) was huge (at one time). Anecdotal findings seemed to point that there was a causal connection. But there were many other possible contributing factors that could not be very well isolated because the smokers were not formal controlled experiments. Even so, the huge number of smokers provided an overwhelming amount of data. The findings are that a certain <u>percentage</u> of smokers will get the disease, but not everyone. This vagueness troubles many people that insist that there must be an "either-or", "this or that" type of answer. However, statistical information can lead to great conclusions. In the above case – It is healthier not to smoke, just to be safe.

"Soft information" presented as statistical probabilities can sometimes be "hardened up", at least in my own mind, for my own purposes. One way that this has happened is by insights from reading Scripture that were possible only because of the original soft information from other sources.

Direct Personal Experience

Plus reason – Reason is especially important on this one, more so if a person does not have an authentic teacher or adviser on whom to rely.

Personal experiences of a spiritual nature are often thought of as "one-time events" or "non-repeatable occurrences" because that is the way they happen to most people, at least in the beginning. Consequently they can't be proven to others even though they are real to the person who experiences them. This is directly opposite to the physical sciences where repeatability is expected if others perform the experiment under the same conditions. That is, the experiment can be demonstrated over and over, at least by those "skilled in the art".

Reader's Digest, and other literature, has related many stories of such personal spiritual experiences. And some readers believe them to be true, or at least possible, while others are skeptical. And very few readers bother to look further.

One such event is recorded in the New Testament.

> Jesus was talking to the Samaritan woman at Jacob's well about the spiritual "living water" and he peered into her mind and related events in her life.

"The woman saith unto him, Sir I perceive that thou art a prophet" John 4:19 KJV

"The woman left her water pot, and went her way into the city, and saith to the men, Come see a man who told me all things that I ever did: is not this the Christ?" John 4:28-29

And many of the Samaritans of that city believed on him for the saying of the woman who testified, "He told me all that I ever did". John 4:39

Other lesser people than Jesus read other people's minds, even today, and I have had my mind "read" vaguely perhaps – by more than one person, but sharply by one.

One personal occurrence was so unusual – so absolutely "air-tight" – that I will include it as an example of both the experience and the subsequent reasoning about it. See the next essay on "The Myrus Incident". It was a beginner's experience in that it was done to me by the psychic ability of another person and required no effort or ability or initiative on my part.

Cross - Symbolism Congruence

This is my own designation for a method, not of proving things, but rather a way of gaining insights into the meaning of scripture or other religious writing. The insights may then be confirmed in some other way, even at a much later time.

It is like the navigator at sea who determines only his latitude. He may have a vague idea of his position, but if he can also determine his longitude, he then knows exactly where he is on the earth's surface. In like manner, if a person is somewhat familiar with the parables in his own religion and then reads or hears other scripture or other religious works, occasionally there may be an inspiration of fresh understanding from the matching of two totally different descriptions (symbolisms) of a particular point.

That is, there is a coinciding of meaning – a congruence – across the two different symbolisms.

I don't struggle to find these points; it would be nearly impossible. Rather I let them happen by inspiration or coincidence and then use reason. I have not had this happen yet, but you might even coincide symbolisms from three sources.

Obviously, this method is of no use to those people who honor only their own scripture and look with contempt upon other religions. It would be of no use to those who believe that their own denomination is already the sole possessor of the "real truth" and the only truth. It would be of even less use to those who insist on literal interpretation of scripture and who do not look for any underlying meaning in the parables.

A Problem for the Spiritual Seeker

Jesus pointed out (Matthew 13:13) that he spoke to the multitude in parables for only those "who had ears to hear". In other words, his message was too precious to be given to everybody, but was only for those who had some degree of "spiritual refinement", "for this people's heart is waxed gross" (Matthew 13:15). He went on to say that he could speak straight out to his disciples (Matthew 13:11) "because it is given unto you to know the mysteries of the kingdom of heaven, but to them it is not given". **Now it is not clear whether the information that he gave to his disciples was ever recorded in the Bible.** Actually, in several religions, including Christianity, there is a "tradition" that there is an oral teaching that supplements and clarifies the meaning of the written scripture. The ancient Jews supposedly were to convey this only to a righteous person.

Fortunate is the person who can be initiated into these divine secrets by "someone who knows". But for the rest of us, at least for myself, it helps to gain spiritual understanding by studying more than just our (my) "home" religion.

But for the real seeker:

Truth is wherever you find it!

However you find it!

And truth is seamless!

Final Note

The first three sections (on reason, methods of science, methods of soft science) are mostly useful in discerning intellectual truth and proving it to one's satisfaction and confidence in order to use it as needed. But intellectual understanding is only a beginning of the "way", a foundation on which to build a more solid spiritual consciousness.

"The way" to higher levels of spiritual consciousness is covered in the great writings of history, some ancient, some modern. Some are the sayings of a great teacher, like the "Sermon on the Mount". Others like the Hindu writings seem to be the compilation of many contributors, like our Old Testament. In fact Hindu sacred writing is so voluminous as to be mind boggling, almost useless for westerners in its entirety, requiring selection of well-known tid-bits by an expert.

It is said that when a person really desires to find spiritual understanding, a suitable way for that person will become apparent.

The 'Myrus' Incident

It was a cold, dreary, rainy afternoon, mid-November long ago at our house in a semi-rural part of Kirtland, Ohio. I was dejectedly looking out the window at an "out building" that I had been building during the summer. It was like a big garage designed to house mowing equipment, garden tools and a small sailboat. To my eye, it was a beautiful piece of architectural design (my own) and construction except that there was no roof on it. And the heavy snows of winter in that part of the country were almost upon us. Everything but the roof was finished and the equipment had already been moved inside, if you could call it that.

The roof was to be made of heavy corrugated steel panels which fitted well into the design of the building. I had prudently ordered the material back in June, and the panels had been cut to my specified length at the factory in a nearby city. They were about to be shipped when a nation-wide strike of the steel workers union shut down just about everything connected with the steel industry. After many weeks, neither the union officials nor the mill executives gave any hope for a settlement. I had just about given up hope for a roof.

Without warning that afternoon, my sister-in-law Julia breezed in from a near-by town, all excited because she had two tickets to the "Myrus TV show". This was a 15 minute, locally produced show at 6 PM on Channel 8 in Cleveland, Ohio. Myrus was a middle-aged, bespectacled (if there is such a word) unassuming man who had a mind reading act. His real name never came out. I had watched him a couple of times, but the program didn't have much showmanship so I had little interest.

The format was simple. Before the actual show started, people in the audience could write a question on a card for Myrus to "divine" an answer. The cards were put into a fish bowl and he would draw one and hold it to his forehead. After a few meditative moments, he would say something like, "This is from a lady over in this section" and he would point.

"Yes madam, your expectant daughter will have a boy." A woman would raise her hand and gush out some words of thanks.

"So what", I thought.

The dumb questions were all like that and there was never any possibility of confirmation. Myrus could have said anything, and the people in the audience that answered might have been "plants", a common practice in old-time stage shows.

My wife Isabel saw things differently, however. She had been doing volunteer work with the relocated American Indians in Cleveland. Families that were new to the area from various tribes were trying to get a community center started, but one of the men was very vocal and bossy. This behavior was so out-of-character for Indians that Isabel was concerned that he might be an impostor. Falsely claiming to be Indian was a serious matter in that circle. So Isabel was jumping at the opportunity to ask Myrus, the mind reader, if the man was truly Indian. It never would have occurred to me, the engineer, to use this method to determine authenticity. Never!

Since it was getting dark early and there was possibility of snow, the two sisters wanted me to drive them into Cleveland so they could attend the show.

"What am I supposed to do in the meantime?, I asked.

"Wait in the lobby," was the answer. I had already expected something like that.

So off we went.

The small lobby was soon jammed with expectant audience-participants in winter coats. An usher appeared and said that seating was limited so that only people with tickets would be allowed in. But when he opened double doors, the excited crowd pushed right on in taking me with them.

The two sisters rushed down front and got seats in the second row. Without a ticket, I sat toward the rear on the aisle in case I would be asked to leave. Soon the question cards were passed out and then collected for the fish bowl ritual. I didn't bother with a card as I had no question for Myrus, and the chance of any one person's card being picked was pretty small.

As show time drew near, the audience was asked for absolute silence, so that when Myrus entered there would be no disturbing "swirl of confusing vibrations". Anxious to avoid making any such swirl, we sat silently with our thoughts in the near darkness with only a little light from the stage.

I felt a gentle tap on my shoulder. I looked up in the dim light and recognized Myrus himself standing there. He had entered at the back of the studio.

"Do not worry. The steel strike will soon be over", he said quietly, and then proceeded down the aisle to the stage. WOW!

He had actually read my mind and addressed my concern as casually as if we had been chatting over coffee. With a prediction yet.

So — Myrus did have the uncanny ability to actually "see" into other people's minds. There was no question about that! I had not put any question in the fish bowl; I had spoken to no one. No one knew that I was coming to the show. There was no gimmick involved. He actually did it.

21

It turned out that the steel strike did end about four days after the show. Maybe that was an actual intuitive "divination" and maybe it wasn't. Myrus could have had inside information about the strike. But about reading my thoughts, there was no question that he was authentic.

But that's not the end of the incident, however.

Myrus went through the usual dumb questions that had interest only for the person who had asked, and as usual, the questions were of the type that could not be confirmed.. Finally he said that there was time for only one more question. He held the card to his forehead and meditated.

"It's from a lady in the front row" — and then he hesitated.

Terrible disappointment in the second row! Isabel realized that her card would not be drawn that day. Her question about the Indian would have to be resolved some other way.

Myrus struggled. His previous smooth mental flow — from the card held to his forehead to the intuited question to the "divinated" answer — was not working. The audience held its breath wondering what was troubling Myrus. I did too.

Finally Myrus blurted out, "I can't receive the question from the lady in the front row because the lady in the second row is thinking so hard about her question."

Then looking right at Isabel, he said, "Yes Madam. That man really is an American Indian."

I don't know about Isabel, but I was absolutely flabbergasted! Isabel had projected her thoughts to Myrus in a more powerful manner than he had used in "reading" the questions from the audience. She obviously felt desperate for an answer. And got it.

The show ended. Later, it turned out that the man was truly an Indian and had papers to prove it.

******

Comment:

People that I have met, actually just a few, could "read minds". When they "see" that I am not troubled by it, they have let me know that they too have the ability to read people's minds, my mind included. And when this happens to you a few times, there will never again be any question that it is real.

Fortunately these have been kindly people who use the ability to help others when they "see" the need for it. But **never again will I imagine that I have any secret thoughts.** In general, some people with this ability seem to be unhappy. Why wouldn't they be? It can be disheartening when they can tell what others really think of them behind an insincere outward smile. And what boss wants an employee who can see through him.

Worst of all for them, to use the ability tends to disclose it. So, a person must be very "comfortable with himself" to enjoy this ability, keep it mostly to himself or herself and suffer the consequences of knowing what people think. On the other hand, it is easy to imagine situations when such an ability could save your life.

When I have related the Myrus story to friends, some have become very upset to think that their thoughts could be picked up. They ask if I can read their minds, and I have to assure them that I do not have the ability, never cared to have it, and would not study to develop it, if that is even possible.

But these experiences brought about a change in my thinking and in my activities. It isn't just God who can see what we are doing, as parents have warned their little kids, trying to scare them to be good. Ordinary looking people can do it too. And I soon realized that my spiritual teacher could "see right through me". This opened the possibility to some very personalized lessons. But I had to be willing to be spiritually "transparent" — feeling almost naked. And there was no point in pretending about anything.

The great sages say that if a person can delve deeply into his or her own soul, then they can be in touch with other souls, usually ones that they are close to and have a strong rapport with.

This story is about only a tiny part of the world of the spirit. But it is simple to understand and was an interesting benign early experience. I then found that there is much more.

Be Careful of Your Thoughts!

In our spiritual quest over a period of several years, wife Isabel and I attended many classes, lectures and we associated with several groups that had similar interests.

One such meeting was put on by the "Spiritual Frontiers Fellowship" organization with which we were not familiar. It was an all day series of lectures at the Carter Hotel in Cleveland, Ohio. And in the evening, the featured speaker was to be Arthur Ford, a "psychic" who was well known in certain circles around the world.

Ford had written an autobiography of sorts titled "Nothing So Strange" and I had read it. One thing that caught my attention was mention of his college fraternity. In passing, he said that the secret password "for that year" was such-and-such. It identified to me, my college fraternity, and the password was not just for that year only. A sneaky way to identify his fraternity affiliation without actually mentioning the name and sounding as though he had not given away any secrets. The pass word was supposed to be kept secret, as passwords usually are.

At the hotel, I was surprised to meet a family that I had met at another study group that belonged to this SFF organization. I believe they came all the way from Indiana. And there were people that I knew from "Shadybrook House" the non-denominational retreat house in Kirtland Hills, Ohio that I will mention elsewhere.

The lectures droned on as lectures frequently do and I can't remember anything about them.

The evening session was open, at a reduced fee, for people to attend after work.

This was when Isabel got thoroughly shaken up. The men that had attended the day-time sessions were dressed in business suits and tie as was customary at that time. And the women were comparably dressed.

A large man in a lumber jacket appeared at the door, stopped to pay the fee and then strode rapidly across the entire ballroom toward Isabel. Right in her face with a certain amount of animosity he said,

"You don't have to be well dressed to be able to read minds!" And walked away.

Isabel was in a state of shock because he had "extracted" her exact thoughts from her mind. She didn't say much for the rest of the evening.

Although I never had this natural psychic ability myself, I knew from past experience that some people can read minds. And so especially in this setting I was careful to "think kind thoughts" or even to keep my mind in neutral, as best I could. Perhaps Isabel learned a lesson that evening that no lecture could teach.

I never particularly cared to "be psychic" myself or to learn to "read minds" if that is even possible to learn. However it is supposed to be one of abilities that might come spontaneously with the development of the "higher consciousness".

On the other hand, it might save your life. A man that I knew very well for many years related this incident just after he got out of the hospital. He had a heart attack and at that time it was customary to supply oxygen to the patient in a transparent plastic tent around head and shoulders. After a while, one cylinder of the life-giving gas was used up, so he rang for a nurse to come and switch the pressure regulator to the full tank which was connected through a series of valves. She fiddled with the apparatus for a couple of minutes and then in frustration **thought to herself,**

"I never did understand how this thing works. It doesn't matter — he's a goner anyway."

My friend picked up her thought — he had this ability to a remarkable degree — and he had no intention of dying. He had been a radio amateur for many years, and with the call button under the blanket, began ringing out "SOS" in Morse code. The nurses at the call station were annoyed at all this noise since a nurse had just answered his earlier call. Fortunately a doctor heard the distress signal and understood. As my friend lapsed into unconsciousness, the doctor rushed in and saved his life. He recovered and we remained good friends for many more years.

The real lesson here is that we might think that we have secrets that only God knows. But somewhere there is a mind reader who can see us as we really are — just as though we are transparent. Better to live life with this in mind. It is truly easier than trying to be devious. How useless to be a hypocrite of any kind. And so we can get on with our spiritual studies without taking any further thought about keeping up a false appearance.

Thoughts Leak Out – Thoughts Can Do Things

My "given talent" was with mechanical things. Even in my early years, I could look at machinery and, pretty soon, have it figured out. So, early on in childhood, I knew that I wanted to be a mechanical engineer, even though I had only a hazy idea as to what that meant. As a kid I built model boats and airplanes, then bigger boats to sail on Lake Erie with brother and friends.

But most other aspects of life were not just a mystery; actually, I was completely unaware of them. A "blessed ignorance", you might say, that enabled me to concentrate my efforts on what I could more easily understand. Later I found that this tends to be typical of many engineers.

In the so-called spiritual aspects of life, I was totally inept. Thirty years of attending church didn't help much with that either. No one that I knew during all that time intimated that there is any reality to the stories in the Bible although on Sunday most paid a casual lip service to the idea before going out to play golf. It was only when I met Rev. E. L. Crump "who knew" and really understood spiritual truth that there was any glimmer of understanding in my mechanically-oriented mind. See the following essay on "Reverend Edward L. Crump and Katherine Calhoun".

After some initial study, I began to realize that I was getting acquainted with people that really did have an interest in the spiritual side of life because they too were beginning to believe that there was some reality. And so I treaded very cautiously in this new area of life as I developed some small abilities. This essay is about some little events in that regard. At first glance they may seem odd to be associated with spirituality but they do illustrate one little corner of a great truth, as you will see.

Some years ago on TV, a woman guest claimed that she could communicate with animals by mental telepathy. I wish that I had taken her name [1] because she made an interesting presentation. In one case that she related, she was called to find out why a race horse was doing so poorly on the track. After 'listening' to the animal, she interpreted her impression of the horse's thoughts this way:

"Run, run, run! That's all they want me to do. I'm tired!"

This 'message' to the trainer caused him to put the horse out to pasture for a suitable time to rest up. The horse soon responded in its old form.

Many people, of course, are skeptical. Can a dumb animal have thoughts? And actually express them by telepathy? Actually a few sensitive people appear to be so successful in doing this feat that they now call themselves "Professional Animal Communicators" and can charge for their services. Imagine how useful this could be to a veterinarian in diagnosing an ailing animal.

1. One such person is Debbie McGillivray who has become well known in certain circles as a "Professional Animal Communicator".

What I am leading up to, of course, is my own personal experience. Without this publically acknowledged story that I just related , nobody would believe me. In fact, no one has ever believed me anyway when I have described these two simple little experiments. See what you think.

Some individuals in my spiritual study group, who were more advanced, began telling me that thoughts can have an effect in the physical world as well as in our minds. And so I tested this idea in these little ways, as a researcher in any subject might set up a "scientific" experiment.

The Horse

I was taking a few lessons at the riding academy run by the wife of a fellow engineer at B-L-H Corp. in Lima, Ohio. I should have taken flying lessons instead (which I did later) because operating an airplane seems more natural to me than "operating" a horse. But I did learn some things, for example, a real appreciation of the skills of the stunt riders in the movies. And an empathy for the old time cowboys, horse wranglers and cavalry who made a living trying to stay on a galloping horse. Also I did learn something about horses that was astounding to me.

The first lessons were on a gentle but tired old mare that should have been put out to pasture. I was to just guide the horse around a short track; give it commands to start and to stop. When the instructor saw that I was competent enough not to fall off (the most important part), she left to allow me to practice by myself. The old mare and I were soon well acquainted. She saw that I didn't want to go faster than a slow walk, which at her age, was as fast as she cared to go anyway.

I began to notice that she seemed to pick up my thoughts of what I wanted to do next without any signal by verbal command or from my body language. It was only two commands — start and stop. But what a surprise — or was it just my imagination?

Ever the amateur scientist/engineer, I decided to experiment. When the instructor would leave, I would start and stop the mare just by telepathy. It was real! No doubt about it! It went like this:

Holding my body and the reins absolutely motionless, I concentrated my thought sharply and 'projected' the thought toward the horse and the horse would comply. We got so good at it that I forgot that you are supposed to "tell" your mount what to do with body movement and reins. My mind and the horse's mind were in unison. This was incredible, I thought; I have control over this big horse because she is willing to listen to my thoughts. Naturally I didn't mention this to the instructor, but she might have had similar experiences to share had I done so.

The riding lessons progressed to a more spirited horse. I soon found out that this animal required firm control by reins and my knees against its sides. Telepathy didn't work at all. At least not from the level of thought power that I had available. Even so, I had personally discovered something. The cowboy of ages past was said to be in tune with the mind of his mount — to a far greater degree than others who customarily rode horses in that era. Perhaps telepathic?

Can a dumb animal really be sensitive enough to pick up telepathic thoughts? I proved it to myself that it can — beyond any shadow of a doubt!

The Dog

When I lived alone at the Kirtland, Ohio house with just our dog "Schroeder" (daughter Marsha's choice for the dog's name), the dog and I "became quite close". He was a mixed breed, friendly, but not too smart as dogs go. Although he was a good watchdog in the daytime, he was a very sound sleeper and did not like to be awakened after dark.

One night as I sat at the drawing table in my shop (part of the house), Schroeder was sound asleep nearby, perhaps 12 feet away. Recalling the telepathic communication that had taken place years before with the riding horse, I wondered if I could "throw" a thought toward the dog.

I projected a thought to wake up. He did! Schroeder looked up rather annoyed and maybe mystified at what had awakened him. After a quick look around, he went back to sleep. Stupid with sleep as he was, he was able to pick up my telepathic message and respond.

In the following weeks, I repeated this several times to make sure that it was not just coincidence, but not enough to disturb the dog's sleep habits.

Having experienced these little "tests", silly as they may sound, I know that concentrated thought is real and can be projected and can have an effect, even on the "lesser" minds of animals. In both of these tests, I had a strong rapport with the animals, a sort of an emotional affinity that is a necessary part of "the hookup". For most situations, it requires much time together.

Animal lovers have always known that when they project love toward their pet, the animal responds in kind. Part of a dog's love may be from its anticipation of dog biscuits, part from scratching of ears, but I believe a good bit of the interchange is simply telepathic love.

The Phone Call

At one time, I became "close to" certain people in a religious study group that I took part in. We apparently had developed a close rapport without even thinking about it. We would talk on the phone and sometimes they would rattle on at great length about some subject that we were studying. As long as I would concentrate intently on what they were saying, they would keep talking. But the instant that I let my concentration drop they would abruptly stop their discourse and ask "are you still there?" Obviously, some part of the communication that they were making was telepathic, and they could sense subconsciously if the telepathic connection was disrupted, whether they were consciously aware of it or not. My rapt attention had been maintaining the psychic connection alongside the regular phone connection and they could feel the break. The conversation appeared to be going over a dual connection— one, the standard electrical telephone connection provided by the phone company, and the second an 'etheric' or mental connection between two minds connected in some strange way over a distance of many miles.

A telepathic connection that worked for a horse and a dog also worked between men! Astounding, yet known to happen often in crisis situations when people drop all extraneous thoughts and concentrate on the crisis. This also implies that any communication can be strengthened by concentration on the part of one or both parties.

Since then I have found it to be expedient to learn how to consciously make such a connection. And even more important, how to break off such a connection. I have noticed that busy executives are good at this — sometimes using the ploy that they have a call on another line.

The Man

A person who can stay calm can actually calm others. I knew just such a man at a small company in Monrovia, California. He was a foreman and when he approached a heated situation, the anger of the people just melted away. He never had to say a word! The workers didn't just suppress the anger because he was the boss. Anger just disappeared. This man was a living antidote to anger.

Actually I could feel the "peace" that surrounded him. People liked to just stand near him. I did too. Alas, I never asked him what his "secret" was. I wondered whether he was naturally that way or whether he had deliberately become the "new man" mentioned by Jesus. [2]

Conclusions:

Imagine the implications of these little experiments and observations.

If our thoughts can be received by dumb beasts, how much more so could a person pick up what we are thinking. It is known that a close rapport between people is normally necessary; for example, family, loved ones, even co-workers. And the person 'throwing the thought' must be concentrating sharply. And a little burst of energy helps.

2. Ephesians 4:24 to 32.   Colossians 3:10 to 17.

Unfortunately, the circumstance that most often combines <u>energy and concentration</u> (for the average person anyway) is when they are **angry** at someone. People receiving angry thoughts from some one may not be consciously aware of this because their own defensive thoughts cover over what their subconscious mind may be receiving. But they can be hurt by the anger.

All of this is nothing new. The great sages and spiritual teachers down through history have pointed out these subliminal truths. And they all recommend that we do not send out anger and hatred because other people receive it. Sometimes even innocent bystanders receive such thoughts and form angry mobs or panics.

And the sages urge a person who "approaches" the spiritual life to eliminate the negative tendencies lurking in the back of the mind <u>before</u> learning the techniques for concentration. Such a "cleansing" is necessary to avoid hurting others — and to avoid hurting themselves.

And so, I try to be careful as to what I think. Oddly enough, I never "used" this "secret of life" of the animals in any other way; but put it in the back of my mind and forgot about it.

However, some people who learn about this "human ability" want to use it to control others for their own advantage. The teachers of spiritual knowledge make it very clear <u>that it is wrong to do</u> <u>this</u>. It probably harms the target and it <u>definitely harms the perpetrator</u>.

I take that lesson to heart!

Even Through Granite Walls

Our kids seemed to enjoy traveling and usually traveled well.

Wife Isabel and I took them on various automobile trips, on an airplane flight from Cleveland, Ohio to Disneyland, USA (as five year old Marsha described it) in Los Angeles. We even took a 'sleeper' on the railroad to St. Louis, back when the regular trains still had such amenities.

The particular incident that I want to relate took place during summer vacation when Carol Ann would have been 14, Bill 11 and Marsha Jane 9 years old.

We were on our way from our home in Kirtland, OH driving to Cincinnati and were just then passing through Columbus. The multilane by-pass freeways had not yet been built and so old two-lane Route 42 went right through the city. But near the center of town, road signs took us off the main street to a side street.

Up to that point in the trip, the three kids in the back seat of the car had been "good as gold". Suddenly they became very agitated and began arguing and poking one another. Isabel turned to the kids and angrily told them to quiet down, a reaction that was all out of proportion to the situation.

I said to Isabel, "Don't you feel what I feel? The kids do."

And after a pause I added in a loud but calm voice for all to hear, "Look over to the left."

No one uttered a peep because they were startled by what I said, and because they were puzzled by what I meant.

"That gray granite wall is the Ohio State Penitentiary We are all feeling the negative vibrations from the people inside."

The evil feeling that we were all receiving was not overpowering. But apparently it was strong enough that we could be aware of it, and the kids were reacting to it even though they did not realize or understand. I had never knowingly felt anything like that before — although I had heard people talk about such things.

"The granite walls can keep the prisoners inside but they can't contain the anguish radiating from the people," I said, trying to sound wise, as we moved on down the street a block or two.

Not wanting to make a big deal of the experience, I said no more.

31

The negative "emanations" from any single prisoner, of course, would never be felt. But the total from the hundreds incarcerated in the many buildings inside the walls combined to create a real "cess pool of evil" surrounding the prison in the world of the spirit.

We were soon "out of range", the wife and kids quieted down to a normal state and we drove on. The entire experience was quickly forgotten.

Now if I were to relate this incident today, many people would say,

"The kids were just getting tired about then, that's all" — Maybe so....
"Isabel was probably tired from preparing for the trip, that's all" — Maybe so....

But nobody can 'talk away' or erase the feelings of anguish that I experienced in that one or two blocks alongside the prison wall in Columbus, Ohio that day!

Over the years since that incident, my further studies of science, philosophy, metaphysics and the deep meaning of religion make clear some of the lessons that might be inferred from the experience.

"Evil" people (in the usual sense of that word) exude evil "vibrations." If they are not so bad, they might just be referred to as "negative vibrations" rather than the strong pejorative word "evil".

Perhaps we all exude "vibrations" (a form of energy) of some kind or other according to our own nature or state of spiritual development, to the level of our intensity of feeling and emotion.

The feelings of anger or hatred that someone directs toward us can cause us to feel anger, hate, or at least agitation unless we can be aware of what is happening, as I fortunately became aware when in proximity to the State Penitentiary. Sad to admit, I have been caught off-guard many times before and after that incident and have reacted just as the kids did. But I am learning to be more spiritually awake — more aware of such things.

The feelings of anger or hate that we may direct toward others can cause them to feel anger, hate toward us, or at least agitation in return. It never helps to spread these negative forces. It is also well to protect ourselves from these things by becoming informed and staying aware.

What strikes me as even more odd than the above story is:.......

that these "lessons" inferred from driving a block or two down a street
in Columbus, Ohio are included in the teachings of the major religions.

It must all be real!

The inmates have committed crimes (most of them) and this "atmosphere of evil emanation" is an additional punishment that they receive from each other, although not by a judge or jury.

And the idea that we can affect others nearby by the "atmosphere" that we exude is something to become aware of, to study and perhaps modify. More will be said about that in later essays.

This Ohio State Penitentiary was closed in 1990. It was torn down a few years later to build a soccer stadium on the same spot.

Energy – From Me to Him

In my young adulthood, I missed many opportunities to learn from others. Each was a personal loss and would have required only a listening attitude on my part. This story is one such about an unusual aspect of the spiritual world.

I worked part time for a small company while I was pursuing a Masters Degree in Mechanical Engineering at Case Tech. The company fancied that they needed only a draftsman and advertised on the Case bulletin board for one to make drawings for a new road-building machine that they had in mind. I grabbed the job because it had flexible hours.

I soon saw that they needed much more than a draftsman — a real design engineer and so I did that. After the first machine was built according to their ideas and failed in every respect, (as I told them it would), it was obvious that they really needed an inventor. Someone who could come up with a completely new concept and who could carry it through. So I did that – working full time now, coming up with one creative aspect after another.

But the point of this tale is not about machinery.

"W. P.", the owner of the company was 74 years old and one time we went on a two day business trip from Cleveland to Columbus, Ohio. I drove because he was a terrible driver. He intended to get the Highway Department at the State Capital to allow the use of the new machine by modifying the existing road building specs. Since I had invented it, designed it and understood it, he took me along to explain the principles of the process to the highway engineers.

We stayed overnight in the old (even then) "Southern Hotel", in beds on opposite sides of the same large room. After W.P. said his evening prayers in a loud stage whisper, he turned to me and said what was a most puzzling thing.

He related that he had gone to a religious retreat many years before and a priest had taught him how to "transfer energy". I didn't have the slightest idea what he was talking about. I didn't know anything about priests and didn't even know (at that time) what a religious retreat was. He didn't add anything to that and I didn't ask him what he was talking about. Perhaps I was tired from driving and the days efforts at the Highway Department. But more likely I just didn't pursue his line-of-thought because I was not in the habit of doing so. Thinking about the next day's work, I soon forgot all about the incident.

Time passed. I designed improved versions of the machine, the little shop out back built them and they sold for use in the construction of highways and turnpikes. I designed other types of road building machines and often went out into the field to show contractors how they worked.

More time passed. Much to my surprise and the considerable disapproval of his son, W.P. married his secretary who was also in her 70's. Now the two of them spent much less time working, more time cavorting around town, and so I had to assume more responsibility in running the little company. Then the strangest thing began to happen. At first I didn't recognize what was going on. When I began to suspect, I found it hard to believe. And I doubt that you will believe it either. But I do now. Here is what took place:

I would open the office in the morning at a normal starting time. The boss's son, crippled from polio, would struggle in some time later to begin the bookkeeping. At that time we were the only two in the office. About 10:30 the newly-weds would come in and the boss would flop down in his chair in a little separate office. He had no pep, no energy, hardly any life left to keep him alive.

He would putter around for about a half hour or so and then the two of them would miraculously be full of life, full of energy, and with a quick good-bye, would go bounding out for another day on the town. It was as though they had taken a shot of adrenalin or some such.

Except — now I was suddenly exhausted! Thirty one years old at the time, strong, in good health and in the prime of life — even so, I wondered how I would make it through the day. This went on two or three days a week because, fortunately for me, they didn't come in every day.

Eventually I recalled what W.P. had said in the hotel in Columbus so many months before. Apparently this is what he meant by "transferring energy"! Somehow he was able to plunder my life energy for his own use. But I was not very smart about such things — I had never heard that such things could be possible. I still can't imagine how anyone can do it. But whether I understood the phenomenon or not, I carefully confirmed to myself that it was indeed taking place. He was able to "extract" life energy from me for his own use. It was an actual transfer of energy from one person to another, making one energized and the other depleted.

That's when I decided to get out of that company. As a stop-gap while I planned my future, I made a point to have some urgent business out in the shop whenever W.P. and his new bride came in the office. The distance between us seemed to somewhat limit his connection to my energy.

Then W.P. had a long bout in the hospital with a serious disease, so I stayed and kept the company together. When he returned for an occasional day at work, I made immediate plans to leave. He died a month after I left, perhaps missing his "outside source" of life energy.

Could this be the basis for the vampire legends? Sucking life energy rather than actual blood. Some years later I began serious spiritual studies. Over time I met a couple of people in study groups who, I suspected, were trying to consciously plunder my energy for their own benefit.

Forewarned, I tried to never again let it happen. However, there may be people more clever at this despicable practice than I can detect. So I try to be aware, but I still get caught off guard repeatedly. Usually my attention is on something else that is important to me, and only later do I realize that my energy has been taken. Furthermore, I would never care to learn how to do it myself, if that were possible, because it is obviously dishonest and probably damaging to the Soul of the person doing it. It is stealing! Stealing the most precious thing in the world — someone's life force.

After much reflection, I realize that I should not be so incredulous about the possibility that our life energy can leak out — or even be projected out by ourselves consciously or unconsciously — or absorbed from others. For example, at sporting events people say that "you could feel the energy" as fans direct their desire and good feelings to their own team. It could be the principle behind the well-known "home field advantage", or part of it at least.

It might also have something to do with the observed phenomenon that players occasionally are able to perform "above themselves". In recent years, athletes have recognized this marvel and call it "being in the zone" [1] And in the theater, there is occasionally an "electric performance", for want of a better descriptive word, where there seems to be an exchange of energy between audience and performer. But if you watch it later on a recording, the spark does not come through. I have experienced this myself several times and have concluded that the performers are projecting "something" to the live audience that audio and video recorders can not pick up.

Also as a general observation, extroverts seem to be energized by just being in a group of people while those with an introverted temperament could be "drained". Have you experienced this?

And in hospitals and sick rooms, it has long been noticed that certain visitors can deplete the energy of the sick person, often dangerously so. Perhaps out of their own fear of death or just their own pessimistic attitude toward life, they unconsciously "connect" to the helpless one and pull them down even lower. And the length of the visit may not be any safeguard against this!

In a similar way, there are rare individuals that can buoy up the sick — more than just "cheering them up" — actually "giving them life". Perhaps the great medical "healers" (doctors) in modern times like the Mayo brothers in Rochester, Minnesota and the Criles in Cleveland, Ohio had just such an ability, even on an unconscious level, that augmented their medical skills.

I leave it to you to decide.

1. The slang expression "In the zone" is derived from the TV program "Twilight Zone" which had spooky, unearthly music and stories. It ran from 1959 to 1964 according to Wikipedia.

Reverend Edward L. Crump & Katherine Calhoun

Everybody called him "Rev". He was the greatest teacher I have ever had! Katherine was a great teacher also and the two worked together as a team extremely well. They were both natives of Tennessee. They taught week-end classes in several cities throughout the Mid West. under the auspices of the "Concept Therapy Institute" of San Antonio, Texas.

Rev was infinitely patient, was kind to everyone, was loved by all who got to know him.

He taught each person at his own speed---- with little glances of eye contact to a particular individual when a particular point was important to that person. No matter what kind of a problem-person was brought into a class for help, he handled the situation. That is, he taught four ways: he taught individuals, he taught the class, he taught the subject and he taught by healing (spiritually) some pretty sick people that came to a class for help. If a person wanted to learn, Rev would teach as much as the person could grasp.

Katherine was adept in the world of the spirit, but it took me, as a beginner, some time to realize what a remarkable person she was. I took classes with other good 'Concept Therapy' teachers. But Rev Crump was the greatest teacher I have ever had.

Brief Bio:

As an outstanding electrical engineering student, he was selected to work briefly with the renowned Charles P. Steinmetz at General Electric Co. under a mentoring program. Then after working some years in the electric power industry, he went to seminary and became a Methodist minister. His first appointment was pastor of a small back-woods church. Although nothing was mentioned in his ministerial training about healing the sick through prayer, he became adept at doing so out of necessity as there was seldom an available doctor. Then with a larger church in Memphis, he still pondered the mystery of how spiritual healing worked. Eventually he met Glenn Clark, founder of the "Camps Farthest Out" organization, who told him that the "Concept Therapy Institute" in San Antonio, Texas taught about that very subject. Rev went there for study and then became a teacher and taught, with Katherine, spiritual subjects on several levels for many years. With his background in Christianity, he understood in depth. Of all the people that taught the Christian message, he was the first one that I met who could actually demonstrate any part of it, and with an apparent ease.

During two decades of teaching, He and Katherine taught thousands. They could "pour love" over the people in their classes, something that I had never witnessed or experienced previously. They were deeply loved by the students. I studied with them over a 13 year period.

Truth is Better Than Belief

There is such a thing as spiritual truth. Even a small amount of it gives added meaning to life. The fact that it is real is a major premise of this book. It is more than a comfortable set of beliefs, undoubtedly deeper than what we were taught as children or in church.

Some people seem to naturally feel the reality of it while others such as myself must search for it in the teachings of the great prophets. Then only by confirming it in our own life experiences do we know that it is really true.

With the mind of a true engineer, I was very much at home in the physical world, the discoveries of science, the design and operation of the marvelous machines of the last 150 years or so.

It was only when I met teachers who understood this more advanced area of human knowledge that I was able to understand any of it. Their patience as teachers was remarkable ---- at times heroic. Any subject is best learned in small increments, especially so with this subject.

"There exists such a thing as spiritual **truth**, as opposed to only **beliefs**" ----

finding that out was the greatest thing that ever happened in my life.

In an opposite vein, it brings to mind the lament of St. Augustine *

"Too late have I loved you, God"

Except for the dedicated efforts of my teachers it could have been,

"too late have I <u>found any reality</u> about you, God"

* St. Augustine of Canterbury, died c 604. Appointed missionary of England by Pope Gregory 1, became the first Archbishop of Canterbury in 601. From Lexicon Webster's Dictionary 1989.

Know All About the Bible

or

Know What the Bible is All About

In my serious spiritual studies over a period of 50+ years, I have, of course, studied how our Christian Bible came to us. I never dreamed that I would ever write anything about it so did not keep track of references. So I leave it to you to search out and verify anything written here as it interests you.

The job of the dedicated Bible scholar is to provide some meaning to essentially every significant part of the Bible. That is their job. And Christian clergy are then trained to be able to teach it.

As a seeker of Wisdom, thank God I don't have to do all that! I only have to understand, (at least as well as I can) the overall meaning of it so that this knowledge can be of some real use in life.

Jesus taught the multitudes, obviously speaking the Aramaic language that they all understood. Then at some later time, his disciples and other followers wrote down the gist of his teaching and the examples that He used, with which we are familiar today. Some of the learned ones could have written in Hebrew just for the Jews. But the manuscripts that have come down to us were written in Greek so that the teaching would be available to a broader range of people than just the Jews. [1]

This led Wilhelm Nietzsche (b 1844, d 1900) a German philosopher who also studied religion to exclaim in anguish, "If God wrote the New Testament, He certainly did not know much Greek."

The reason for this strange statement has become clear in later years. For centuries, Bible scholars and translators had studied the classical Greek language. So did Nietzsche. Yet they saw that the early manuscripts that had been gathered together from various places to be translated were written in a somewhat different form of Greek. And when the King James Version was translated, as well as the English translations that preceded it, Bible scholars believed that this was a special form of Greek that had been used only for writing holy literature. They were very mistaken!

In the Twentieth Century, continuing study showed this form of Greek to be the "business Greek" of Biblical times. It was a simpler, limited form of the language that had become useful as a "second language" among traders from many different parts of the Middle East. Now designated as koine´ Greek, it has become better understood in recent times as computers have analyzed old business records saved from biblical times. Meanings of some words have been revised or expanded.

1. While some wanted to "hoard" the Teaching just for the Jews, St. Paul realized that it was "too big" for the Jews to keep to themselves. Jesus taught for Jew and Gentile alike.

It is known that this condensed form of the Greek language, while sufficient for trading, did not have words available for the nuances and shadings of meaning that Jesus undoubtedly used. This would have been no problem for early Christians neophytes, since there were enlightened ones who could expand the basic teaching in study groups that were probably "home churches".

When translations were made into English and other vernaculars, however, any expansion of meaning was done by the translator (or committee) and the nuances and shades of meaning were added by the translators using the customary language of **their** times. How about that!

In the last 150 years or so, there has been a large number of new translations of the Bible. Some are revisions of older versions; some are totally new. Some are word-for-word translations, some are thought-for-thought and some are paraphrased to save time in reading. Perhaps someone has kept count of how many of these have been published, but I have not.

This has brought about a situation today that some consider to be a dilemma and others see as an opportunity for greater insight.

If these many Bible translations have considerable differences, **which one is right ?**

Some people hang on to the "old King James Version" because it is time honored by 400 hundred years of use and counting. I like it myself but I won't tell you why till later in this essay. Others must use a translation approved by their church if they even care to study the Bible at all. And I wouldn't blame anyone starting out in Bible study today to go for a translation that is written in a modern form of English.

But which **one is right?**

Actually, that is not a valid question. There are no known original manuscripts written by early Christians. What we have are copies of copies of copies. A few of the early copies might have been made by learned scribes, most of whom were dedicated Jews rather than early converts. Many of the copies were undoubtedly made by amateurs who wanted a portion of the Gospel or Paul's letters for their own home church. Maybe certain aspects were emphasized, others aspects omitted. Errors certainly crept in. Only some time later, perhaps a couple centuries, did a more organized church have "professional copy makers" who, we are told, took great pains to avoid error. With all of these many known Greek manuscripts, the parts that are the same in each may be more nearly correct, and the parts that are different could well be errors.

Bible scholars know, for example, that the venerated King James Version has some known errors taken from earlier translations, also has some passages that were added at the behest of Popes in order to reinforce particular beliefs. Perhaps these details are important to you or your church, as they certainly are to Bible scholars. To me they are only little obstacles **to be worked around**. The only thing of importance to me is to learn spiritual truth. And this can be done by skipping over many of the details and letting the big ideas to shine through. [2]   So, for me —

> "It is better to know what the Bible is all about,
> than knowing all about the Bible."

I use several Bibles and also look up particular passages on the Internet in many translations. But my standard reference Bible is the King James Authorized version for these reasons:

1. It's true that the old English language and idioms are a little hard to get accustomed to. However, Luke 17:21 is translated accurately. This verse is more important to me than many other things about Bibles. It tells where you should look for the Kingdom of God. My later essays will discuss this one thought in considerable detail; it is part of the so-called "higher teaching". If a more recent translation can't get that right, and many do not, then how can you trust the rest of that translation? When I pick up an unfamiliar translation, this is the verse that I look up to get a quick appraisal of the accuracy of the translation. I realize that my judgement based on only one verse might seem severe to many Bible readers.

2. The several errors in the KJV are known and most are minor. Scholars are working to refine this translation in informal writings that you can access on the Internet. There are also obscure scholarly books about the errors.

3. The KJV translation of Matthew 6:22 (and a couple of early translations based upon it) is profound. More about this in a later essay, but it leads me to believe that there was at least one member of the KJV translating committee who had a very high level of spiritual insight. If so, this is in great contrast to modern translators who appear to be mostly "word people", which is necessary, of course. But an ideal translator would be a master of the <u>subject</u> as well as master of two languages. And that is asking a lot. This is one reason to study several translations and to try to get the best meaning.

One other thing about **my** Bible reading for which friends and ministers scold me: —

Jesus put the **Great Truths** in a new context which He called the New Covenant or the "new wine" which (He said) could not be put into old wineskins". That is, He brought new concepts that were way beyond the existing ideas of the Jews — something totally new. They were new meanings that had to be understood as new. Not just a touch-up of the old. Since I am searching for the Great Truths in the modern era, why then should I wrestle with the old muddled context of the ancient Jews and their writings in the Old Testament? So I don't "wrestle" and I approach the OT only lightly.

2. And by confirming, confirming, confirming by whatever means are available, perhaps for a lifetime.

41

The Old Testament used storytelling to teach spiritual truths, a method well suited to the level of education of the people in those ancient times. Jesus pointed out that the ancient Jews had killed off their prophets; so who could explain the stories in the Old Testament and the deep spiritual meanings they were meant to teach? Jesus could — but nobody I know today.

If the Old Testament had been working for the Jews, Jesus would not have had to come to earth to teach, or so it seems to me.

Although the Old Testament contains much accumulated human wisdom as well as the spiritual teaching, the teaching brought by Jesus is an update, so to speak, of the "Ancient Wisdom".

In the light of this, the direction of my spiritual search is to follow the teaching of Jesus. The New Testament has the great teaching! Why look elsewhere? I have never met anyone who understood it from studying <u>only</u> the Old Testament, but would love to chat with anyone who feels that he has unlocked the great spiritual meanings just from that source.

However, each person begins a search from a different starting point and has a somewhat different path to go, so in your particular case — take note of the above, but follow **your** heart.

Jesus Process

Jesus came on earth to teach a _process_ for spiritual enlightenment. It is a process of _evolution_ of a person's soul to higher levels of spiritual consciousness.

These few words, when understood in depth, outline a life's work for the person who is serious about his spiritual well being.

In section three there is another essay that takes a deeper look into the above brief statement. This is just a glimpse of some profound concepts to come.

The Spiritual "Players"

In our everyday practice of religion, there are three distinct functions carried out by the following three classes of "providers" or workers. It is well for church-goers to understand the function, the responsibilities and the limitations of each of these three classes. They are:

1. The cleric - works directly with people, usually in a church setting, performs rituals, teaches, advises, consoles.

2. The theologian - develops the belief system used by the clerics through a systematic study of God. Some are professionals and some have been rank amateurs.

3. The mystic - Provides the initial spiritual insight to the theologian through the process of spiritual illumination. There have been very few of these throughout history.

The clergy, especially when young, may not have first-hand knowledge of all of the deep religious and philosophical questions of life. People should not expect that of them. They may well be working diligently on their own spiritual quest, and as a result of that, have a broader knowledge than others who may be more oriented toward church business or politics. But they are constrained by the official teaching of their church affiliation. In some churches, an individual may be promoted into what is more of a managerial function, then only partly spiritual.

The theologian has the responsibility of providing a "valid" belief system based on something more than just some flight-of-fancy. But there are some amateurs who seek to merely satisfy the whims of their followers with a "prosperity theology", for example. Others are urged to develop a variation of belief for a splinter group. Theologians often work in a conference to delineate the doctrine of their church, or to update it. Since they work directly with the clergy rather than the congregations, fewer theologians are needed than clergy. Sometimes however, they are called to clarify a doctrine directly with the congregation as St. Paul had to do.

The mystic is relatively rare in the world and usually has contact with a group of limited size. Historically, they have allowed their disciples to write down their "sayings", often in an unorganized fashion. They speak of things and concepts far removed from the average person's understanding and must therefore use terminology that is puzzling to all but the serious theologian. They teach of the realm of the spirit rather than the physical world. While most people think of mystics only in antiquity, there are active ones today who mostly support and confirm the teachings of the mystics of old.

The above three are the professionals. And it might be tempting to leave the work up to them since you and I are the reason that they are in business. But we have the biggest part to play — to listen, to learn, to study, to validate, to change ourselves, to evolve and to grow spiritually. It may be extra hard for us because we may be householders with the duties of job and family in addition to being spiritual aspirants.

Such is the way that it appears to me.

The Blind Men and the Elephant

There is a story that everyone has heard about a group of blind men groping an elephant to determine its shape, each forming a different interpretation. It sounds like a fable of Aesop, but 'Wikipedia Dictionary Website' says that it came from India, although other countries had similar tales. And that the best known version in the West is the delightful 19th Century poem by John Godfrey Saxe, transcribed here. Published 1873.

The Blind Men and the Elephant
John Godfrey Saxe (1816 - 1887)

It was six men of Indostan
To learning much inclined,
Who went to see the Elephant
Though all of them were blind,
That each by observation
Might satisfy his mind.

The First approach'd the Elephant,
And happened to fall
Against his broad and sturdy side,
At once began to bawl:
"God bless me! But the Elephant
is very like a wall!"

The Second, feeling of the tusk,
Cried, - "Ho! What have we here
So very round and smooth and sharp?
To me 'tis might clear
This wonder of an Elephant
Is very like a spear!"

The Third approached the animal,
And happening to take
The squirming trunk within his hands,
Thus boldly up and spake:
"I see," quoth he, "the Elephant
Is very like a snake!"

The Fourth reached out his eager hand,
And felt about the knee.
"What most this wondrous beast is like
Is mighty plain," quoth he,
"Tis clear enough the Elephant
Is very like a tree!"

The Fifth, who chanced to touch the ear,
Said: "E'en the blindest man
Can tell what this resembles most;
Deny the fact who can,
This marvel of an Elephant
Is very like a fan!"

The Sixth no sooner had begun
About the beast to grope,
Then, seizing on the swinging tail
That fell within his scope,
"I see," quoth he, "the Elephant
Is very like a rope!"

And so these men of Indostan
Disputed loud and long,
Each in his own opinion
Exceeding stiff and strong,
Though each was partly in the right,
And all were in the wrong!

(continued)

So oft in theologic wars,
The disputants, I ween,
Rail on in utter ignorance
of what each other mean,
And prate about an Elephant
Not one of them has seen!

This story has long been told to illustrate how people dig in the heels of their ego to defend a personally selected position about which they may have little or only partial understanding. While it may be understandable in cases that are still in the realm of opinion, it becomes ridiculous in areas that are known and can be verified. I suspect that the "Guiness Book of Records" was originally compiled to provide one such source to settle arguments.

But the main point of the story illustrates an additional foible in the realm of human thought processes. And that is the tendency to grasp at the first thought that a person may have about something, with the satisfied assumption that their first thought is all there is.

Psychologists explain that many people have a strong need for "intellectual closure". They do not like to have an unanswered question dangling in their mind. And so they grab onto some explanation that gives even a small degree of comfort. That is probably why myths, legends and superstitions have been created to assuage the intellectual uneasiness of not knowing. For us today, the various sciences have explained so much of the nature around us that we might forget how frightening "not understanding" was in earlier ages. And it still is frightening today in "areas of unknowing" for many people.

You can see this process in how people interpret Scripture. Despite the fact that sages have pointed out for centuries that there are great hidden meanings in Bible stories, many readers grab only a literal interpretation, are satisfied, and don't bother to look deeper. The person who is able to progress spiritually and intellectually is normally open to additional explanations, open to anomalies — open! But then must be careful to authenticate the issues sooner or later.

The longer I have been involved in spiritual studies, the easier it has become not to jump to conclusions just to have something to "hang on to". It seems that the more reality I "have under my belt", the less is the psychological need to build a complete, but flimsy, belief system. I can leave some unanswered questions for tomorrow. The more that I truly **know**, the less is the need to **believe** something that may not be true.

Man Overboard

Lake Erie is a great place for small boat sailing. There are no sharks to nip you and the water gets warm in the summer. Unlike salt water, the spray doesn't burn your eyes or corrode metal fittings. And it's large enough that you can't see the other side, about 56 miles across.

I built a little canoe when I was 12, bent ribs and canvas covered. Brother Ed and I outgrew it in one summer. Then a 10 foot sail boat at 13 and finally a 14 foot sail boat when I was 14. The kids in the neighborhood, Ed and I sailed it for seven summers. I loved it! World War Two came and went.

Many years went by and I bought a "Sunfish". Not much of a boat, only 13 + feet long, one sail, little more than a surf board. Mostly for one person, but it would hold me and two of the kids when they were small.

Mostly we sailed at Fairport Harbor, Ohio. In rough weather we could stay inside the breakwater, and in nice weather we could sail out in the lake. I loved 'day sailing' in a small boat.

This incident happened on a glorious sailing day. The wind, parallel to the shore, was smooth and steady. There were no motor boats around to make waves for the sailboat (a fun game for them, not so much fun for the little sailboat). Actually there were no other boats in sight at all, odd for a Wednesday afternoon. I had been sailing straight out and back and was at least a half mile out from the breakwater — just enjoying being on the water.

Then it happened!

I just slipped out of the boat! My body was heavily coated with suntan oil and I was slippery as a watermelon seed. I still can't understand how it happened, but there I was in the water.

No problem I thought. Without the weight of a person in the boat, it is supposed to tip over. You swim to it, pull it back upright and splash some of the water out of the little cockpit. Climb in, get up some speed and the automatic bailer empties the rest of the water. No problem.

But the boat didn't tip over. The wind was not quite strong enough. No problem, I thought. Without me holding the sheet (the rope that trims the sail) the sail will just swing out, flap in the wind and the boat will stop. Swim to it. No problem.

But there was a problem. The sheet rope apparently tangled around the little canoe paddle that was in the cockpit. The boat sailed away without anyone sailing it! Impossible! I had read stories of "ghost ships" back in the days of sail that sailed along without a crew that had somehow been lost. Here was my own little ghost boat created by my own doing.

I couldn't possibly swim fast enough to catch it. And my expensive life jacket was lying right there on the deck — in arm's reach if I had only been in the boat.

Now I realized that I had a real problem! It was too far to swim to shore.

And this is the purpose of this little story.

I turned my thoughts inward — as I had been accustomed to doing in situations like this. I said in a most concentrated, intense, desperate way, "I need help". Essentially, I was making an input to my subconscious mind for some kind of a solution, as I had learned how to do to a small degree.

Instantly, a "knowingness" said,   (I won't call it a voice because it was not)

"Swim for the intercept point"

And it gave me a "feeling" as to where that point might be.

The diagram on the next page shows my predicament.

Obviously my subconscious was using this concept of an intercept point to tell me something. It was from my Navy training at sub-chaser school where we calculated on a circular graph how to meet a supply ship or an enemy submarine that was on a known course and speed. The intercept point would be the expected rendevous. In a small way, we had a similar situation here.

Somehow the subconscious part of my mind was able to put together in an instant all of the details of the situation, then calculate a survival answer because that is what I asked for (directed it to do). Some part of my brain "thought" like this:

The boat is sailing away even though it is not supposed to.
Bill can't possibly swim fast enough to catch it.
The boat should eventually head up into the wind and then drift downwind.

And so I swam as fast as I could toward this imaginary intercept point with complete faith that I was doing the right thing. Rather than swimming toward the boat where it was — which is what many would do and never catch it.

Looking up at the last minute, there was the boat coming toward me, drifting stern first, driven by the wind, sail fluttering. Just as it went by, I reached up and pulled myself back into the cockpit. Unbelievable! The boat and I had reached this imaginary point in Lake Erie at the same instant.

Shore – another half mile

Fairport Harbor Breakwater
Half mile away

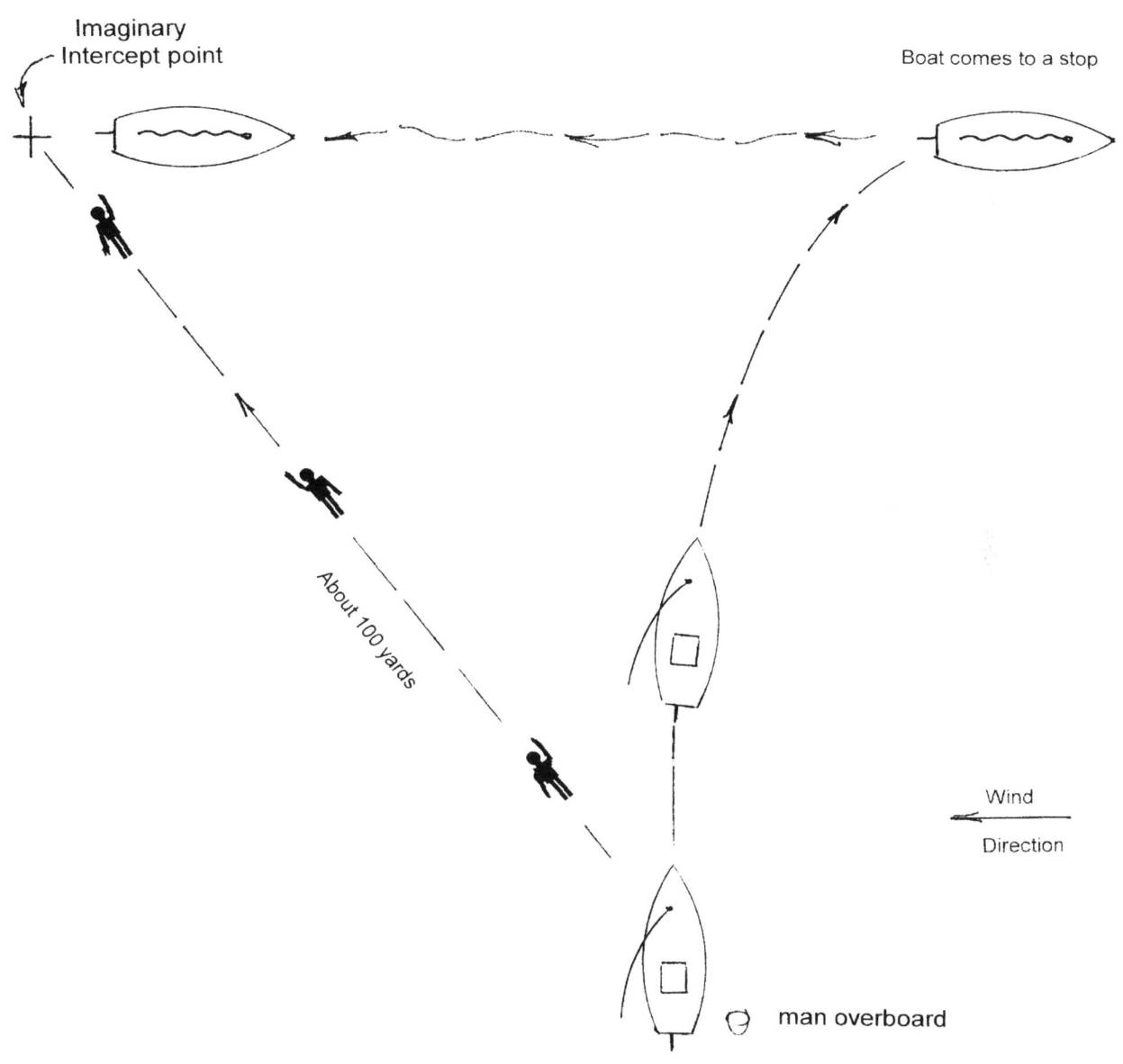

Imaginary
Intercept point

Boat comes to a stop

About 100 yards

Wind

Direction

man overboard

If I had taken any other action, I would have missed it and been left in an awkward situation. (I would not have drowned, but the boat might have been lost.)

Back in the boat, getting collected and underway again, I reasoned that I should take the boat home. One scare should be enough. But it was such a beautiful sailing day — and this embarrassing (maybe semi-life-threatening) ordeal had only lasted about ten minutes, so I continued sailing for the rest of the afternoon. Maybe not life threatening because sooner or later other boats would have to come by. But I would have been chilled and waterlogged.

After all, I thought, if something else should come up, I still have my subconscious mind to give me an answer — if it worked once, it should work again when I need it. (Keeping in mind not to over extend my luck).

Needless to say, in the several years of sailing after that, I was careful not to get too greased up with suntan oil. It also dawned on me later that if I had been **wearing** the bulky life jacket, I never would have been able to swim fast enough to meet the boat at the intercept point.

-------------------------------- # --------------------------------

This was an incident of turning to my subconscious mind in an emergency situation. But Thomas Edison used it deliberately to solve problems in his daily work, as we will see in the next essay. And more people are learning to do this now in all walks of life. You can too.

Many people think that looking inward to the subconscious mind is spooky, some are even terrified at the mention of it. But it is part of the human abilities, and it is largely unused in a <u>deliberate</u> way in our culture. But we will see as we go along that it can be incredibly powerful and useful.

It is the seat of all inspirational creativity; And it is continually reported as being useful in crisis situations such as the one in this story. Some people put a religious connotation on this part of our personal makeup and it may well have some such connection. In any case, it is part of us and the benefits can be useful to the person who is aware of it and who practices the use of it where it is appropriate.

Thomas Edison and the Creative Process

The previous essay related the use of the subconscious mind in an emergency situation. It worked because I had been studying and practicing how to use my subconscious, and because I felt that I was in a desperate situation. Desperation can concentrate thoughts and intentions sharply.

In this essay we will look at the creative process involving the subconscious mind that can be deliberately used in many aspects of life to solve problems, create new ideas and inventions. First let me say that I consider "artistic creations" to be more "expression of the artist" rather than a creative product. But I say that merely because many people think of "creativity" only in connection with the arts, whereas it is much more.

As pointed out above, the subconscious part of our mind is the seat of all inspirational creativity. However, it is below our normal threshold of awareness so that it doesn't interfere with our normal life. The subconscious controls much of our body functions, is the seat of our emotions and it stores our deep memories, some of which we might like to forget. In addition, it has an ability to carry out "orders" from our conscious part and can do other things as we shall see.

While we might think of the subconscious part of our brain as an **entity**, it is not a particular **part** of the brain. However it is convenient to think of it as "the basement of the brain" with our conscious awareness as the main floor. Some people envision a protective layer over it which might be temporarily penetrated by the conscious awareness in emergencies for some sort of direct help. But to be of any deliberate use in non-emergencies, we must poke a few little access holes which we can then open and close as desired. This can take some thought, will be covered in a couple of later essays on how to do it, and can take some practice. There are also books on how to.

In my years of doing creative engineering work, I studied everything that I could find about creative mind processes. Many problem-solving methods in the literature were more adapted to the use of the conscious part of the mind, such as bouncing ideas around a group. However these mthods may trigger subconscious thoughts, sometimes with the result coming at a later time.

By studying the biographies of the great inventors, I saw that there were simple things that they did that could be reduced to four requisite steps. Later, I found a slim obscure book in a university library that described a similar idea. It was written by an inventor and I knew it was right. The creative process based on this idea could justify an entire book, even more than one. However, it will be best understood in connection with the lessons of several essays in this book.

It is worth learning this four step technique of creative thinking. In my early years as an independent inventor, I would have paid "big bucks" for this information, had it been available.

The steps are:

1. Create a "data base" in your memory. Ordinarily this is done by our usual education, by accumulated life experiences and perhaps by an intense interest in some specialty. This provides bits for the subconscious to combine into new forms in ways that you might never think of consciously.

2. Concentrate intensely on a problem or some desired result or solution. This is best done while working consciously on the problem also. Intense thought in a narrow direction activates the subconscious to "help you" by providing a solution. Sometimes the intense thought need take only an instant, sometimes an extended period. Sometimes many inputs.

3. Step back from the work. Stop all conscious thought on the project. Allow an "incubation" period while the subconscious works, albeit beneath your awareness of its presence. Often, just going home at the end of a work day can provide this. Or perhaps as soon as a few steps to the water cooler. Or it might take a weekend or longer.

4. Have a quiet time in your activity. Let the mind be "in neutral" to allow the sub conscious to "deliver the result without being trampled to death" by other activity — mental, physical or emotional. Often called the "Eureka experience when a solution just seems to appear out of nowhere. Archimedes, who first shouted Eureka, reportedly was in the bathtub when he got the idea for specific gravity (because it is related to water). A physicist at the Battelle Memorial Research Institute said that he got his best ideas (that is, step 4 took place) in church. Others get the result while showering or shaving or other routine, gentle situation.

Just at the instant of awakening is a good time for many, or just at the instant of falling asleep. It is vital to make notes, sketches, etc. at that time because often a great idea can drift away and may or may not ever be retrieved. Also, some people have purposely developed a meditative state of mind that they can call on when they feel the sub-con has "an offering". And several famous inventions have come to their inventors just as they have given up the project as being hopeless. But it doesn't have to come to that if you "get this process into your fingertips".

Let's look at how Thomas Edison used this process in creating some of his great inventions.

When he was a traveling telegrapher, he had only a suit of clothes and a trunk full of books about electricity. This was a subject of great interest to him and he **saturated** his mind with the basics that were known at that time. In doing this he was **creating a "data base" in his mind** of this new technology. Learning things that later might be combined into a new result. **Step 1 of the process.** Still a young man he began his inventing. He would concentrate strongly, energetically on the project at hand in his lab. He would often continue into the night with meals sent over from his house. Such was his interest and intensity. **Step 2 of the process**.

At times, Edison would be stumped. The problem seemed unsolvable. He would then deliberately take a nap. He would just lie down on a workbench, and since he was totally deaf at that time, the shop noise did not bother him. **Step 3 of the process**. Stepping back from the problem. An incubation period for the subcon to work. Edison chose to take a nap, which he could easily do because he slept less at night.

After a half hour or so, he would awaken, and in his own words, "like as not, I would have the solution". **Step 4 of the process.** He took this useful nap when ever the need arose, and as his conscious mind slowly came out of the sleep state, the subconscious would "present" a result.

Most people choose a way that appears different, but gives the same effect. Even in a high level research lab, the boss might frown on people lying down for a nap. But some years ago, a large corporation provided their research facility with a swimming pool and other ways for their engineers to relax, hopefully to garner some Eureka moments for the company. Step 4 of the process. It wasn't long, however, until teams were organized for competitive water sports, perhaps because quiet relaxation is too difficult for some. Step 4 of the creative process went down the drain!

This process for creativity can be useful to those who are willing to practice it and learn to work with their sub conscious mind. But your results probably won't match the wonders of Edison. Mine never did, although I did get some great ideas. Still — we will have an additional "arrow in our quiver" whatever type of work or activity that we do.

<u>Edison had a very unusual mind</u>. He was different even from other intelligent people. And nothing illustrates that better than an often told story about his younger years as an itinerant telegrapher.

He had developed a skill for speed and accuracy with the telegraph instrument. One time he applied for a job, and for a test, the boss contacted a telegrapher in another city who had a reputation for phenomenal 'sending speed' in order to give Edison a real workout and put him in his place. Back then, newspaper text was sent manually by telegraph from city to city at night. During the test, the sender telegraphed page after page of newspaper to Edison at high speed. Edison realized what they were trying to do to him; he copied the message with no trouble and kept it up until the sender was totally exhausted. Depending on who told the story, it was three hours of intense work or maybe even five, and then Edison sent back the insulting message "Now send with your other <u>foot</u>", implying that the text was sent slow and sloppy while he was taking the lengthy message with no sweat, even ready for some more. That skill by-passed thinking about the Morse telegraph code altogether while the subconscious mind connected the clatter of the telegraph sounder directly to his writing hand. A skill used even today by those who still communicate with this method.

I relate this story to demonstrate that Edison showed a highly unusual mind even before he began inventing. And that his mind along with his use of the subconscious part of it contributed to his success.

Here is something that is still "secret".

Difficult as it may be to believe, nevertheless it is true; a final creative result can be "composed" of a lot more than just the data base that you put into your mind. Strange as it may seem, the sub con has the ability to go outside of your own being to find necessary information. This is a more advanced aspect of inspirational creativity that works for some, and can best be understood after you ponder some of the essays in Sections 2 and 3 of this book.

The above simple four step technique, that can be used by most people, is just the basis for some of the greater things to be covered in later essays.

A peculiar incident —

Years ago, when I sold an invention to a corporation in California, the head of the company asked me how I got my inventive ideas. I suspected that he was thinking of "golden goose" possibilities. I absent mindedly said that my system of creativity used the sub conscious mind. A look of terror came across his face. I was too surprised at his reaction to say anything else. He never mentioned it again. Nor did I.

Another peculiar incident —

At the Cleveland Engineering Society, I taught "Methods of Creativity" in evening classes for several years. About half of the class of 20 or so would be people who wanted to increase their ability in creative engineering work. The rest were executives who were looking for insights into the so-called "creative personality" in order to more easily schedule and control their creative employees.

After I covered the part about the use of the subconscious mind, at the next recess the "head honcho" (as he described himself) of an aircraft parts manufacturer grouched, "So that's why these 'nerds' are so far out". So I smiled and said nothing, thankful that I did not have to do creative work in that company. Like most executives, he would like to schedule the work flow of the research department in a manner similar to that of the production department. The difference, of course is that production is repetitive and the creative work has never been done before.

54

Many people doing creative work <u>are</u> using their subconscious mind, perhaps without realizing that they are doing so. They just feel that they "are creative" and let it go at that. And as long as they are functioning well, I also would let it go at that.

Despite the superstitions of some people, there is nothing to fear in learning to work with the subconscious part of your mind if you care to. An exception to this would be those people whose lives are in turmoil, especially those burdened with guilt or fear. Obviously those who have serious mental problems have more immediate priorities.

Even though the previous essay related the use of the subconscious mind to get through an emergency, it is best to learn about it before experiencing life's emergencies, just as you would learn to swim before venturing out on a surfboard. Creative use of the subconscious mind can be an every day useful skill.

I leave it to you to interpret

Intuition

Knowledge by means of intuition is somewhat similar to the creative problem-solving process of the previous essay, but without the first three conscious steps.

There was a time when intuition was considered to be a special mental disposition or ability — a direct mental pipeline "to the essence of things". It was accepted by philosophers as a way to knowledge. Unfortunately, it seems that engineers and others are conditioned by education and environment to neglect intuitive thinking in creative living, and to rely entirely on step-by-step analytical reasoning. But then a few of us do also use the four-step method as well.

This bias is regrettable, for many great scientists and inventors depended strongly on intuition for their insights. Edison, for example, had the remarkable ability to generate useful "hunches" which, when tested, turned out to be right. He learned to completely trust the feeling of certainty accompanying his intuitions. Similarly, Einstein said: "I believe in intuition and inspiration .....at times I feel certain I am right while not knowing the reason." In much of his work, Einstein did not take the slow, painful, step-by-step path to solution, but relied, instead, on "feeling" his way to the right solution.

Other great thinkers have pointed out these similar ideas. Some that I particularly like:

"The intuitive mind will tell the thinking mind where to look next." Jonas Salk
[I really like this quotation by this contemporary medical researcher because right in the beginning it combines intuition with the thinking mind. WLH]

"Intuitive knowledge rates above empirical knowledge." Spinoza

"All human knowledge begins with intuition, proceeds thence to concepts, and ends with ideas." Immanuel Kant

"By intuition is meant the kind of intellectual sympathy by which one places oneself within an object in order to coincide with what is unique in it and consequently inexpressible." Bergson

"It is by logic we prove. It is by intuition we discover." Henri Poincaré

"The healthy understanding, we should say, is not the logical, argumentative but the intuitive; for the end of understanding is not to prove (see below) and find reasons, but to know and believe."
Thomas Carlyle

"Strictly speaking, there is hardly any completely logical discovery. Some intervention of intuition issuing from the unconscious is necessary at least to initiate the logical work.

Jacques Hadamaar

"In the complicated situations of life, we have to solve numerous problems and make many decisions. It is absurd to think that reason should be our guide in all cases. Reason is too slow and too difficult. We frequently do not have the necessary data or we cannot simplify our problems sufficiently to apply the methods of reasoning. What then must we do? Why not do what the human race has always done – use the abilities we have, our common sense, judgment, and experience. We underrate the importance of intuition." --Irving Langmuir

"It is the intuitive reason that grasps the first principles." ---Aristotle

I have collected these quotations over a period of many years for my own use and have lost their source. Frequently many writers have copied from each other and it is difficult to pin point the original speaker and give credit. In any case I appreciate the collector's effort that wrote them where I could read them.

There is one important thing left out in these clever statements. These quotations were first lifted by somebody from original works to illustrate the importance of the use of intuition. The original authors **may have also pointed out** at the time that it is equally important to **prove** what is arrived at by intuition. The method of proof would, of course, be selected to be appropriate to the intuition. People often overlook this most important aspect of the intuitive process, even **not realizing that proof is really necessary.**

The last quotation above by Aristotle does bring to mind that he did not bother to prove many things, sad to say. And because he was "an authority" in his own day, people followed his sayings for a thousand years without ever confirming or questioning. Only when science began to awaken people from the dark ages was Aristotle proved wrong in many things.

I have known some people who sincerely believe that even their most fleeting thoughts are direct communications to them from God, and can be acted upon without further thought. Unbelievable! And if an "important" thought occurs to them, they term it to be "a word of knowledge" and they consider it to be an absolute. To me it is absolutely astounding that anyone would base their life on such a flimsy way of gathering knowledge. As an engineer brought up in the strict testing "mentality" of science and technology, I find this simplistic way of thinking to be appalling. Equally appalling to me is that **these folk** could not see anything vague or doubtful about that fuzzy type of thinking. Is it any wonder that there are "differences of opinion" on every subject.

As you observe and become aware of this mode of thinking, (if you haven't already) you will notice 'wacko' thinking of all kinds in many situations that could be easily tested before use. This type of thinking misses only the additional important step of **checking out the intuitive insight** in some appropriate way before "running with it".

On another aspect — to consciously improve your ability in receiving intuitive impressions, here is an important principle that is worth considering. Just knowing about this will not help very much, but there are books and courses of instruction that can expand on it, and later essays here will touch on it also. It is not simple to do and it takes much effort. A teacher helps.

It was mentioned in the Edison essay that we can deliberately build a "data base" in our subconscious mind. But in addition to that, we also normally accumulate, especially early in life, impressions that dissolve into a "glob" deep in our subconscious mind. This can become a thick layer of thoughts mulling around <u>beneath the level of our awareness</u>, and apparently it is "thicker" and more troublesome in some people than in others. Memories of guilt and remorse are traditionally thought to be especially painful. In addition, trauma of all kinds in childhood can hurt long after the causative event has been forgotten.

The higher teaching of religion says that this layer is **one** factor that separates us from our deep inner selves — the "Know Thyself" part of ourselves — the very place within our being that is in contact with God. And so methods are taught to:

- temporarily punch through this layer, as we might do anyway in any emergency. This might also be useful in attempts at spiritual healing, for example.
- work over a period of time to permanently reduce the thickness or tightness of this layer. Such a course of action is a common part of religion, and can be done know- ingly as it is done in some groups, or just talked about as in other groups.

In many religious groups, the method used to lighten up this burden of memories is to willingly "confess one's sins, be forgiven by a compassionate deity, change one's erroneous ways for the future, forget and go on." If a person thinks that he or she doesn't have any "appreciable" sins, some can usually be pointed out for them by friends, co-workers or spouse.

A secular approach is more like Socrates admonition "that an unexamined life is not worth living". And the secular approach through "depth psychology", or some such, does not have the con- notations of "good and evil" that has become so wrapped up in the religious approach. This has put off a lot of people in our present society who might otherwise give up some of their so-called evil (negative thoughts and memories) and adopt a little more of the so-called "good".

Another factor that separates us from our deep inner self is the Western habit (as opposed to India, for example) of looking outward into the physical world rather than looking inward some of the time, as the teaching of Jesus advises us to do in the four Gospels. With the advent of 24 hour entertainment via television and its many electronic derivatives, we can spend all of our leisure hours effortlessly looking outward. And with the typical goal that so many have of enjoying (or satiating) the stimulation of physical senses, we can completely obliterate any awareness of a deep inner self. To do so, however, is our own loss of a greater life.

Those aspects of life are easily lost today that were possible, say, to a shepherd of ancient times guarding his flock under the dome of blazing stars on a pitch black night of desert-dry air. Such an environment can be conducive to the <u>deep double solitude</u> of being alone only with one's self and God. For most of us, any such environment is rare today — sad to say.

The uncomfortable part of working on one's self in this manner is that some submerged memories might be very painful, and if brought to light, can upset a life that is functioning at a tolerable level. And there **are** those who should either be under the guidance of an expert or "just leave well enough alone" when it comes to working on or with their subconscious feelings and memories. Use good sense, especially if "teaching" others about it.

But for the rest of us "level headed people" ---- this is why we should look more deeply into religion (or the secular approach that addresses the same concepts) than the average person ever does in our Western Culture. The benefits are many.

And when done, even a little bit can improve our intuition.

Table of Contents

Levels of Understanding [1]

In Spiritual Matters, there are many levels of understanding — WLH

There was a lull in the auction. So I spoke to the Amish man near me.

We were at a farm auction, in Geauga County, Ohio where there is a sizable Amish community. Normally, the Amish stick to themselves, but an auction is almost a festive occasion in their lives and I apparently did not seem intimidating.

"Are you a builder?", I asked because I noticed that he was not bidding on any of the farm equipment. Traditionally farmers, some Amish men had gone into building houses and barns, logging and even cheese making.

"Blacksmith" he said, and after a short pause, added "I don't shoe horses."

Man and boy I had loved working with metals and although I had studied metallurgy, I thought I might pick up some practical tips from the blacksmith.

So I said, "Do you ever harden steel by dropping it red hot into water?", a basic operation, but tricky to do on a blacksmith level.

"Heard about that – tried it – didn't work", he said as though he was saving words for some other occasion.

Without thinking, I began explaining, "You probably had low carbon steel, but you need high carbon steel like a buggy spring if you want to harden it." Buggy springs he knew, but carbon he didn't. From his expression I saw that this was over his head. After all, the Amish go to school only to the sixth (some areas to the eighth) grade and consider that to be enough. It does not include the subject of chemistry or things like carbon.

Then the dumbest thought occurred to me. Fortunately I didn't say it or he might have thought I was crazy. But I intended to say, "You know the black soot that gets on the inside of a lamp chimney from a smoky wick — that's carbon. And the more of it that is in steel, the harder the steel can be." It dawned on me just in time that – to me the black soot on the lamp is nearly pure carbon. But to him – soot on a lamp chimney is just soot.

1. I have used the properties of metals here for an analogy. If this is an unfamiliar subject for you, just skip to the last two pages to see the purpose of this essay. Then maybe come back and skim from the beginning, if you like.

63

The auction resumed; he moved away. This blacksmith was working with steel on a low level. You heat it red hot. It gets pliable. You hammer it into a useful shape. That's it. Period.

I have thought of this incident many times over the years and finally realized that my understanding of metals on several different levels would be a marvelous analogy (for me and other engineers at least) of other things that might be understood on more than one distinct level.

My father worked with metals on a higher level than the blacksmith. He became a self-taught metallurgist. Let's call this **Level Two** of working with metals; the blacksmith being **Level One**.

In metallurgy, the study of the crystalline structure of metals is all important. One technique is to polish a small sample, of steel for example, then etch the surface with acid. This would make the crystalline structure visible under a microscope. By analyzing this, heat treatments can be improved to make steel stronger, better casting methods can be developed, etc. Much progress in the usefulness of metals was made during the Twentieth Century with the science of metallurgy.

Level Three

When I was in high school physics class, we studied the atomic structure of matter. This was a new science at the end of the 19th century but was beginning to be better understood and led to the development of atomic energy. When I mentioned this higher level of understanding in connection with metals, Dad didn't think that this was "necessary". After all, you can't even see an atom with the most powerful microscope. However, <u>visualizing</u> metals on the atomic level has led to the development of semi-conductors and all of the electronic wizardry that has come from that. It has enabled metal alloys to "be designed" rather than discovered by chance, one of them being a magnetic material more powerful by far than any previous material.

Level Four

Scientists began working on the sub-atomic level. They "imagined" (how else can you describe it) that atoms of matter, metals included, are constructed of incredibly small charged particles, the particles being held together by electrical attraction. And that a heavy metal, like some types of uranium, can be broken down with a conversion of part of it to a tremendous amount of energy. On the basis of this science, atomic power plants operate. And new elements that did not exist in nature, such as plutonium (a mixed blessing at best), have been created.

Level Five

A part of science that is still rather vague; scientists say that these tiny sub-atomic particles (as many as 26 different kinds or shades of them) that form the atoms are really just <u>energy in a "congealed form"</u>. Note that in the case of looking at metals as presented here, that each and every level under-

64

standing has a usefulness of its own for the particular need at hand. All are "good" and all are "correct". But what has all of this got to do with our daily life and especially our spiritual life. Plenty! When seen as an example of an analogy, even if it's a complicated analogy.

As I said, it is an analogy. And the purpose of an analogy is to more easily understand the unfamiliar by seeing similarities with something that is familiar. It is commonly pointed out that analogies are normally "imperfect".

There are many things in life that can be seen on different levels of understanding, just as I have outlined in the above study of metals. But in much of education, we learn more and more about a subject, but usually on the same level of understanding..

Notice in my analogy that each higher level delves **deeper** in understanding. **The only thing given up in going to the next level is the idea that you "already understand it all"** when you are on any particular level. Understanding on a higher level may not be easy. And in the matter of the spirit, God is probably the only entity that "sees" all levels of the subject. We "see through a glass darkly" as St Paul said, [2] but we can progress a **long way** even as Paul did.

But imagine trying to explain to that Amish blacksmith that, on some level of understanding, the hard steel with which he works is nothing more than electrical charges. The Amish do not accept electricity anyway, and he most certainly would believe that somehow you are associated with the Devil or were just plain crazy.

And if you tried to explain that the hard steel is actually made up of separate atoms that are too small to be seen even with a powerful microscope, [3] he would simply ask, "How do you know that they are there?" And would go away satisfied in his logic, again sure that you were associated with the Devil for even saying such blasphemous things.

In our secular schools, from kindergarten, through grade school, high school, college and graduate work, we are very familiar with the basic idea of levels of education. And that the lower teachings must be learned first in order for the higher teachings to be understood. Eventually we see that the higher levels can be immensely higher than the beginning levels.

However in much of our church and religious teaching, the idea that there may be many levels of understanding seems to be overlooked. For example, if you attend Bible study class, you just absorb more and more of the Bible stories without realizing that there may be many levels "deeper" than

2. First Corinthians 13:12
3. Outline of some molecules are now being seen in the laboratory, maybe atoms will be seen someday.

just the literal interpretation of the stories. Or that the real purpose of the story is to teach a "deep" meaning, rather than merely relating an event that happened long ago. As in the above analogy of "seeing" the various levels-of-understanding of ordinary metals — so in this collection of essays, I have tried to convey that there are many levels of understanding of spiritual truth. And that a person **can** delve more deeply than most will **ever** do, if he or she chooses to do so.

Now just as each level of understanding has a usefulness in the world of metals, so it is with spiritual understanding. Each level has a usefulness for the particular need at hand.

It helps to think of levels when you run across this situation in your spiritual studies. If you read something that is written at your existing level of understanding, it "makes good sense". But the ideas in a book written at a lower level will seem simplistic, whereas ideas at a higher level might not make any sense at all. Teachers help to bridge the gap to the next higher level of understanding, and they are invaluable. They make the "too-simple" seem like much needed review, and what you already know, they reinforce. Then you are ready for the new stuff that may be strange and puzzling at first.

Without the teacher, there is a strong tendency to stick with what is already understandable — what is comfortable. This is especially true in spiritual studies where the great sages of history ask us to change the basis of our thinking from the physical world to the world of the spirit — an incredible jump in itself for most of us. Even a small change in this direction, however, begins to make the Bible and other spiritual literature come alive in their true meaning.

If you are puzzled by the foregoing analogy based on the subject of metals, **here is the same idea** with a more familiar subject — a living person. We can view a person in their everyday outward appearance. We could call that 'level one'. With a little medical knowledge, we can think of the person as having internal organs, several complex systems, skeleton, etc. That would be 'level two'. In recent years, medical research is looking at the body on the cellular and even molecular level. That would be 'level three'. And if we have some spiritual insight, we can view the person as a soul of spirit made in the image of God.[4] That would be 'level four'. Again, the purpose of this "living person" analogy is to point out that there are levels in the world of the spirit that vary from the simple to the most profound.

Why is the realization of levels so useful — so important to our thinking?

As pointed out, many things in the world, many things in life — and most important — many things in the world of the spirit can be understood on more than one level. Yet many people will see only the surface. And on the surface of things, people tend to interpret life's endless controversies as "this or that" arguments. They might say that "it" has to be one or the other. On a basic level, such controversies can not be resolved — so sides are chosen for a standoff.

4. My spiritual teacher could actually see students in the class as souls of spirit if he chose to do so.

66

But from a higher level — that is, a higher perspective — the "this or that" argument often resolves itself. By "looking down" from a higher level, you might see that both sides are right and that they are "just opposite sides of the same coin" in the total scheme of things. But those still thinking on the lower level will never come to agreement. Even shooting wars can bring annihilation without bringing agreement.

Stated as a general principle: Controversies on a particular level of understanding can often be resolved only when viewed from a higher level.

Example:

In reading the Bible, many people make a literal interpretation — they say that scripture "says what it means and it means what it says." Their church might insist on just that interpretation. And so they might argue at school board meetings, in politics, etc. that such an interpretation is the correct one, the only correct one. And they will live their lives based on an interpretation at that lowest level.

Still, the Bible and particularly the New Testament has deep shades of meaning beyond the literal reading. And the higher the levels (that is, the deeper insight) that a person can understand, the fewer are the controversies in his or her mind about the world of the spirit, as well as other things. **Life is better with less inner conflict and fewer unresolved thoughts since our inner spiritual level affects the physical level of our daily lives — profoundly so.**

At the highest level, there is only God and so (I would imagine) there should be no controversy or ambiguity there. We can strive to become closer to that level, to some degree at least.

We will look at several 'things of the spirit' on different levels in coming essays. It is part of increasing our spiritual consciousness.

Sorting Knowledge — Especially One's Own

An unexamined life is not worth living — Socrates [1]

It is as true today as it has been for centuries. Most people (including myself from time to time) have a muddled mixture in their minds of:

beliefs, fantasies, real facts, pseudo-facts and emotions.

Very few people care to even try to sort out this mixture or to even see that there could be some benefit in doing so. Many (including myself at one time) might even feel insulted if it is pointed out that they don't have everything exactly clear and straight. In fact many people become angry just at the suggestion, some extremely angry.

Apparently, that's what happened in Socrates' day. In the study of philosophy, I never felt very confident about the details of what Socrates said or meant. He never wrote anything. We know of his teaching only from what Plato and others wrote about him.

"He was not good looking, but his friends knew that he was glorious within," Plato said, "the most upright man of that day." [2]

"He was a man of deep piety and believed himself charged with a mission from God to make his fellow men aware of their ignorance and of the supreme importance of what is for the Soul's good." [3]   That is, "he did not suffer fools gladly". Wow. How to lose friends!

He questioned beliefs that were considered normal and common sense of that day, and he apparently did not do this in a kindly or patient manner. Naturally, the authority figures hated him. Nobody likes to be told that his ideas are wrong, inadequate or inferior. No wonder Socrates was tried by a court and condemned to death "for disturbing the youth". Obviously the elders were disturbed more than the youth.

But it is wise to examine one's own beliefs. And "Socrates had to admit that he was wiser than others just because he alone was aware of his own ignorance." [4] His words quoted at the top of the page seem to be addressed to individuals and that is where the greatest benefit can occur. In today's complex society, with its heavy demands on our intellectual abilities, sorting one's knowledge can help in almost everything we do.

1. Socrates of Athens   b about 470 BC. d 399 BC Philosopher, teacher, political critic.
    Encyclopedia. Britannica.   2, 3 & 4 Quoted from the Encyclopedia Britannica.

Even so, the following ideas are not meant for everyone:

- not meant for people who live primarily for physical activity in work and in recreation, satisfying as that sort of life may be for many.
- not meant for those who live primarily in their emotions as many do.

It can be of great usefulness, however, for those who base their lives on an intellectual understanding of the world, life in general and their own life in particular.

It can be of special benefit to those few who pursue a deep understanding of religion— that is, the true meaning underlying religion as contrasted with the outward forms.

The idea presented here comes from the teaching of Dr. Thurman Fleet. [5] He may have been influenced by Socrates and others. But the standard philosophy books that I have read treat these ideas in vague generalities with no real thought of using the wisdom of Socrates in one's own life. Dr. Fleet, on the other hand, teaches the following method in some detail. I have found this method to be useful in my life as will be explained. It does take some effort, however, and many people may not see the wisdom in it or care to do it on a continuing basis.

- - - - - - - - - - - -

We all live by our basic beliefs; there is no other choice. Different countries have varying sets of beliefs, ethnic groups have sets of beliefs and sociologists study them because there are these differences, often big differences. Yet to the individuals that are brought up in these various belief systems, immersed in them from a young age, they seem to be right despite the fact that members of other religions, other countries may think differently.

In a similar way, families have sets of beliefs to live by, the accumulated family wisdom, covering many aspects of daily life: work ethics, religion, interpersonal relationships, etc.

I began to notice when I was growing up that kids from other families had considerably different beliefs from what I was being taught. And some families seemed to have much better belief systems than others. The homogenizing effect of television, good books on every conceivable subject, better schools and the Internet had not yet arrived.

5. Dr. Thurman Fleet. b 1895 d 1983 Chiropractor, writer, teacher. Founder of the "Concept Therapy Institute", San Antonio, TX

Just as an example:

> During summer vacation from grade school, we kids spent a lot of time at the beach. Sunburn was a problem. Sun screen lotions and tanning oils had not yet come on the market. My mother cautioned my brother and me to expose our pale skin for short periods to gradually "get a tan"; avoid getting burned. Some of the other kids were operating on a different idea. They were taught that, with their fair skin, they had to get sunburned, put up with the pain, let the damaged skin peel, and then there would be a tan underneath. (Decades later, some still believe this.)

> Since my mother was a Registered Nurse, I was sure that her/my method was correct. Oddly enough. the other kids thought that their idea was correct. At that time, no one was concerned about long-term skin damage because no one knew. We were going on beliefs, not on fact. But facts are obviously better than beliefs, if they are available. But even without facts, some beliefs may be better than others.

If a person compares some of his own family beliefs with those of other people, he might find that many of them are just concepts that he has been brought up with. But some families certainly have better beliefs than others as in the sunburn story above. And that better beliefs can make for a better lifestyle. But there is more!

Francis Bacon, English statesman, philosopher and essayist [6] said that knowledge is power and that knowledge is the force that drives history. But at one point in his life, he lamented that he "had all this knowledge and would now have to find out how much of it was true". So he began to classify his knowledge into three categories.

I don't find Bacon's classifications to be very useful and won't mention them here. Incredible progress has been made since his day, some due to his genius. So we can see things from a different perspective now. But his idea that knowledge should be examined is still basic.

The categories that Dr. Fleet taught are simple, to the point and useful to everyone.

What you know to be:	FACT
What you hold as:	BELIEFS or THEORIES
What you have found to be:	FANTASY

I have added for myself:	FEELINGS or EMOTIONS that could color the above.

A grand purpose of an intellectual life is — to sort one's personal knowledge according to these categories — by whatever means are available over a period of time. To examine one's beliefs and move them into the FACT category or into the FANTASY category, or if necessary, continue to hold them as beliefs till later.

6. Francis Bacon (1561 – 1626), From Lexicon Webster's Dictionary 1989 Lexicon Publishers, NY.

Fortunately it doesn't have to be done in a hurry or all at once. Once you get used to thinking in these terms, you can sort your store of knowledge as additional information or experience becomes available. Many things will turn up to help you see the distinction.

This idea is especially useful for a person engaged in spiritual studies in order to clarify religious beliefs — to distinguish factual knowledge that you really know from beliefs that you may have accepted "from authority" and mistakenly taken to be facts whether they actually are or not.

Now for the details:

FACT:

In your own thinking you can make the"fact" category as strict as you want. Dr. Fleet, in his thinking, was extremely strict. He said that if you would not be allowed to testify something in a court of law, it should not be fact to you. That is — anything that you know only as hearsay cannot really be considered to be fact.

The example he used was that he had never been to a certain foreign city. So a court of law would not allow him to testify that he "knew anything"of his own knowledge about that. Anything that he might have accepted about a foreign city from a book or geography lesson was "hearsay", actually a belief. I find that, only sometimes, is such a strict definition useful. But in those cases, it can be.

BELIEF or THEORY:

We all live our lives based more or less on our beliefs. Nothing wrong with that! Even research scientists shape their work according to the theory that might be true, hoping that their experimental efforts eventually might prove it to be true.

Examination of beliefs is especially important in religion. Many people "believe" that religious beliefs are the essence of religion. Not so! Beliefs are only a step along the way of learning. Eventually, many religious beliefs can be "turned into" religious facts, just in your own knowledge, of course. And you may eventually see some of your early beliefs to be fantasies. Hopefully, some of the essays in this collection will point the way. But to the first-time reader, they will, of course, be beliefs and theories. That's where we start.

FANTASY:

From childhood on, we continually discard our little-kid ideas as fantasy without even thinking about it. But things like Aesop's Fables and fairy stories, no matter how delightful or how useful in illustrating a point — are still fantasy. So is much of classical literature, of television, some of politics, some of economics, etc. In our serious thinking, when some part of a previously held belief is turned into fact, often some other part will drop away as fantasy. It can be simple and painless.

FEELING or EMOTIONS that could color the above.

As we absorb beliefs, we often have unconscious feelings connected with the incident. We should not allow such feelings to sway us to cling to non-useful beliefs or fantasies. Only you can be aware of this. Just because "my daddy tol' me" something does not make it fact.

Unlike Socrates, I don't feel that I have any mission to tell people, even friends, that they are mistaking beliefs to be facts. In fact, years ago I couldn't even convince one friend that my engineering knowledge (I was an automotive engineer) was truer than his lunatic fantasy about his automobile. His belief was that his car couldn't run on a certain brand of gasoline because "it tightened the clutch". Brands of gasoline might not be identical, but they all do have to meet industry specs. So I gave up trying to convert anyone's "beliefs" to "fact".

I find the idea of "sorting knowledge" to be useful for myself. It would help the human race immensely if more people would do it. Isn't that pretty obvious?

One immediately useful tip from the idea of this essay is this observation:

> People, groups, or governments seldom argue facts. Most arguments are about beliefs. Dr. Fleet pointed that out. If one person (or one side in the argument) has the facts, he usually sees that it is pointless to argue with someone's mere belief. So the one with the facts usually just walks away, or "disengages". You have done just that on occasion, I am sure.

> When I feel that I want to argue with someone else's ideas, I realize that I am doing so from the basis of a belief, my belief. That takes the heat (my heat, at least) out of my argument. I can then examine my belief when I get a chance, and perhaps make some effort to prove or disprove it. Lacking that, I can still be aware that I am keeping it as a belief. It may be a useful belief or perhaps a belief that I just don't want to part with — just yet.

My thanks to Dr. Fleet for this great idea.

While my main interest in using this intellectual exercise is in the pursuit of my spiritual studies, it is surprising how it can also simplify "human relations".

Difficult to Change One's Beliefs

As explained in the previous essay, it can be useful to scan one's beliefs from time to time just to see if they have some basis in fact. This can be especially pertinent when we come up against another person's beliefs that might be in opposition to our own. Then we wonder, "Why is it so difficult for this guy to see the validity of MY belief?"

And then, "Why are people so reluctant to change their obviously wrong beliefs?"
A couple of such beliefs come to mind..

The Airplane Wing Theory

As the early airplane developed, people who were interested in that sort of thing wondered how the wings produced a lifting force. There was an almost plausible explanation that was taught to WW One pilots and it was in all of the school books when I was in grade school. It was derived from a horrible misinterpretation of early scientific data and was taught as though it was valid. It was not! Aeronautical engineers must have cringed if they saw it.

Thankfully it died out and was replaced by an explanation that has lasted perhaps for 60 or 70 years. This too is wrong — almost totally wrong. Yet it was taught to WW Two pilots, student pilots ever since and high school kids. Even scientists at NASA believed it — one of them was a classmate of mine from engineering college who stoutly defended the theory.

You may have studied it too, so I won't go into a lot of details. Briefly it says that the wing shape is curved on the upper surface and flat (or flatter) on the bottom. At one time, many airplanes, large and small, were designed with a wing section, called a "Clark Y", like this:

The particular shape was developed by Verginious E. Clark in 1922 and does have good flying characteristics for moderate speeds. [1] And it had space for internal structure that did away with the previous external bracing wires, eliminating the drag in the air that the wires produced. The "explanation" says that airflow "has" to go faster over the longer upper surface than on the shorter flat lower surface. And that this difference in speed produces lift according to known scientific principles. (Bernouli's theorem, if you want to look it up) That is, supposedly it is the particular cross-sectional shape of the wing structure that is necessary to produce the lift that supports the plane in flight. This effect alone might produce a slight amount of lift, but never enough to get off the ground. The big lift comes from forcing air downward due to the "angle of attack" of the wing.

1. Wikipedia entry on Clark Y airfoil

I first heard of this explanation when I was in the seventh grade and I knew instantly that it was not correct. Why? Because such a wing can fly inverted? I had been to many air shows and had seen planes of this design (which were common in that era) and they flew inverted, did loops and other incredible aerobatics. The flat bottom wing produced upward lift even though the flat was on the upper side. Even a kid could disprove a scientific-sounding explanation!

This explanation might sound very plausible, but only if you had never seen inverted flight.

Let me digress a little here to describe just such a stunt at "The National Air Races" in Cleveland, Ohio many years ago. At one end of the runway two men, each holding a long bamboo fishing pole, stretched a string high in the air across the runway. On the string was a hanky. The announcer said that the pilot had a hook on the wing tip of his biplane and would try to snag the hanky. We were to hold our breaths, of course. Along came the plane inverted, flying the length of the field with the pilot's head "almost scraping the ground". He then "rolled out" attempting to catch the string and the hanky with the hook while the wings were vertical.

He missed. A nearby spectator said, "they always miss the first time just to make you think it's hard to do." Good grief. It was hard to do! The second pass was successful and I thought, "what a risk just for an air show, and for those guys holding the poles too". But it did burn into my young mind that a flat bottom wing can fly just as well inverted, even if not as efficiently. Later I saw the parked airplane up close. The hook was a wire coat hanger that was stuck to the wing with tape. As a little kid, I mused that two poles, a string, a hanky and a coat hanger were all that was needed to do the stunt, if you had a plane, the skill and desperation enough to try it!

Oddly enough, it was Louis Bleriot, French aviation pioneer, who wondered what would happen if his plane "tipped over" as boats tip over. Wouldn't the wing that mysteriously produced lift in the normal manner then pull the airplane down? He had just flown a history making flight across the English Channel in 1909. So he then fitted a plane with seat belts so he could try inverted flight at a safe altitude. Alas, his wife pointed out that he was father of several children and would not be doing any more flying. So he hired what was probably the first professional test pilot who found that he could indeed fly inverted, loop and do other tricks — even with a primitive airplane and without the safety of a parachute that had not yet been developed for the airplane.

Now to the point:

When I was taking flying lessons, I would listen to the "hangar flying" that pilots and mechanics would do in the hangar after work. I hoped to pick up some useful tips. Eventually someone did bring up the "flat-bottom-wing theory of flight" as though it was the true explanation for how an airplane can fly. By that time I knew that many airplanes had wings with the **same identical curvature on the top and bottom surfaces,** the B-17 bomber of WW Two for example; thousands of them were built. There were no flat sides on their wings. Same for the P-51 fighter plane.

By this time the old flat bottom wing theory should have been forgotten, but the hangar flyers were still believing it. I introduced myself as a fledgling student who hadn't even soloed yet (therefore could not know much about flying). But I just casually wondered out loud, "How can the flat bottom wing fly inverted?"

Would they be willing to consider that? Perhaps question the old theory in their own mind? Perhaps discuss the need for a better theory that might actually explain what we had all seen. Did not happen! No way—

The pilots and the mechanics were furious that I had exposed the flaw in their belief. They jumped up and ran out. That was the end of my hangar flying. I did not dare go back. Such a change in belief was too abrupt for them to make in just one sitting. And of course, no one likes to be proven wrong, and in this case by such a simple and air-tight proof given by a "nobody".

As similar situations have arisen over the years, I have tried to be more gentle and gradual in mentioning the fallacy. Still I haven't met anyone willing to even consider the shortcomings of the old theory. Most have become angry. Such is the difficulty of changing one's beliefs. The sad part is that the true explanation of flight is so very simple and applies to all wing shapes.

My Spiritual Teacher Did It Better

When I have a belief, sometimes even a treasured belief, that has been questioned in the glare of someone else's greater knowledge, or their greater understanding or even a contrary belief, I try to learn from the experience. Easier said than done. It is not always comfortable, especially in matters of spiritual belief. Still, I try to train myself to at least consider, rather than reject out of a habitual reflex as I might have done in the past.

But my teacher [2] gave me this valuable experience:

One day, he explained something in class that apparently conflicted with my existing understanding. At the recess I asked him to explain it further. He could see that I was troubled by the new idea that he had presented.

Rather than launching into any explanation, he just asked, "How do you see it now?
I proudly explained how I understood the matter and he agreeably said,

        "That's a good way to see it ---------------- for now."

2. The teacher is described in the earlier essay: "Reverend Edward L. Crump and Katherine Calhoun"

His timing was perfect. The pause allowed me to puff up a bit for a second or two at my "learned discourse". And the hesitated "------ for now" was a nice way of implying that I was holding onto a shallow understanding, but that he was going to allow me to keep it as long as I wanted to keep it.

I immediately realized that my purpose for being in the class was to raise my understanding with the help of the teacher who had a greater understanding. Why not accept his more lofty vision? By not going over the class work again during the recess, he had "sacrificed" that particular lesson in order to teach me a greater lesson, knowing that I would eventually learn what I needed.

Still, he had mentioned right at the beginning of the course that students in the class should just skip over any troubling thoughts. They could be considered later if desired.

So I am saying here:

If there is any thing in these essays that you find troubling, just skip over it. Hopefully there will be many such sticky questions as we get into the deeper aspects of spirituality.

Consider them again later if you care to. Sometimes a difficult new concept does not seem so daunting after you have learned other things that round out the whole idea.

Useful Attitudes

Whenever I am wondering about my own concept of God or when I am discussing concepts of God with others, these four "attitudes" or "ways at looking at things" have been very useful. And the "attitudes" can be useful in discussing other aspects of religion too. I have them in my mind ready ahead of time, although I sometimes get caught off guard and maybe forget one or more.

1. The word "belief" as it is used in religion is similar in meaning to the word "theory" that is used in science. Both of these words describe situations in which the actual facts are not yet known. Both the religious belief and the scientific theory provide a working hypothesis for the purpose of further study or investigation. And both in science and religion, seemingly different or even conflicting beliefs and theories can sometimes be useful. But believing is not the same as knowing, just as a scientific theory is not the same as proven fact. And these two levels of thought should not be confused with each other as we saw in the earlier essay "Sorting Knowledge".

2. Whatever concept we may hold of God, or that others may hold, must of necessity be limited and fall far short of the total reality.

    God is considered to be infinite. And it is difficult — actually impossible — for a finite human mind to grasp anything that is infinite. Or to imagine a picture image of an infinite "being".

3. Most individuals who "believe in God" hold a partial concept of that portion of the Infinite God that seems plausible to them, or that fulfills some human need of their personality. For example, "you are in good hands" of God or "God will show us the way", or that God has gender as 'He' in Christianity [1] and 'She' in some other religions.

Recall the earlier essay about the blind men and the elephant.

1. The Hebrew language of Biblical times had only two genders, masculine and feminine. Their patriarchal society chose HE rather than SHE as the gender of their God concept. Perhaps their God might have been named IT if there had been neuter gender in the language. In modern times, some do think of God as IT.

3. (Continued) In our limited comprehension of God, most of us are like these blind men. Each of us has a limited personal perspective, not necessarily because we are "blind" in some way or other, but that we are all limited in our direct experience. With only a limited or slight contact with the spiritual side of the Universe, we "see through a glass darkly" as St. Paul described it.[2] But our individual egos might cause most of us to defend our own limited concept of God as being the totality.

Oddly enough, those few people who have been closest to God in their direct experience are the very ones who argue the least about the nature of God. (I have met a few such people at religious events over the years.)

4. In the course of one's lifetime, a person can strive to enlarge his or her concept of God to make it closer to the reality of God.

   Enlarging one's concept means "giving up" an existing limited belief. And most people hate to give up any of their basic ideas, even for a greater one. Consequently, most of us are stuck with the limited concepts that we were taught as children. And the more basic and important that the ideas are, such as our concept of God, the more we tend to cling to what we have already.

The best way for most of us is to modify our ideas gradually based on increased knowledge. This appears to be easier for some to do than for others, but I have not found it to be any easier for myself than it is for most.

2. First Corinthians 13:12.

Symbolisms

Authentic religion teaches profound spiritual truths.

These truths are taught using <u>symbolisms</u> because there is no other way to teach them.

The trick for the spiritual seeker is to recognize the truths without getting hopelessly tangled up in the symbolisms.

Real authentic religion
contains a bunch of spiritual truths wrapped up in a bunch of symbolisms.

There seems to be no other way to express or to teach these truths except by means of symbolisms. The process for the teacher or the writer is to bring ethereal, intangible truths of the spirit to the minds of people who normally live in the physical world, and are accustomed to seeing only tangible things with their own eyes. This is especially so when the truths are to be conveyed by writing — in Scripture, for example.

If you have a strong desire to know: —

The trick is to learn what the truths are without getting hopelessly tangled up in the symbolisms. Many people I have known, and myself included at times, cannot get beyond the symbol to the truth and are not encouraged to even try to do so by their church or their belief group. Only by realizing in the beginning that the symbols are just symbols can one expect to see beyond. More about this in the essay "One Little Word" coming up later, still in Section 2.

A good bit of the Bible and essentially all of the New Testament is about man and God and the possibility of "man's oneness with the Father". There are also some obscure metaphors, obscure passages in the Bible that have been interpreted in many ways by various writers, by various church groups. If you, in your studies, interpret this type of passage in the light of the main theme, that is, "man's oneness with the Father", then the interpretation is more likely to be accurate.

It also seems to me that there is an evolution of thought and belief all through the Bible. This has been pointed out by others too. The continuing story goes from the chronicle in the Old Testament of a primitive people who sacrificed animals to propitiate a fierce God — to a God of love in the New Testament giving unearned grace to a wayward humanity if they would only accept it.

Although the great truths apparently were taught in the stories of the Old Testament, where are the teachers today who can explain what the stories were meant to teach?

We now have this New Covenant with the teaching of Jesus. Why should we bother with the old obsolete covenant? There are wonderous "advanced concepts" that Jesus taught that won't be spelled out in detail in this essay. But they are in the Gospels.

These "wonderous teachings" are, for the most part, overlooked in our churches today for two reasons, at least:

1. Until a "holy person" appears, who can actually demonstrate the reality of these things — to some degree at least — it all seems unreal and long ago.

2. Those few people who might understand the reality of it — to some degree at least — find it too steep a path to climb in its fullness. So churches must work on the level of their congregations or they would lose all of their members.

It is said that in ancient times, some few devout Jews had great spiritual knowledge. They kept it a closely guarded secret from the barbarous people of those times. This knowledge may well have been similar to the ideas I have expressed above.

These secrets were to be conveyed only to a righteous man at the proper time when complete trust and worthiness had been established: [1]

> In a lonely place
> In the dark of night
> In a quiet voice
> With mouth to ear

Jesus came to teach these very secrets (some of them anyway) to a larger group of people. But not to everyone in the crowds listening to him, which is why he spoke in parables so that "only those who had ears to hear" could really understand. Then He pointed out to his disciples that He spoke straight out to them. And Bible scholars have wondered ever since whether this 'straight out' instruction got written into the scriptures. Whether it did or not, the instruction is still available.

---

1. From the secret mystic doctrine of the Jewish "Kabbalah". Encyl. Of Religion Verginius Ferm. There are several different spellings for Kabbalah currently in use.

I have found that these so-called secrets, ancient though they may be, are not so secret anymore (some of them anyway). And people long before me knew this to be true and guided me and many others through the years. But the "secrets" are available today only for those who are willing to look for them and to strive for them. There is an interesting story that illustrates this point in the essay "Greatest Secret - Greatest Revelation" on page 123. There are still lots of people who do not care to know the "secrets", or don't know that they exist, or prefer to direct their minds to more "worldly things".

Nothing wrong with that. "Each to his own way" as they say. Jesus allows it [2]

2. In Revelations 22:11   Please look this up. Many devout church people do not "buy" this idea at all. They feel that they must proselytize anyone that they encounter, even to those who do not want to hear it.

Preface to the Ancient Wisdom

Let's jump ahead, a little out of order, with the next three essays about the Ancient Wisdom. Some authors would put such important chapters at the end of their book with lots of details guiding the reader gradually to the understanding of it.

I like it closer to the beginning in case you don't read the entire book. If it is too tedious, you might skip some of it and return later. And if it seems too unreal in places, skip over that too.

The several groups with which I studied each had their own particular expression of the great truths. Some were couched in old classical biblical language and some were in a more modern idiom. It was only after some years of study that it became apparent to me that each of the study groups had parallels of expression with each other for the same truths. When teaching truth, how could it be otherwise? **Truth is seamless.** But at first look, they appeared to be talking about totally unrelated subjects. And some writers even pretended that they had some exclusive new truth never before revealed to humanity. Not true, although they may have had great new insights for expressing the old truths.

After a while, the different approaches began to gell into a really coherent understanding — not a compilation of unrelated ideas that I might have selected along the way to put together a "new religion" — rather they were different ways of expressing the same basic truths.

It then took another while for the various **symbolisms** that had been learned to be "allowed to step aside" to reveal their hidden true meanings in the world of spiritual reality.

I finally realized that I was studying something called "The Ancient Wisdom" and was trying to understand it in a coherent manner that was connected to reality.

So I am inserting three essays on this great subject at this point to give a glimpse of what all the rest of the essays hopefully lead to. You can refer back to them many times if you like, because there is a lot of substance in them. I know it is more than I could have grasped in just a few readings. But then again, I started with a scientific mentality rather than natural spiritual insight that some people are blessed with.

And you might choose to check other sources for confirmation as you go. I do not expect any reader to believe everything (or anything) written here just because it is written here. It really requires the tentative attitude of the researcher rather than just unquestioning acceptance of what you read or are told.

The Ancient Wisdom

There is an unusual body of knowledge that has been known since ancient times.

It is called by various names — "The Ancient Wisdom", "The Wisdom of the Ages" and "The Ageless Wisdom".

It is about the relationship between the individual person (like you and me) and God. It has also been described as the connection between man and the 'world of the spirit' or the 'domain of the spirit'.

It is not ordinary stuff!

It is not the usual folksy platitudes that are frequently described as 'wisdom'.

According to "those who know", this knowledge was kept secret by priesthoods and small groups 'in the know' for some thousands of years. Maybe so. But there have also been writings about it from antiquity for those who cared to study it. And it is extremely important to the human race that it be properly understood. It is equally important that it not be misunderstood.

Millions of people world-wide still see it in terms of superstition, awe and fear. But it need not be that way for anyone willing to study the teachings of the great prophets.

The Ancient Wisdom is the underlying basis of all true religion. However, religions have tended to surround the teaching of the Ancient Wisdom with rituals, beliefs of various sorts, ceremonies and long histories of events connected with their particular group. A spiritual seeker can get lost in irrelevancy; interesting stuff perhaps but not the heart of the teaching.

Portions of the Ancient Wisdom have permeated our culture over a period of many centuries. So there are many people teaching bits and pieces of it, perhaps without being aware that they are part of this great teaching.

So here, in this essay, only an overview is described, with the belief that it might be beneficial for some people to be aware of the existence of the Ancient Wisdom, even though they might not choose to learn it to its full depth. But many may choose to go part way, at least, hopefully so.

The Ancient Wisdom has been taught in many different formats at different times to match the culture of the people. For example, the theme of it runs all through the ancient Jewish writings, part of which Christians see in the Old Testament. But I do not know of anyone who has actually been able to learn it directly from this source. Apparently a teacher and an oral teaching were needed to explain the written text. And would still be needed today. Fortunately, we now have clearer teachings with which to work and study.

The value and desirability of the Ancient Wisdom are referred to in the Old Testament in the Book of Proverbs, verses 3:13-18 [1] (paraphrased here)

> Happy is the man that finds wisdom
> And the man who gets understanding;
> For its benefits are better than the profits of silver,
> And the gain thereof than fine gold.
> It is more precious than rubies,
> And all the things that you can desire
> Cannot be compared to it.
> Length of days is in its right hand,
> And in its left hand riches and honor.
> Its ways are ways of pleasantness,
> And all its paths are peace.
> It is a tree of life to them that lay hold upon it.
> And happy is everyone that retaineth it.

And as frequently happens in the Bible, the lesson is repeated for emphasis, in this case in Proverbs 4:7-9 KJV —

> Wisdom is the principle thing;
> Therefore get wisdom.
> And with all your getting, get understanding,
> Exalt it and it will promote thee;
> It will bring you honor, when you embrace it.
> It will put on your head an ornament of grace;
> A crown of glory it will deliver to you.

Notice that these passages from the Old Testament promise something of incredible value — things that people today search and strive for in all sorts of other ways — often to find that they bring only temporary satisfaction or none at all.

1. The ancient Hebrew language, in which this was written, had only two genders, masculine and feminine. In these verses, "wisdom" is described as feminine. Since it sounds strange to our ears today, I have taken the liberty of converting it to neuter, as it would be written today, and paraphrasing some of the words. Although of no consequence in these verses, in some other parts of the Bible, a change in meaning might result from the ancient Hebrew "two gender" writing on our present-day "three gender ears". Book of Proverbs is said to have been written between the 10th and 6th century B.C. Obviously the wisdom that is described here is truly ancient!

Unfortunately few people today look in the direction of the Ancient Wisdom because it is not taught very well in our Western culture. But it can be learned — to some degree at least. And to whatever degree one learns it, it can give a perspective to evaluate the confusing thought and shallow "ministries" that are so prevalent on TV, the Internet and radio today.

Many people, especially in our Western culture, find the idea of a "world of the spirit" to be a strange concept — more imagination than anything else, while some others of "a more sensitive nature" might feel familiar with it in their own experience in church or in the quiet of nature.

Does it seem that something invisible might be of no consequence? An analogy or two might show a skeptic or a doubter the **possibility** of unseen things.

Consider radio waves. They surround us, carry information, even pass through our bodies and brains. Yet we cannot feel or even be aware of this entire "world of information" by ourselves. Seemingly ethereal, radio waves actually are real, "in their world", as we all know by our daily use of them.

Also consider the microscopic "plant and animal kingdom". Imagine the disbelief that ordinary people must have had when researchers with crude handmade microscopes discovered the existence of this incredible unseen world around us. And imagine the consternation among doctors and others when Louis Pasteur [2] showed that wine was made by microscopic creatures that could also spoil the wine, or make bread moldy, or cause disease in humans, tiny and invisible to the eye though they maybe. It **was** unbelievable that some **invisible** bacteria could "bring down" a huge man.

In a similar way, the world of the spirit seems to have a resemblance to the spectrum of radio waves once you strip away superstition, strange beliefs and misinformation from the uninformed.

An expanded analogy of the radio wave idea in connection with the world of the spirit is in the later essay titled "The Essence of the Teaching of Jesus". Please take a look, keeping in mind that analogies are only approximate — a way of 'sort of' getting the 'feeling' of some unseen concept.

Jesus came to teach the Ancient Wisdom in a new context to a larger group of people than the closed priesthoods of an earlier time. Whether you consider Jesus to be an emissary sent by

2. Antony Van Leeuwenhoek, 1632 - 1723, made simple microscopes of a single lens and on Sept. 17, 1683 "saw with great wonder" live microbes in the plaque from his teeth. Louis Pasteur, 1822 - 1895. studied processes of fermentation during period of 1860-64. Developed 'pasteurization' to stop fermentation. Discovered that some forms of yeast made wine, other forms spoiled it. Developed vaccines for rabies and anthrax. Demonstrated bacterial cause of some diseases, later confirmed by Koch.

God or to be a part of God itself, you will agree that He did do a magnificent job of teaching and demonstrating.

His stated purpose was so "that we might have life, and that we might have it more abundantly." [3] (that is, we might know spiritual life and benefit from its effect on physical life). So much so that He and his teaching have had more beneficial influence on the human race than any other person or teaching before or since. So the quotations from the Book of Proverbs cited above have come true to some extent.

> The Holy Bible is many things to many people.
> But its most basic, noble purpose, underlying all other
> uses, is as a textbook to teach this Ancient Wisdom.

Once a person is aware of the Ancient Wisdom, many of the so-called prophecies in the Old Testament seem to refer to the Ancient Wisdom coming to the individual rather than a prediction of the coming of Jesus as so many Christian Bible scholars believe. However, several passages in the Book of Isaiah, written about 750 BC, may refer specifically to the coming of Jesus [4].

It was this knowledge that enabled Jesus to actually do the miracles that are attributed to him. [5] And it is this **knowledge that could enable an individual to do the things today that He said that we would be able to do** — not only the things that He did — but "greater works than these shall he [we] do; because I go unto the Father." [6] More about this later.

Sad to say, people today think only of the magnitude of these incredible miracles and believe that they 'were allowed to happen' only during the Biblical era. Actually some pretty miraculous things are still done today, but are kept quiet or within small groups because of disbelief in such things in our Western culture, or worse — the possibility of antagonistic reaction by the uninformed out of fear. Lots of examples of this have occurred.

3. Paraphrased from John 10:10 KJV
4. One such is Isaiah 9:1-7. The virgin birth is predicted in Isaiah 7:14, although to me it is a rather hazy prediction as so many old time predictions were. You will interpret them according to your basic belief. I would not argue the point either way.
5. Some yoga masters in India have allegedly done miracles similar to those of Jesus, although none (as far as I know) ever claimed to return from the dead as Jesus did; however, they may have 'appeared' after death to their disciples. And Jesus giving sight to a man blind from birth, John 9:1-25, appears to be unique.
6. John 14:12 Please read the entire context as well as the particular verse.

Note that the **important factor** in these miracles, as attested to by Jesus, was the idea of **'going unto the Father'** whatever that means. And what it means is being able to contact the power and energy existing in the world of the spirit.

And the ability to 'go unto the Father' is the great secret of it all.

How to do it is what the teachings are about, whatever the particular idiom in which they are presented. There are many books to provide you with the details which are beyond the scope of this essay. And an authentic teacher is a God-send, but they are rare.

For a person trying to learn, it helps to "start small" just as in any field of endeavor, 'you learn to walk before you try to run'. There are small miracles happening daily from the 'workings of the spirit' that most of us don't realize. With understanding, more of these will become apparent. With understanding, more of the good can be brought into our lives. It is real!   More about the Ancient Wisdom in the next two essays.

More Ancient Wisdom - The Heavy Stuff

Sometimes, this subject is divided into what is called the 'lower teaching' and the 'higher teaching'. While there is some overlap between the two, there is a natural transition point from one to the other in the progress of a spiritual seeker that we do not have to define here.

Naturally a student begins with the lower teaching. But here we will look briefly at some of the higher teaching first since we are looking only for an overview.

One of the basic precepts of the Ancient Wisdom and also the teaching of Jesus is that:

A person is a soul of spirit residing in a physical body.[1]

That is: A person has a two fold nature. His or her **apparent** self is a physical body that can be seen by others. But even though the soul may be invisible to the eye, it is actually the real 'self' of the person. In other words: you **are** the soul — you **have** a body.

Many church teachings describe the inverse of this great truth. Since everyone can be aware that they have a body, it might "seem more real" if that is presented first and followed with the idea of "having a soul" because the soul seems rather etheric and intangible, and maybe even imaginary.

It is more accurate, however, to envision yourself as the soul and that you have a body. And a person can more easily understand the Ancient Wisdom, or any other spiritual idiom for that matter, from this perspective as stated above. It is a more profound perspective and can help a person in many aspects of life.

My teacher gave me the incredible experience of actually 'seeing' or becoming aware of my spiritual body. Although I cannot describe it here, I then knew for a fact that what Jesus taught and what St. Paul said is truly true — "There is a natural body, and there is a spiritual body" [1]

Some of the later essays explain this further. Suffice it to say: a 'spiritual master' might be able to see the soul of a prospective student. And some people are able to occasionally see just the outline of a person's spirit body when they observe a person's aura.

Yoga was one of the early forms of the Ancient Wisdom, perhaps three thousand years old. Although the words of Yoga may seem strange to our ears, coming from a distant and ancient culture, there are higher forms of Yoga that are a parallel to Jesus' teaching. The goals are identical even though some of the practices are different. Many Christians rush to deny this, preferring to

1. I Corinthians 15:44 KJV

believe that only they have **the** unique set of understandings and beliefs. But once you truly understand the teachings of Jesus as well as something about Kriya yoga or Raja yoga, you will see the similarities between these two great dispensations of God's spiritual knowledge.

Concerning the feelings of exclusivity that Jews might have, and that Christians might have:

> Think about it — "Is God's arm so short" [2] that He cannot teach Wisdom and extend salvation to more than just one little local sect (the Hebrews) on this great planet?

If you haven't heard these ideas before, it might take a while to digest the possibility that it might be true and it helps to have an experience or two so that you can begin to know. In any organized spiritual teaching, the pace is purposely made gradual. So just take a breath and remember that this essay is an overview just to show the existence of the ancient teaching and that there could be some great possibilities in your life if you choose to pursue them.

Another lofty idea of the Ancient Wisdom and also of the higher forms of Yoga is that:

> The purpose of life is to discover the divinity that is within one's self.

And that is **also the exact teaching of Jesus in the four Gospels!**

But you might laughingly say that none of your relatives or friends show any signs of divinity — within or without. You might even make a more derogatory appraisal of their worth even as human beings. That certainly is our perception with our limited (or more likely — non existent) spiritual vision. But Jesus **saw these things** which we cannot see; and spiritual masters, as well, see the divinity in people even today. That is one reason that they dedicate themselves in such a selfless manner to teach. But most of us can't look beneath the personality or the physical appearance of people to see the 'divinity' for the simple reason that we are not spiritual masters. We do not have spiritual insight to 'see' into the world of the spirit unless we spend the effort to develop it.

"Seeking one's own divinity", in Christianity or Yoga or other path, can sound as though a search for divine wisdom in one's self could be a selfish goal — pursued even for some sort of self-centered ego satisfaction. However, those few individuals who have actually accomplished this exalted level of existence — whatever "way" they have followed to get there — always seem to express an altruistic life. How could they do otherwise?

---

2. Paraphrased from the Old Testament, Numbers 11:23 KJV, a little out of context here.

There is more to this incredible teaching:

Find God — Teach Others

Traditional Yoga aphorism

This terse statement of spiritual purpose explains in four simple words what a person is going to do after his (usually long) personal struggle to attain the divine wisdom. It couldn't hurt to expand the idea a little as

First experience God yourself — Then teach others

Church and secular writings down through history have documented many cases of individuals who have done just that. Some are considered to be saints. How could these people not want to teach others? Knowing the greatest things that a person can know, could they keep it a secret to themselves?

They have learned the greatest secret, and like lighting one candle from another, sharing the knowledge does not diminish it in any way. However, you can be sure that a teacher does not disclose all of the secrets till the student's soul has evolved to the desire of being a "servant to humanity" rather than being a servant just to himself, or worse, having some evil intent.

Keep in mind, however, that even **part of the understanding of the Wisdom** can enrich a person's life (including your life) and the lives of those around him or her (you). Dedicated students of the Bible, in church, or on their own, often receive great insights about the world of the spirit, only to settle for a portion, not realizing that there is much more.

"Finding God" is certainly a strange sounding phrase. As is often pointed out: 'God is not lost — we are'. So "finding God" really means finding the connection within one's self to the "Father" that Jesus talked about [3] or another way of saying it — establishing such a connection.

This whole idea seems so distant and unattainable to most of us. Just trying to make a living takes so much of our time and energy, how can we even think of 'finding God'. Yet some few do, and many come close, and some very close, and they all do have a tremendous impact for good on the world.[4] And each one adds proof that the ancient teachings are valid!

3. See Luke 17:21 KJV. The King James Version has this verse correctly translated from the Greek. Some of the recent translations mislead on this. One of the most important sayings of Jesus wrong? Incredible! More about this in the essay on "Essence of the Teaching of Jesus" See also First Corinthians 3:16.

4. See Matthew 11:11 and Luke 7:2.

A reasonable course to pursue for a spiritual seeker brought up in a Western culture would be to study Jesus and western interpretations, but to also be aware (even if vaguely so) of Yoga in its higher forms in the Eastern tradition. And for a person brought up in an Eastern culture, best to study the higher spiritual teachings of that culture, but to also be aware of the teaching of Jesus.

Such an approach has three benefits (at least):

1. A particular idiomatic teaching of the Ancient Wisdom is shaped to the culture of the people being taught. It can seem to make more sense to them than some other teaching in a different idiom from some distant culture.

2. A view from two (or more) perspectives can help to interpret the symbolisms of one's own religious teaching in a correct way. Just as latitude plus longitude determines an exact position on the earth that either one alone does not. Remember my idea of "Cross Symbolism Congruence" from the essay "How Do I Know?".

3. Being aware that there is more than one valid "way" might reduce a person's egotistical belief that he is part of a divinely chosen group singularly selected to receive the instruction. The hindrance of egotism (and all that goes with it) has been pointed out in every known spiritual "way". It is included in the Beatitudes of Jesus. It is one of the central human characteristics to be overcome in a person's spiritual quest.

Keep in mind that we are talking about the essence of other religions, not just the descriptive level of the study of "Comparative Religions" that may mix in quaint 'folk' religion and false beliefs.

Some Christian authorities see this as a destructive process. They say that you are "forcing a combination of their true religion with an inferior pagan religion" Not so! We don't have to combine anything! We only need to see the real TRUTH in Christianity as it is shown to be the same real TRUTH in other teachings. Then TRUTH will truly prevail in our personal understanding; then we can actually prove it in our own life.

I suspect that 'authorities' of other religions might hold Christianity to be inferior to their own in a manner similar to the above paragraph. Such is the tribal allegiance of the human race.

To sum up this particular argument:

The Ancient Wisdom is the greatest teaching that human ears can hear. Jesus came to teach it. He did a great job because He could demonstrate it! Others have also come to teach it — but in other idioms. Enough said.

These things take much careful study. In the beginning few people understand that spiritual truths can be proven just as scientific truths are proven, although the methods of proof are not the same methods of proof that are used in science. Spiritual truth is more than just "religious belief" as so many of us have been taught; it can be demonstrated. Once this idea is accepted as 'possibly being true', a person can begin to study with a totally new and different perspective. Verses of scripture should eventually take on a deeper meaning.

God blesses anyone who sets foot on the "Path of Spiritual Attainment".

The Wisdom — A Place to Begin

In the previous two essays on the Ancient Wisdom, there are some pretty lofty ideas presented. They may seem to be totally out of this world. However, it is important to be aware of them, even though most of us have other duties and commitments that may make it impractical to pursue these lofty goals many hours of the day or to aspire to go all the way.

So here lets look at some of the simpler aspects of the Ancient Wisdom in the 'lower teaching' that can be immensely useful to everyone.

Sometimes this is called a "secret", but it's in the teaching of Jesus in the four Gospels if you look. It might sound simple, but it is profound and it separates the successful people in life who use it from the unsuccessful in life who don't.

The so-called secret:

1. A person is a creator "in life" by using his or her thoughts. That is, the thoughts that you hold frequently and **strongly** direct your life in general. Is this too farfetched to believe? Just daydreaming, however, does not do it, at least for anyone that I have known. Nowadays some untutored person might present this idea as his belief only to be laughed at for believing worthless superstition. But Jesus taught that you are vastly greater as a 'child of God' than most people can possibly imagine. And this process is part of it. The Gospels, however, do not expand the teaching with very much detail.

2. What you **strongly** and **consistently** think about now is creating some part of your future.

3. What you think about and feel strongly about attracts to you the things and situations that you think about. (This is more subtle than it might appear, more details later).

4. This process can be haphazard (as it is with most people) or it can be controlled to your everlasting benefit if you think correctly about things that are appropriate to you. This includes stopping thoughts that can be disadvantageous or even harmful to you.

Whether we like it or not, whether we believe it or not, this process is truly true and has been truly proven. It has apparently been used knowingly for millennia by a few. And it has been used unknowingly by the rest of us, sometimes to our great disadvantage.

Does this idea seem strange? Many people would think so. Why? Because it does not seem to match the experience of most people. The answer below:

It's true that this process has some 'heavy' implications that we might not like at first glance. It means that we have attracted and created the life that we presently have, to some extent at least. The person who considers his life to be 'messed up' usually would rather blame it on something else like "circumstances" or bad luck, and he would likely deny the validity of the whole idea. A typical human response (my own included at times).

And it takes away the randomness of why we have 'good luck' sometimes and 'bad luck' other times. So a comfortable superstition that absolves us of responsibility crumbles. There is an extension of the 'luck idea', commonly believed, that if you have had a seven-year run of bad luck, you are entitled to expect a seven-year run of good luck. And I have been told in great seriousness that a double-seven year, that is 14 years of bad luck, will bring a double-seven of good luck. How sad that people believe these things, especially when they don't match everyday experience.

Other people describe the 'events of life' as **fate**, whatever that means, or **Karma** accumulated from past lives [1], or **predestination**, Kismet, and even shallower vague explanations.

Psychologists explain why these seemingly inexplicable things happen to us. Important!

> In our early years, the subconscious part of our minds (often called the 'unconscious') does get programed with all sorts of things coming from training by our parents, interaction with siblings, our own observations from our surroundings (often times a misinterpretation from a child's limited perspective). Additionally, some children are traumatized by natural disasters, crimes committed against them and so on.

> As we grow, all of this 'dissolves' back in our subconscious mind as a basic 'feeling of life'. We forget the earliest details completely and tend to forget even the later ones unless they are traumatic.

Now note this, **because it unlocks a great mystery**. It has incredible value to the individual (you).

The psychologists who study this phenomenon point out that we tend to (choose to) do the things in our grown-up life that recreate this **general feeling** of our younger years, **not because it is beneficial to us but because it is familiar to us.** And because the events that are chosen later might be totally different from the early events, the **connection** between early years (**feeling of life**) and **events chosen later** has been missed until recent years. On the other hand, you can be sure that spiritual masters have seen this clearly for ages.

1. If you feel that accumulated Karma is affecting you, you can overcome it by the method explained here. But in our scientific culture, it is only when psychologists have made careful observations of many individuals over long periods that we will believe. In other words, only when it has been recently proven to our conscious minds will we believe what has gone on in subconscious minds for millennia.

Let me state this basic idea again:

We recreate in adult life the **feeling that was formed in early childhood**, not because it is good, but **because it is familiar**.

With some individuals, this behavior can be completely self destructive as we see in the daily news. Others are more fortunate. And some are blessed with beneficial early impressions.

We can see how important it is to form this 'good feeling of life' (not identical to 'self esteem') in a child. Parents not only create a new human body, but they also create the kind of psychological life that this little person will have for many years in the future. How sad that many parents overlook the terrible effect of some TV programs as they pour crap into a little mind that has not yet developed reasoning censorship. The image that the eyes see is what is retained — not the words. And there are many images on TV that are very destructive to a little kid's mind.

Important!

> The incredible thing about this understanding — this old knowledge of the spiritual masters — this same knowledge recently new to psychology — is that we can do something about it in our own lives by taking thought.

Many books have been written about this in recent years. Some authors stretch it out to fill an entire book. Unless you look carefully through all of the filler material, you are liable to miss the jist of the important principle. On the other hand, the possibilities of the simple procedures on the following pages do justify an entire book.

This is especially so when our beginning efforts don't show immediate results, our natural human impatience makes us doubt the validity of the entire idea. We might need the reinforcement of some examples that have worked, or some expanded explanations. It could help to read some of the current books on the subject or the four gospels in the New Testament.

A few paragraphs above, it states that we choose events (or create situations) that activate this process. However, there is an even more important aspect to this great principle and it is automatic.

You have experienced it, no doubt, and it is like this:
You may 'feel' that some person is 'evil' even though you know nothing about them, and so you avoid them. This is a valuable human survival mechanism; some people rely on it more than others.

And you might also feel that you like a person even though you do not know why. A common everyday experience. The explanation is this:

Our life energy 'bubbles up' through this stuff in our subconscious mind and 'projects' an energy field in the space that surrounds us. It has been likened to a slide projector where the light is our life energy and the picture on the slide that is being projected is the imprint in our subconscious mind. It is an 'aura'[2] that all people project.

Some people are more sensitive to feeling it than the rest of us. Perhaps women are more aware of it than men (just an opinion), and executives of all types are reported to be more sensitive. This explains why they seemingly can work with people by using their 'gut instinct' more than their reason in many situations.

What most of us are blind to, however, is that we ourselves are projecting just such an aura of our 'spiritual profile' (distinctive energy, if you like) into our surroundings.

> And it is our projected energy field that tends to attract certain
> types of people and certain types of circumstances into our lives.

It is a fact that we may actually feel this phenomenon from others and use it to our advantage and safety in daily life. Yet we overlook the fact that we are projecting who we are to anyone else who is the least bit sensitive to the 'world of the spirit'.

> The effect of this energy field works both ways; it can attract or repel.

If a person is attracting certain things into his or her life, they can be obvious, especially if they are harmful. People sometimes recognize this even if they have never heard of the spiritual principles outlined in this essay. But the sad part of this is that the situations and the people that we repel may not be obvious at all because they are not being brought into our lives. A spiritual master would be able to discern the shortcoming in a person's life if asked, but the rest of us would be baffled.

> Something to think about — and if it is hampering a person's
> life, it can be changed with 'work on one's self'.[3]

2. This is not exactly the 'aura' that some spiritually sensitive people can see that also emanates around all people. What we are describing above is like a subtle cloud of energy that many people do feel. Think back about the essay "Even Through Granite Walls" in Section One, a powerful example.

3. Epistle of James 1:22, 2:14 and 2:17. This is some of the work that James means when he says that "Faith without works is dead, being alone." That is, just knowing about the principles and believing them does not accomplish anything unless you work at it.

96

It does require you to learn a very difficult trick — controlling your thoughts. Most people don't even try, but it is worth the effort, and naturally takes some practice in everyday situations.

Socrates said, "An unexamined life is not worth living"

Here's your chance. This is a new way of living a life for most people — and it can be a better life.

How To Make it Work For You —

- Be careful of what you habitually think about, especially if you feel strongly about it.

- When you have some peaceful moments, think about what you really want in your life.

- Hold the thought as a 'picture image' in your mind. Don't bother with a lot of words, because words do not work very well in this process — really! God understands pictures better than words. So if you think in words, as many people naturally do, use the words to form a picture in your mind.[4]

- Put intensity into the picture image. It does take focus and mental energy. One intense mental input can accomplish wonders, as people have demonstrated in emergency situations. Few people can make such an intense thought at will, but the process also works with an image of lesser intensity if the image is repeated often. But this lesser intensity must still be over a certain 'threshold of background noise of the universe'[5] in order for the picture to "go out". Who knows where it really goes? But many believe that it goes to God, others say it goes to "the Universe" but it also goes to the subconscious part of our mind.

Here is a physical analogy to the above "threshold" idea:

Imagine you are driving a spike into a timber. A single blow with a heavy sledge could drive it in. Or several blows with a smaller hammer could do it. But tapping the spike with a little tack hammer could go on forever without budging it. Because there is a certain threshold of friction of the nail in the wood that must be overcome for any physical movement to take place. Experience shows that the process with thought that is outlined above works in a similar way. A sharp, intense mental input is necessary to "crash through" the threshold.

4. **This is an incredible "secret"** that verbally-oriented people not only miss, but might dispute. True nonetheless, and a later essay will explain why some prayer works better than others.
5. A 'threshold' might sound like some punitive barrier. But it is actually a God-given blessing. Otherwise, our every fleeting thought would manifest something. We would soon be smothered in stuff created by our own uncontrolled flitting thoughts. As others did the same, the world would soon be in chaos, wouldn't it?

- Successful people do not fritter away their valuable energy, because they know intuitively that they need energy to make this process work. Not feeling up to par? Work on that first. This may be one reason why Jesus healed the sick. It is the first step to having vital energy.

- The closer we are to the God that is within us, the more powerfully this type of prayer works. It might be that the less "subconscious garbage" that our prayer has to go through, the less energy it takes to make the direct contact. So 'getting close to God' is the first big job. Meditate on this!

Notice that these are things that many people do "naturally". And some are successful even though they have never heard of the 'world of the spirit'. But it is easier and quicker if you know why! You just begin to do the right thing automatically after some practice.

Why This Process Doesn't Work For Most

- Most people do not bother to think intently (it takes effort) about anything except when they are angry. This, of course, brings to themselves what they really do not need or want. Other strong emotions, often destructive, do the same. Strong emotions are easy and commonplace.

- They think conflicting thoughts. — one thing for an instant, something else the next. Sometimes it is desire alternating with doubt. Constancy does count. Doubt nullifies.

- The intensity of their desire does not get over the minimum that is necessary. That is, above the threshold of the 'background noise ....' Usually because of lack of focus and/or lack of energy. And it takes energy!

- If they think a big image, like winning the lottery, their common sense tells them that the odds against it are so great that they automatically nullify the image. The image must be logical to the person or their own doubt cancels it. Most of us can doubt and cancel even small ideas..

- Many people feel separated from the God within because of personal guilt. Jesus had much to say about that and how to correct it. He said that this stuff (this process) is your birthright!

Many have made this work! Perhaps you have too! It is one of the processes of life — especially a powerful life. But it is not something that a person can learn overnight. And it is best to learn when there is no crisis in your life. Like learning to swim; it is a little late when you fall out of the boat. Yet so many people turn to God and prayer only when a crisis arises in their life. Or they only have their church pray for the sick when they know it is too late. Better then than never, of course. But better to learn this grand process ahead of time. Then use it the rest of your life.

However, there are some churches that actually teach that you must have a crisis in your life before you really turn to God. And there must be an actual distinct turning point. While that may have happened in some (or many) cases, you do not have to wait for a crisis to begin learning about any subject, including this one.

There are, inevitably, other people in our lives that exert influences on us, some good, some invigorating, but some may be energy depleting, and some may be pulling us away from the path we know we should take and some may even be downright evil, Only by becoming aware of these additional inputs to our lives can we be whole. And only by controlling the effect of these inputs can we make spiritual progress.

Just this brief mention of using one's own subconscious mind can be unsettling or even scary to some people. But working with this part of the mind in a positive way can be of immense benefit to daily life. Guidance from a good teacher can be a great help and such a teacher would not apply this process to a psychotic person or even a deeply troubled person. Getting well should be their first concern.

More could be said — but these are the basics. And this is only a small part of the Ancient Wisdom.

The Secret Path

The "Secret Path" is an allegory for the process of working on one's own spiritual understanding and attainment. And so it is also called "The Path of Attainment".

Jesus called it "the way".

It is said to be secret because it is done in one's mind and soul, not obvious to others, although as a person's life changes, it will be apparent to others. In our Western culture, not many have followed the path until recent times so it has not even been known by most. And perhaps, the higher levels may even be kept somewhat secret by "those who know" so that it doesn't fall into the wrong hands.

The great sages down through history have taught that all of the wisdom that a person could desire is within themselves. And that one's "inner sanctum" is the proper place to look for it. Scripture teaches about this!

Some people do, of course, feel that they must trek off to some faraway place like the "Holy Land", India, Tibet or Egypt. The idea of "pilgrimage" to "look for something" outside of one's self is an ancient longing.

Fortunately for us today, others have brought the ancient wisdom of faraway places to our own doorstep via books and local organizations. Translations have been made and re-made. The great truths may be in other idioms — may be strange to our ears. But the basic spiritual truth is the same the world over. So we make "the journey" within ourselves and can do it wherever we are.

Some people that I have met envision this so-called path to be like the following picture — dark, foreboding, leading into unlighted, uncharted mysterious depths. Something to be avoided out of fear. Some churches teach this!

I have found it to be otherwise. More like the picture on the page following of a lighter path. With "flecks of light" to show the beginner that there is a path. And then the path becomes well-marked by the previous travel of others. And the farther one goes, the more apparent is the light at the end.

God blesses all who sincerely set foot on the secret path

.

In the Old Testament book of Isaiah, I ran across three verses that seem to refer to this same sort of a Secret Path.

Isaiah 35:8-10 KJV

> "And a highway shall be there, and a way, and it shall be called The way of holiness; the unclean shall not pass over it; but it shall be for those: the wayfaring men, though fools, shall not err therein.
>
> No lion shall be there, nor any ravenous beast shall go up thereon, it shall not be found there; but the redeemed shall walk there:
> turn, and come to Zion with songs and everlasting joy upon their heads: they shall obtain joy and gladness, and sorrow and sighing shall flee away."

You might also see these same verses in the: New King James Version
New International Version and
Holman Christian Standard Bible version
or other translations

The verses are much easier to read and easier to understand in translations other than the KJV quoted here. The verses can be found on the Internet in many translations.

One site is www.biblegateway.com.

As you can see, it is not easy to interpret the writings of the Old Testament because they are written in a semi-poetic style about an unfamiliar subject. Undoubtedly, a teacher often helped to explain these things in the ancient Jewish tradition. However, once you understand the meaning as expressed in modern language, it is possible to recognize the meaning in the encrypted tongue of the ancients.

How Do You "Read" the Bible?

In chatting with people about Bible study over the years, I see that many have preconceived ideas as to what Scripture is about. And so they "go at" their reading with a particular mind-set and they "get" different interpretations, sometimes vastly different meanings, one person to another, from reading the same passage, depending on their preconceived starting point and thought structure.

I believe that it can help a serious religious student to be aware "ahead of time"of these common preconceived ideas. Because a person can easily pick up these various concepts almost sub-consciously from friends or clergy, and may influence years, or even a life-time, of one's Bible study.

Some of the common ways I've noticed that people "read" the Bible:

- As history
- As literature
- For moral guidance and as basis for law
- As prophesy of things to come
- As a guide to higher spiritual consciousness

Of course, some readers may have more than one of these ideas in mind, either at the same time or by shifting from one to another over the years as their spiritual understanding grows.

In addition to the above, a beginner may be instructed by his religious guide that:
- the Bible is to be read literally and understood literally because "God's word means just what it says", or conversely —
- that much of the Bible is written in allegories that have deep hidden meanings that must be interpreted or de-coded in order to be understood.

Let's look at each of the first five in a little more detail and you can add your thoughts from your own perspective as you read along.

But before that:

I will not keep you in the dark as to how I myself "see" the Bible, especially the New Testament. After listening to years of sermons in church (actually decades) I absorbed the idea that the Bible was about religious history and it was mostly for our moral guidance, and of course, judgement after death. That was all well and good as far as it went. But it missed the important teaching of Jesus that many churches do not seem to know or teach. Knowledge that I hope will show through in some of these essays. And so in my mature years, I read the New Testament, as a guide to **higher spiritual**

consciousness. I wish that I had been aware of this a few decades earlier, but did not know that was such a thing as "higher spiritual consciousness".

As History

In the neighborhood church where I grew up, there were some people who could relate most of the stories of the Old Testament by heart. They knew the characters, the family relationships, the strange events, etc. They learned all of this in the same manner that other people studied the great stories of classical literature.

But some also studied the ways of life during Biblical times, the geography of the Biblical lands and so on, in order to get a better understanding of the stories, a better understanding of the peoples and a better understanding of the times,. They seemed to feel that doing all this made themselves "more religious". Some of these people hoped that they might visit the Holy Land. Innumerable books have been written on these subjects. I am glad that someone, not me, took the time to do it.

Try as I may however, I could not see then, and I cannot see now, how knowing all of this stuff can enhance one's religious well being. Although I realize that by going through the old stories, you can run across gems of wisdom here and there. But all of these gems have been extracted and used repeatedly by present-day writers, lawmakers and others. Some are familiar to just about everyone.

And then there are the archaeologists who search the Bible for clues about ancient lost cities. One such was J. E. Taylor who discovered and began excavating the ancient city of "UR" about 1919 in what the ancients called Mesopotamia.

In the Bible, it is called "UR of the Chaldeans". (Genesis 11:31 KJV, written between 1491 - 1451 B.C.) It was the home of Abraham, father of the Hebrews. UR was in present-day Iraq, about 140 miles south of Babylon. [1] When an ancient city like UR is found, it does confirm a historical aspect of the Bible. And many people feel that this "proves" the Bible in all other aspects. It does not prove the spiritual teaching, but there are other proofs of that and they are more meaningful.

As Literature

Many Universities have courses titled "The Bible as Literature". Many books interpreting the subject are available to the student. But, oddly enough, the only people I know who have actually read any of the Bible "as literature" on their own are atheists. And it puzzles me why anyone would want to read a religious book "as literature" because many of the stories make little sense when read literally. If, on the other hand, you look for the deep, underlying, symbolic meaning of the stories, then you are doing more than just "reading literature".

1. Information from Internet site "www.mnsu.edu/emuseum/archaeology/sites/middle_east/ur.html"

106

For Moral Guidance and As Basis for Law

The morality of the Old Testament historically brought an unruly people into becoming a more civilized society. The Ten Commandments are so basic that they could be used as a basis of law, with the exception of the religious parts, for any country, anywhere, any time, till end of time.

But there is also the "eye for an eye, tooth for a tooth" [2] idea that is still the basis for much of our criminal law. Ancient Jews just meant that the punishment should fit the crime. I don't believe that they used immolation although it's hard to tell just by reading the passage. But even today, people who do not understand this justify this vengeful idea in a literal way "because it's in the Bible". Down through the centuries, Jews have called it "justice" while modern politically-correct society calls it "closure". But vengeance is not the teaching of Jesus.

"Thomas Jefferson believed that the ethical system of Jesus was the finest the world had ever seen".[3] In order to isolate the moral teachings from what he considered to be the supernatural aspects of the story in the four Gospels, he cut up a Bible (KJV) and pasted his selections into a blank book. In one of these "Jefferson Bibles", he had parallel verses in English, Latin, Greek and French.

His thinking along these lines must have influenced his input in the writing of the U.S. Constitution (adopted in 1787); one idea that comes to mind is the prohibition of "cruel and unusual punishments." However he didn't actually begin his Bible project until 1804 and then was so busy in Washington that he didn't finish it until 1820. Some libraries have copies of the "Jefferson Bible". My library had to order it "on loan" for me; now I have a copy of my own.

Sad to say, Jefferson seems to have missed the deep spiritual teaching of Jesus while concentrating his attention on the moral teaching.

As Prophesy of Things to Come

Many churches teach that the Bible predicts events that will take place sometime in the future. One such event is the "second coming of Jesus". And many churches today believe that this will happen in the near future. More about this in an essay in Section Three.

I used to talk many hours with the representatives of such a church during the 1970's. Their church had calculated from various passages of the Old and New Testaments that 1975 was the year (give or take a little) for the return of Jesus, a tribulation and then his thousand year reign on earth. Didn't happen! Naturally they were disappointe. Their group had made the prediction several times before

2. Exodus 21:24, written between 1491 - 1451 B.C.
3. Paraphrased from Eyler Robert Coates, Sr.

and been disappointed. It turns out that people, especially theologians, have been making these predictions from the Bible for almost 1900 years. And they have always been wrong. But that doesn't stop people today from going over the same ground. The arrival of the Second Millennium renewed interest in prophesy and "end times" predictions. It seems to correlate with cultural anxiety.

Personally I don't believe that the Bible predicts literal future events from this time on. The Bible is mostly about spiritual teachings. But this idea puts me at odds with many Christian churches. However, if the predictions do come true — that would be incredible!

But I am not going to agonize over every earthquake and every little war as a "sign of the end" as so many church people are presently doing. And I certainly would not try to influence world events in order to hasten "the second coming" as some church people are doing based on a very tenuous interpretation of Scripture.

As a Guide to Higher Spiritual Consciousness

There are two viewpoints about how to practice religion in general:

- Most religious people are satisfied with a church that is based on beliefs. That is, as long as the beliefs arise from the Bible, they think that beliefs are religion and that there is nothing more. Many do not even realize that their beliefs are just that — beliefs. They tend to accept them as facts "because they come from the Bible". And if you were to question this entire idea, they might say, "Don't you believe the Bible? — not realizing that they have just pointed out that their religious ideas are beliefs.

    (Incidentally, I do believe the Bible, profoundly so!)

- Many of these churches use a literal interpretation of the Bible. They believe that the "words mean just exactly what they say" in the simplest possible way. All of this despite the fact that Jesus pointed out that he hid "higher" meanings by the use of parables. Many churches believe that the teachings of the Bible are concerned more with worldly things rather than with spiritual things. Since their ideas are beliefs, there is no way to validate them – to prove them or disprove them – or to test them in any realistic way.

And so we have churches with a great variety of differing beliefs. Look into the subject if you doubt this statement. Any theological question posed to the Internet will bring hundreds, even thousands, of differing "explanations" (beliefs).

In contrast, a relatively few religious people want to go beyond mere belief so that they can actually experience the things, to some degree at least, that the great spiritual teachers talked about and demonstrated. That is what these few people consider to be the real message of the Bible. The message hidden in parables so that only those "who have ears to hear" would know what they "really" mean. That is, they interpret the Bible as allegory.

What I discovered is that some people do study Scripture in this way. And down through history, some have achieved the experiential side of religion, and then they know it is correct. They have proved beyond all doubt that the teaching of the Bible is valid when interpreted this way. You could say that they have proved the Bible by living it!

But after going to church for thirty years in the earlier part of my life, I did not even realize that this second group existed. Or that it might be possible to actually "experience " religion.

Then I discovered why it is seldom taught, and then only to a few. It is difficult! And there are few real teachers! Teachers that can teach in depth and demonstrate what they teach.

Jesus described the difficulty this way:

- "Enter in at the strait gate; (archaic: meaning narrow as in Strait of Gibralter) for wide is the gate and broad is the way, that leadeth to destruction and many there be which go in there at: Because strait is the gate, and narrow is the way, which leadeth unto life, and few there be that find it.[4]

- Keep the Ten Commandments [5]

- "It is easier for a camel to go through the eye of a needle than for a rich man to enter into the kingdom of God.[6]

- "Be ye therefore perfect, even as your Father which is in heaven is perfect".[7]

Jesus and other great teachers never said that a spiritual life leading to actual spiritual experience would be easy, only that the reward would be great. "Among those that are born of women there is not a greater prophet than John the Baptist: but he that is least in the kingdom of God is greater than he." [8]

Whatever others may believe:

> To me, the important message of the Bible is about man's soul and God and is best interpreted in that direction.

4. Matthew 7:13,14   Luke 13:24 is similar   KJV   5. Originally given in Exodus 20. Jesus reiterates them in Matthew 19:18 KJV   6. Mark 10:25 KJV   7. Matthew 5:48 KJV   8. Luke 7:28 KJV

The Bible is about the Ancient Wisdom — Apparently God gave the ancient Jews a version of the Ancient Wisdom in story form.

In the New Testament, the teaching of Jesus is explicitly about the "Evolution of Man's Soul" [9] from lower levels to higher levels of spiritual consciousness. The purpose of his teaching is so that an individual can actually experience the Kingdom of God (also called the Kingdom of Heaven) while here on earth, while still existing in his or her body.

Jesus teaches this lofty message in his own words that have come down to us in the four Gospels. And the disciples did it and St. Paul did it. So have others down through the ages following His teaching.

How then, can a serious person do this now? In modern times the process is often called "the way" (from the Bible) and just as often called "the work" because it involves work on one's self. It is not easy for most of us! It requires us to "become a new man" to a very high degree.

In our Western culture, however, few people ever work on themselves in this direction because the meaning of Jesus' teaching has been almost lost, or at least covered up by other interpretations. These other interpretations have become part of our religious culture and have been widely accepted as being "the" message of Jesus the Messenger.

The Sermon on the Mount, as well as other sayings of Jesus, point the way for a dedicated person to do this, although some of the details may be missing. A sizable literature, in addition to the Bible, is available to those who might be interested in seeking (to some degree at least) this high purpose. But first we must realize that this is what it is all about. That is my purpose in writing these few pages. Others have written the more worthy books to guide a person in the details of really living "on the way". These books can be judged for authenticity once you understand the jist of what the grand purpose truly is.

9. "Evolution of the Soul" is the title of a book about this subject by Dr. Thurman Fleet, b 1895, d 1983, chiropractor, educator, writer, lecturer, founder of the "Concept Therapy Institute", San Antonio, TX.

One Little Word — One Big Change

Some churches teach that the Bible is all literally true or else none of it is true. And some people say that in the Bible, "God says what He means and He means what He says". So that any interpretation then is to be done literally on the simplest level of understanding. I mentioned that earlier, but here I want to take a different look at only the first few chapters of the Bible.

The first five chapters of the Christian Bible are often referred to as the Pentateuch, 'penta' meaning five and the root of the rest of the word coming from 'to teach'. The Pentateuch is the same as the Jewish Torah, and so there has been an immense amount of study by both Jewish and Christian scholars as to its meaning. It was originally written in ancient Hebrew, and it is still used in that form in Jewish services so that shades of meaning will not be lost in translation. Even though the Torah is one long scroll in Jewish tradition, it is five separate books (the Pentateuch) of the Christian Bible. Christians have it in many translations, old and modern.

I am not a professional Bible scholar and know only a word or two of Hebrew. So it is with great humility that I approach this subject and must rely on the findings of others who have dedicated their lives to these particular subjects and how to interpret them.

One such scholar was Rabbi Moses Maimonides, a medieval Jewish philosopher who was one of the greatest interpreters of the Torah. He was born in Spain in 1135 and died in Egypt in 1204. [1] He wrote extensively expounding on the meaning of the Torah and other Jewish holy writ. Jews with whom I have talked hold him in very high regard even these centuries later.

He was also a physician and wrote about medicine. In recognition of his monumental work in this area, a large hospital in Brooklyn, NY is named the "Maimonides Medical Center". There is also a "Maimonides Society" of doctors and dentists in the U.S.

His writings are so voluminous that you could spend a lifetime studying just the parts that have been translated. For my purpose in this essay, there is a simpler way to understand the broad teachings of Maimonides. After the rabbi's death, his son Abraham was urged to write about his father's basic teaching. Abraham was also considered to be a great scholar, and he did write a moderately sized book praising his father titled:

"Abraham Maimonides' War of the Lord and the Maimonidean Controversy".

This book, about 800 years old, has been re-published in recent years and translated into English. The controversy, of course, was the clash of the new, expanded ideas against the old. More specifically, it was a clash between use of reason versus just faith.

1. Dates are from Wikipedia online.

When I read this book, several things popped out that became new lines of spiritual study. As a result, some of my concepts were modified and others were firmed up. For what it may be worth to you, I present them here.

Maimonides repeatedly said that Torah is not to be interpreted literally. He pointed out that the more unlikely a story would be in the usual sense, usually the deeper is the spiritual lesson that is contained therein. Anyone extracting just a literal interpretation would lose the spiritual meaning and would have to strain his or her credulity to accept the literal story.

Although Maimonides was talking about Jewish Torah, this is the same as the first five books of the Christian Bible. He says that this part of scripture is not to be interpreted literally. He goes on to say, "Man's intellect comes alive in measure as it knows truth. Blemished ideas prevent its activation." And on another line, "My people are destroyed for lack of knowledge, because the priests have rejected knowledge." Remember this is in the late 1100's.

The rabbi had some sharp things to say about clergy ---- "these rabbis who believe that God has a body have never advanced in esoteric knowledge beyond the stage of childhood." And that "Biblical anthropomorphisms are misleading; hence the uncompromising insistence that they be understood as allegories."

And his clarity on the subject reminded me of people I have known who were deeply troubled by these so-called anthropomorphisms and so became confirmed atheists. They were taught by their church that the images were real, yet their reason told them otherwise. They became disillusioned and just didn't bother to ever sort it all out.

I was privileged to tour the Vatican and see the celestial paintings of Michelangelo in the Sistine Chapel. The ceiling had been restored during the 1980's after being blackened by hundreds of years of candle soot. The colors are now vibrant. The 343 figures depicting Biblical stories were actually done by the fresco process which makes it even more astounding. The artist blended pigments into wet plaster one small section at a time, the result being color deep into the surface. Tourists are not allowed to take snapshots of the 65 ½ foot high ceiling — unnecessary anyway with the excellent color photos available nearby at a reasonable price. As I leisurely studied the figures, it brought to mind that Michelangelo had studied human anatomy at considerable length so that his sculpture and painting would look authentic. And he succeeded in this magnificently.

The best known of the many paintings is the "Creation of Adam". If there is anyone who cannot bring this picture to their mind's eye, let me describe it briefly. The image of God is an old man with gray white beard, knotted brow, stern expression lolling in a bunch of angels in the sky. God reaches out with pointed finger, not quite touching the naked Adam's finger, to give him the spark of life.

Although in Genesis verse 2:7, it says that God "breathed into man's nostrils the breath of life." Spark or breath — either way God is pictured as an old man — an anthropomorphism. And little kids are taught in many Sunday Schools at a tender age that this is true, because how do you explain a metaphor to a little kid? Many probably replace this childish concept of God with something closer to truth in later years. And many don't ever. I know — because adults have confided in me that they just can't believe God is an old man. Sad! And the concept of a "God in the sky" put into the mind of a trusting little child can be difficult to dislodge.

Despite Michelangelo's beautiful work, I have never liked the "Creation of Adam" because of its atrocious theology. Talking serpents are another thing, but let's not get into that.

I don't know whether Jewish readers of the Torah forego the advice of Maimonides and read it literally or not. But many Christians do read and digest the Pentateuch literally because they have never been instructed that the real meaning may not be in a literal interpretation. I read literally myself for years, not knowing any different. Indeed, many churches insist that only a literal reading can be tolerated. It strikes me that they're hanging onto the literal Bible "for dear life" and can allow only one interpretation, whereas allegorical interpretation might result in a variety of interpreted meanings depending on the level of spiritual understanding of the individual.

It is not my purpose to dissuade anyone to go against the beliefs of his or her church. But for me, this upgrade of Bible interpretation brought an incredible relief to my religious life. Line by line, story by story, most of the clash between science and religion dissolved and faded away in my mind as I changed from a literal to a deeper interpretive mode of reading. Although it did not improve my understanding of science, (why would it?) it had a colossal benefit to the progress of my religious search and it enabled me to gain a higher level of spiritual understanding.

Another scholar who wrote against literal interpretation was Fabre d'Olivet [2] in his book "The Hebraic Tongue Restored" published in French in 1815. He started out searching for the origin of language. Along the way, it occurred to him that the **Hebrew language that was being used in later years to interpret ancient Jewish scripture** was far from the language in which it was written. The reason being that the Jews spent four centuries in exile in Egypt and that their original tongue was "contaminated" or modified by use alongside the Egyptian language. By going back to the most basic roots of the two languages, he found many words and phrases that needed correction. And he made a new translation of the 'creation story' based on this idea.

2. Antoine Fabre d'Olivet, b 1767 - d 1825 from Wikipedia.

While his book is mainly of interest to language experts, one aspect of the book is neatly expressed by Nayán Louise Redfield [3] who made the English translation published in 1921.

Speaking about the author, (Fabre d'Olivet) she says:

> "He asserts plainly and fearlessly that the Genesis of Moses was symbolically expressed and ought not to be taken in a purely literal sense. Saint Augustine [4] recognized this, and Origen [5] avers that 'if one takes the history of the creation in the literal sense, it is absurd and contradictory'"

These four authorities of long ago — Maimonides, Fabre d'Olivet, St Augustine and Origen — spoke against a simplistic literal reading of the Bible, especially the Book of Genesis. So you see, it is not just a recent idea that has been 'cooked up' to try to adjust scripture to latter-day discoveries of science in order to reduce the conflict between science and religion. Not at all.

Even so, the first page or two of the Bible is still the cause of endless contention between people who have chosen one side or the other of the "religion versus science" argument.
For example:

> Some churches, some Christian Bible schools and some Bible colleges feel that they must disprove science in order to validate the Bible.

> Not necessary —

> The Bible is true when properly interpreted. And there is little or no clash with science if you also understand the methods of science.

The Bible has stood the test of time and millions attest to its validity. Yet I meet deeply religious people who are endlessly trying to prove the Bible to me, (and to themselves) one way or another — because deep down, they find it difficult to resolve the arguments that they have heard and so they doubt. If they took a slightly different perspective, they could see the truth. But it is so hard for all of us to give up the "familiar" — the things we were taught when young.

3. Nayán Louise Redfield - The quotation above is from her 'Translator's Forward', dated October 1918 which is in the 1921 English edition - G.P. Putnam, publisher. Book is in Cleveland Public Library.
4. St. Augustine of Hippo b 354 - d 430. One of the great Christian theologians, early "church father", Bishop in what is now Algeria. Wikipedia.
5. Origen b 184 or 5 - d 253 or 4. Early Christian theologian and "church father". Wikipedia.

For me, not having to believe all of scripture literally has enabled me to begin to understand the incredible teaching of Jesus and other sages, as I will try to relate to you in later essays. The Bible took on new authority as something that is actually real rather than the fantasy that it appears to be to so many people today. A real "sea change", as we used to say in the Navy.

Still — the stories of the creation in their most literal form have entered the culture of the United States, both the religious and the secular cultures. Perhaps also in other countries with large Christian or Jewish populations. In some ways, it is a convenience when referring to certain concepts in the same manner that we use Aesop's Fables for this same purpose. It really would help, however, if we kept in the back of our mind that neither is literally true.

The title of this essay mentions "one little word". You might have guessed by now — that word is "allegory", and you may surmise that I interpret parts of the Bible as allegory or metaphor. As a matter of fact, I do. And so do all of the sincere spiritual seekers that I have met.

But just as a matter of interest, let me point out that:

The word 'allegory' is in the King James Bible [6] whereas the word 'literal' is not!

I leave it to you to decide.

6. See Galations 4:24

Bible Interpretation - Belief and Faith

As mentioned before, I am not a professional Bible scholar — never cared to be one — although I greatly appreciate and respect their work. But with the many "helps" available today, it is possible for any layman to gain much understanding that would have been impossible a couple of centuries ago. As pointed out in the previous essay, some churches interpret the Bible literally, while others interpret the same words allegorically.

Entirely different sets of meanings are thereby derived, depending on the method of interpretation. In my personal Bible study, I tend to the allegorical method of exegesis where it is appropriate.

But the purpose of this essay is to point out that the interpreted meaning of **even single words** can have a profound effect on religious beliefs.

And a second problem in interpretation is that the common meaning and usage of words can shift over a period of just a few years, and from one culture to another. What then about the possible shift of meaning over a period of twenty centuries? Modern translations **should** help in this respect.

And a third problem is that — in a select group of people (such as the early Christians) sometimes a single word is used to convey an extended group of concepts, whereas in our present-day, common language, the same word might be used with just a specific or narrow meaning.

Two words that might benefit from examination in light of the above are commonly used in religious teaching — " belief" and "faith".

Today's meaning in many Christian churches:

> Belief – Believe that the teaching of Jesus is true. That He is Savior and that He is God and that He will come again, etc. In other words, the belief is in the particular teaching of the particular church denomination. "Distinctives" they are called. Correct me if I have left out something from your church.

And many church goers profess to believe these things with great sincerity. Jesus, on the other hand, seemed to have a much more profound meaning to the word 'belief'. He pointed out:

> "And these signs shall follow them that believe; In my name they shall cast out devils; they shall speak with new tongues; They shall take up serpents; and if they drink any deadly thing, it shall not hurt them; they shall lay hands on the sick, and they shall recover." Mark 16:17,18 KJV

(Note: Bible scholars have found that this passage in the Book of Mark is not in the earliest Christian manuscripts. So it is assumed that it may have been added later by some unknown copyist. Not easy to prove one way or the other. But since it is included in the King James Version of the Bible and it illustrates my point, I will use it here.)

Jesus, in this verse, indicates that those **"who believe"** can effectively heal the sick, speak with languages unknown to them and if they are bitten by a poisonous snake (as Paul was bitten while gathering firewood on the Island of Malta) they will be unhurt.

This use of the term "believe" by Jesus indicates a person **who is highly accomplished in spiritual abilities**. It is a level of spiritual ability attained by some Yogi's after some years of dedicated discipline. It is a level of spiritual attainment not found (or seldom found) in our Christian churches. In fact, some churches would expel such a person out of fear of the occult, just as Jesus was accused of being in league with the Devil in order to do his miracles.

He was accused by the Pharisees in Matthew 12:24:

> Jesus healed someone who was blind and dumb. "But when the Pharisees heard it, they said, This fellow [Jesus] doth not cast out devils, but by Beelzebub the prince of the devils." Jesus then had to give an involved defense.

Jesus was accused by the scribes in Mark 3:22:

> After healing many — "And the scribes which came down from Jerusalem said, He hath Beelzebub, and by the prince of the devils he casteth out devils." And Jesus said, "How can Satan cast out Satan?" To me, that is great logic that should clarify the question.

and Jesus was accused by the multitude in Luke 11:15:

> After Jesus had "cast out a dumb devil" and the person spoke (perhaps the same incident as in Matthew 12:24 above) "the people wondered and some of them said, He casteth out devils through Beelzebub the chief of the devils."

And it is probable that some people with these highly developed spiritual abilities were even burned at the stake in following centuries in Europe out of gross misunderstanding and fear. Still the goal of the teaching of Jesus includes the spiritual abilities of the above "signs". And his use of the phrase "them that believe" seems to mean a person who has **achieved** these rather significant spiritual abilities as opposed to just accepting them to be true.

On another occasion, the disciples tried to cure an epileptic man, but could not. They brought him to Jesus, Mark 9:23. Jesus said unto them, "If thou canst (can) believe, all things are possible to him that believeth." Then Jesus went ahead and cast out the spirit of epilepsy from the man, implying that the disciples did not have enough belief.

It is known that such a spiritual feat today requires intense concentration of mind and the ability to 'go unto the Father' who doeth the works. But Jesus included all of this in just the word "believe".

Conclusion:

There are other similar passages in the New Testament where Jesus equates "believing" with the possession of spiritual abilities, and they are rather considerable abilities at that!

In our churches, the present-day usage of the word "believing" absolutely does not indicate the level of accomplishment that Jesus said we could do if we believed. He obviously used the word to convey, as a collected group of meanings, all of the things that a person must do to gain the mentioned spiritual abilities. That's why we have churches full of sincere 'believers' (using the present-day meaning of the word) who wouldn't even pretend to have the afore-mentioned spiritual abilities.

The real harm in this "watered-down" usage of the words "belief" and "believing" to the sincere Christian is that he may imagine that he is more advanced spiritually than he actually is. And that there may be nothing more that he should do for his spiritual growth, according to the Bible.

In other words, he has every right to feel that he has done all that he needs to do to be a "good Christian", at least as far as belief in concerned. I know that I was "sold short" during many years of church attendance because of the modern-day use of this particular word, not realizing that there was the greater reality that Jesus talked about. And that I could possibly learn it from a teacher "who knew". I was fortunate to meet just such a teacher, but how about others who might have 'walked on by' a teacher, not realizing that 'there is more' and that there are those who can teach it.

Another word that Jesus used is "faith".

Remember the incident when Jesus 'walked on water'? The meaning that Jesus had for the word "faith" apparently included several attributes beyond our present-day meaning. Let's look:

Matthew 14:24-31. "But the ship was now in the midst of the sea, tossed with waves: for the wind was contrary. And in the fourth watch of the night Jesus went unto them, walking on the sea. And when the disciples saw him walking on the sea, they were troubled, saying, It is a spirit; and they cried out for fear. But straightway Jesus spake unto them, saying,

'Be of good cheer; it is I; be not afraid.'

And Peter answered him and said, "Lord, if it be thou, bid me come unto thee on the water". "And He said, Come". And when Peter was come down out of the ship, he walked on the water to go to Jesus. But when he saw the wind boisterous, he was afraid; and beginning to sink, he cried, saying, "Lord, save me". And immediately Jesus stretched forth his hand, and caught him, and said unto him, "O thou of little faith, wherefore didst thou doubt?"

To walk on the water in the way that Jesus was doing, Peter needed intense concentration on what he was doing and the feeling of assurance that he could do it. He needed concentration of mind and body like a circus 'flyer' sailing through the air looking to catch the swinging trapeze — or fall — and knowing that he can catch it and knowing that he will do it.

Our present-day meaning of faith in this context would be "trust in God, especially without logical proof." This would be a considerably lower meaning than the admonition that Jesus gave to Peter. A deep trust in God would certainly 'carry Peter a long way' but he would still need intense concentration and assurance that he could do the walking-on-water feat. But it was when he lost concentration by becoming aware of the surroundings that he began to sink. (Boaters and fishermen back in that era did not appear to be good swimmers.) Peter's doubt would, of course, be the same meaning as today's 'lack of faith'.

Yoga masters in India have allegedly done similar feats in modern times. I have read about it but have not met anyone who claims to have seen such a demonstration or could do it himself.

Other biblical words have ancient meanings that are bigger than the present-day definition, but 'belief' and 'faith' are the most commonly used today, and the most important, so it seems to me. Other words, such as these two, may become apparent to you as your consciousness increases.

Proving Spiritual "Truths" To Be True

First the more familiar. The world of the physical sciences:

In the physical sciences, the goal is to explain some puzzling phenomenon and then to prove the explanation. The methodology is to propose a theory that might possibly lead to an explanation and then set up a suitable experiment that will prove or disprove the theory. By this approach, immense numbers of solid facts about the physical world have been accumulated. Former superstitions and false beliefs have been replaced with useable facts to the considerable benefit of the human race.

The basic idea in science is that a proposed solution to a theory can be duplicated by other scientists if they set up the same conditions. This 'peer review' by other scientists sorts out the real from the imagined, and the process is sometimes verbally vicious, and may take much time.

The puzzling phenomena that were solved and proven in the early days of the scientific era were on a level that most people could understand once they were made known, and the benefits were often dramatic in every day life. As science has progressed, however, the things that are still a puzzle become increasingly distant from ordinary life and become of interest only to scientists — frequently only to those in a narrow specialty. Which is where we are today. And it is confusing to the public when the tentative conjecture of scientists is prematurely brought to the public's attention before much scientific progress has been made, as news people often do.

Now the not so familiar. The world of the spirit:

The teachings that are in scripture are about "the world of the spirit". Despite the fact that the 'world of the spirit' is intangible, invisible, and non-existent to many, or most, the teachings of scripture can be, and are, verified by a powerful methodology — although the idea of proof itself is not necessarily the goal, unlike physical science.

Spiritual realities, often referred to as "secrets", are **experienced** and **verified** by anyone who truly follows the teachings all the way, thereby **obtaining a high level of "spiritual consciousness"** — ultimately attaining what is called, in Christianity "the mystic union" with God. When a person **experiences** and then tests and verifies the experience, he or she really **knows**. Telling others, however, cannot convey to them the depth of the experience or the knowingness.

Down through history, however, only an exalted few have "reached the heights" because of the difficulty. But many have experienced part way. And for centuries, many of these people kept their attainment secret out of fear from the established church and from "ignorant masses". We are blessed in recent times that some of these great ones are making themselves known, and it is a surprise to many that these contemporary "adepts" are proving in modern times exactly what the ancient prophets wrote in scripture. This is in stark contrast to the erroneous belief of many today who conclude that the unusual, or even astounding, events of biblical times happened in a one-time, never to be repeated, era in the history of humanity. This imaginary brief window in past time for the 'miraculous' to have taken place lets these believers off the hook from having to even consider doing any of the old teaching themselves.

"The miraculous era is over", they say, "so it would be presumptuous for us to try."

I ignorantly accepted that until I discovered that it is not true. But having an engineer's mind, I started in unfamiliar territory. On the other hand, Jesus said that his teaching would be good till the end of time. If He was teaching "spiritual truth", as He said He was, these truths should be eternal. And wouldn't He mean all of his teaching — the miracles part as well as the morality part. I believe so. And now, I know so! Because of what I have experienced myself. Details later.

Unfortunately, it is not quick and easy for a modern "adept" to adequately convey this high spiritual state to a person who may be on a lower spiritual level, just as the scientist may not be able to convincingly explain to the public what a particular scientific experiment proved so clearly to him and his fellow scientists.

But those few that have found the "ancient truths" to be verily true do tell others and also try to teach a few to follow the teachings and **actually see for themselves.** The most marvelous part is that a person can, in the beginning, knowingly **prove some small part** of the great teaching in his or her own experience. Such an incremental success then can encourage one to believe that other aspects of scripture might be true..... can be true, and to eventually prove these also to be true.

Since this "proof" is individually experienced and can die with the individual, there are those who fear that these understandings may be lost to civilization through lack of interest, or whatever. I have been assured that this cannot happen as long as the human race continues. Down through history, when spiritual individuals have been threatened by church, by government or disdained by the multitude, they have gone underground to preserve the knowledge. Then a few have even become martyrs if the situation called for it from their perspective.

Contrast the above idea of real solid proof of spiritual truth in modern times with what so many still believe today. They look to the archeologist to uncover the ruins of some ancient city mentioned in the Bible as proof that the Bible is true. Such findings might prove something, but they do not validate the authenticity of the **spiritual teaching,** and the spiritual teaching is the only significant reason for studying the Bible. Fortunately for us, that has been proven, as I have mentioned several times, writing from several different perspectives.

However, if these peripheral connections with the Bible, like archeology, make some people more confident in the truth of the Bible, there is certainly nothing wrong with that.

Some things that you can experience in your own spirit life that will prove validity:

- Receiving a clear concise answer to a specific prayer.

- Having an intuitive feeling that was clear and sharp and proved to be true.

- "Performing" a spiritual healing as the result of your efforts. (It must be more than just a person getting well by themselves. Some times, the healing can be almost instant, so then you know it was really from your input). In the beginning it is best to practice on yourself.

- Receiving a creative solution "out of the blue", especially if you feel it is from God.

- The realization dawns on you concerning why certain things have happened in your life, past or present. The underlying cause becomes apparent from your subconscious mind. In early efforts, the realization might appear in a dream. As you develop, it can come to your mind more directly, although dreams can continue to be enlightening.

- Eventually, as spiritual consciousness develops, you might see these causes in others. But if a person has painful memories in his or her own life that they would rather not face, it is ever so easy to look mainly at the lives of others. Jesus recommended clearing up one's own inner self first.

Keep in mind that "Rome was not built in a day" — neither is a deep spiritual understanding.

The Greatest Secret —
The Greatest Revelation

For those people who study matters of the Spirit, there can also be a **great paradox**.

A story[1]
In ancient times, Jewish holy men made profound spiritual discoveries and incorporated them into their religion. Some of the knowledge was hidden in the writings of the Torah (Book of Laws) and other ancient Jewish Texts--- what Christians now call the Old Testament. And some of the knowledge supposedly was kept secret for just a few to know and this was reserved for oral teaching only.

Apparently, it was feared that this knowledge might be misused. Down through the ages, many of these secrets have probably become known. I surmise that these secrets were all or part of the Ancient Wisdom. Wisdom that is being taught today in small groups by those "who know".

But isn't it interesting that these ancient sages lived the "Godly Life" and wrote about it in scrolls which became present-day scripture. And then people coming after for two or three millennia have studied the scriptures in order to find out how to lead a holy life. That is, the ancient group lived "to write the book" and the rest of us even today try to interpret the book to live.

An anecdote that illustrates the paradox. [2]

In India, a Yoga Master was lecturing to a small group of his students, teen age boys mostly. Thirsty from talking in the hot room, he rang a bell to summon his servant to bring some water. Soon the servant came with a pitcher, carefully poured a glass of water and set it on a table while the Master continued.

When the servant had left the room, one of the students appeared troubled and asked , "Great Master, is it proper for a lowly servant to hear the divine truths that you are teaching?" The Yoga Master laughed and said, "I could go out into the busy market place and shout my wisdom all day long. And no one would understand!"

In a similar way, Jesus said that his parables were only "for those who had ears to hear" No one else would understand what he was talking about. He explained that only to his disciples did he speak "straight out"   Matthew 13:11 KJV.

1. From the Jewish Kabbalah. (There are several different spellings for this book in use.)
2. Paraphrased from traditional Yoga anecdote.

A personal experience:

During my middle years, I studied the teachings of the "Concept Therapy Institute" with the teachers Reverend Edward L. Crump and Katherine Calhoun. They had a basic course and several additional "higher level" courses. After listening the first time to 2 ½ days of lectures of the basic course, I thought that I had understood just about everything. When I reviewed the course some months later by sitting through the identical lectures a second time, I was surprised to discover much that I had "missed". Over a period of years, I sat through these same lectures by the same teachers thirteen times, each time gaining insight. Talk about reviewing a subject!

It was a real surprise when I finally saw that the most profound "secrets" of the teaching were presented right near the beginning of the lectures. But with insufficient background to understand, my brain just allowed this great knowledge to go over my head without my realizing that I had missed anything. It became apparent to me that a person can not assimilate a totally new subject all at once. Nothing new about that. Basic concepts must first be firmly understood before additional layers of knowledge can be added. And often these basic concepts might be contrary to what one has previously believed and so the old must be unlearned if it is found to be limiting. This graded approach to new knowledge is, of course, familiar to us in our grade schools. But sometimes a teacher can "stretch" our understanding by mixing some advanced ideas in with the ideas that are just "gently new".

This is the great paradox

Great spiritual wisdom--- great spiritual secrets could be "shouted in the market place" and few, if any, would understand. And the reason is that few people have the basic concepts upon which to build higher spiritual knowledge. And sad to say, most of us are satisfied to stay on the level of understanding that we already possess. It is comfortable that way.

What then is the "Greatest Revelation"?

Ralph Waldo Emerson described it in the simplest possible words. He said,

"The highest revelation is that God is in every man." [3]

I would add, "and it is possible for man to become directly aware of the God that is within."

3. From "The Heart of Emerson's Journals", edited by Bliss Perry, page 79.

Jesus taught that! And so have all of the other great spiritual teachers.

"Ye are the temple of the living God" [4]

"There is a natural body and a spiritual body." [5]

"Know ye not that ye are the temple of God, and that the spirit of God dwelleth in you?" [6]

"I am in God and God is in me." [7]

"Behold, I show you a mystery;" [8]

I have heard these biblical passages, and many others, read in church. The congregation apparently "agrees"that they must be true. After all, they are in the Bible. And yet it all seems so far away or so long ago that it is not really real. It may be theoretically true, but what can we do about it anyway? Besides, there are the more immediate concerns of daily life—everyone has them.

All of this begins to become real, however, when an individual meets someone who actually knows that it is real. A person who can demonstrate in some way that it is real, and can lead one to actually experience some aspect of spiritual reality himself. Then and only then does the "Spiritual Quest" become worthwhile. Then and only then does it begin to be the most important search that a person can make, with the most satisfying results.

And then an immense existing literature becomes "visible" to help a person work toward higher levels of spiritual consciousness.

And an even greater secret and an even greater revelation than the above statement of Emerson begins to appear! I won't mention it here, it is too deep a subject for this essay.

And an immense world opens up.

God blesses anyone who aspires to it.

4. 2 Corinthians 6:16   King James Version.
5. 1 Corinthians 15:44.
6. 1 Corinthians 3:16.
7. 1 John 4:15.
8. 1 Corinthians 15.

Some Unusual Coincidences

The thoughts that we have "in the spirit" can bring about what most people consider to be 'coincidences'. Once we become aware of this, we can often make the connection — see why things happen. A basic part of the Ancient Wisdom. Then again, it might just be coincidence.

The Parking Ticket

Sometime years ago, I parked on Euclid Avenue in Cleveland, right in front of the Church of the Covenant. It was just before Christmas and I knew that the police like to make money at this time by being "excessively vigilant" about parking infractions. So I was "excessively careful" to observe all of the rules.

When I returned to the car, wouldn't ya' know, a parking ticket was on the windshield!

The only excuse that I could see for the ticket was that the 8 foot tall signpost with the "No parking beyond..." sign was leaning about 18 inches forward. My bumper was about 2 inches past the base of the post at the ground level even though it was well behind the actual sign.

If they wanted to split hairs this was enough!

So I went to the "old" police headquarters on Payne Avenue to register my beef. The payment window was on the second floor. At the landing of the marble stairway, there was a large display case of badges of policemen who had been killed in line of duty, perhaps 30 or more.

It brought to my mind our street crossing guard ,"Dick-the-cop", when I was in the early grades. This was before there were 20 MPH school zones and there were only a few guards at the most dangerous crossings, such as at Lake Shore Boulevard by the Commodore Theater. All the guards then were real policemen. The kids loved Dick-the-cop. He would occasionally swing the little kids in the air amid their squeals of delight while waiting for the traffic light to change.

None of us knew Dick-the-cop's last name until.......

One evening, a desperate man held up the box office at the Commodore. There was a shoot-out and Dick-the-cop was badly wounded. His last name appeared in the newspaper, but to us, he was still just Dick-the-cop. Teachers helped little kids write get well cards and we all waited weeks for him to return to his post. Finally he did, but not for long. He was transferred to desk duty.

My reverie was quickly terminated and I found the place to pay the fine. I started to object to the man behind the bullet-proof window about the injustice of it all. His tired, cynical response was,

"Getta lawyer – $20". I saw the futility and paid the $20.

Going down the stairs, I thought, "what a contrast between those policemen that had given their lives in line of duty and the extreme pettiness of this trivial parking infraction. Where is the justice?

At the bottom of the marble stairs, I saw a $20 bill lying on the floor. When I looked around to see who might have dropped it, the place was deserted. I picked it up, smiled and put it my pocket. There was some justice after all!   Or Coincidence.

The Art Fair

The annual art fair is a big thing in Ann Arbor, Michigan. They close off several streets near the university and artists from all over the country set up booths.

At a booth, I saw a man, with a torch, brazing some custom-made jewelry. I said that I did inventive work, was interested in the creative process and I wondered how he got his creative ideas.

He said, "Oh I don't get the ideas. My wife does that. I just do the brazing. I retired just last week from Nicrobraze Corp." I asked, "in Detroit?" He seemed surprised that I would be aware of this small company.

I added, "I was talking with Mr. Peasely (the founder of the company) by phone just last week. And I went on to explain my interest in nickle brazing, the product of the company. We had a nice chat. Coincidence.

In the next booth, I talked to a woman artist, told her of my inventive work, asked how she got her creative ideas. She skipped right over my question and said that she had an aunt who was a patent attorney in Cleveland –"Helen Slough – haven't seen or heard from her in years – I'm sure she's dead by now."

I said, "No she's not dead — I was talking with her just last week." A look of shock, surprise and disbelief came over the artist's countenance.

I went on to explain that Helen Slough, now in her 80's, was still doing patent work and she gave a talk at the Inventor's Club in Cleveland about getting foreign patents, her specialty. That's where I met her.

I added, "Why don't you give her a call? I'm sure she would love to hear from you." Tears came to her eyes. She choked up and couldn't say anything. So I smiled and moved on. I hope she called, because Helen died a few months later. Coincidence.

The Kerosene Solution

Earl Schweitzer, a classmate from Case School of Applied Science, was driving by our house in Kirtland, Ohio and, on the spur of the moment, stopped by with his wife for a visit. I hadn't seen him for many years. We had both studied mechanical engineering, so we talked over old times.

Then I remembered that he had done his undergrad thesis on something in the machine shop and so I asked him about it. It involved a method of machining plastic lenses, new tech at the time. The secret, he said, was to squirt kerosene on the cutting tool as a lubricant. It made a smooth finish on the plastic, just as though the lens had been polished. I couldn't wait for Earl to leave.

For some days, I had been working in my shop trying to machine expensive black plastic for the body of a camera invention. Time after time, the plastic workpiece warped all out of shape from the heat of the milling cutter. I tried all of the usual lubricants for machining metals and nothing worked. Piece after piece was ruined. I had wasted almost all of the big block of material and would then have to order more from Cadillac Plastic Co. in Detroit, more delay, more expense.

Could Earl's idea of kerosene be the magic that I needed? I couldn't wait to try it, so I filled an oil can with it and started to machine the plastic work piece. It worked beautifully! Problem solved! Just from Earl's unexpected visit.   Coincidence.

The Hydraulic Pump

It worked the other way also. Earl's unique knowledge had helped me, and my unique knowledge helped Phil. I was driving along Rt. 6 a few miles from home as I had done hundreds of times. Passing Bill Wilder's place I stopped in just to say hello; he had taken me for a ride in one of his airplanes a couple of years earlier. He had built a large mobile home retirement facility. Not home, but his son Phil was at the maintenance building trying to get an ancient piece of home built machinery to operate. I knew Phil only by name, but he knew that I was an engineer so he asked me about the hydraulic pump on this machine.

"It's got a port for the oil to go in and a port for the oil to go out", he said, "but I've spent all afternoon trying to figure out what this third port is for."

A quick glance showed that the pump was 'WW II aircraft'. They were manufactured in nearby Cleveland, Ohio and "tons" of them were dumped at the end of the war.

"The third port is a 'drain' for the high pressure seal", I pointed out, and went on to explain the need for it on pumps of that vintage, and how to hook it up with just any kind of low pressure hose. Phil appreciated the information. My random visit had solved his problem. Coincidence.

The Junk Man

Working as an inventor, I got an idea for a different way to design a "rack-and-pinion" power steering gear for an automobile. Any usable automobile invention can, of course, be lucrative because the market for cars is so large. To explain a little bit, a pinion is just a small gear. And a rack is a "straight gear". That is, it is a straight bar with teeth cut in one side of it in order to mesh with a round gear. Together they were originally used as a steering gear just for small sport cars because they didn't have enough mechanical advantage for a heavier car. But then hydraulic power assist was added and they became popular for heavier cars too. I decided to make a little model to see how my idea would look. My "Boston Gear Co." catalog showed just what I needed and I selected a small brass rack that would mesh with some gears that I had on hand. I wrote down the catalog number "Boston G583" and planned to buy a couple of pieces at their Cleveland store when I got to town. A strange feeling of delight came over me, that I might have a good invention. Days went by while I worked on other things.

Then a junk man struggled up our driveway with his pitiful beat-up old truck. He asked if I had any scrap metal that he could have. I pointed to some junk in the weeds by the tree row and while he was loading it, I looked over the stuff in his truck for metal that I might possibly use.

Wow! Here was a keg with assorted junk in it including some brass rack that looked something like the stuff I planned to buy. I offered to pay the man, but he said to just take what I wanted. There were several pieces and if I could use it, I would not have to drive to Cleveland to buy any from the Boston Gear Co. From Boston Gear it was rather expensive, from the junk man it was free.

Imagine my surprise, and believe it or not.....

This brass rack from the junk man was made by Boston Gear Co. and the catalog number stamped on it was "Boston G583" , exactly the number I had written down days before.

The invention didn't pan out, but the extremely unlikely chance of finding the exact type of gear material in the junk truck was stupefying! Dozens of sizes were in the catalog. Coincidence.

The Punch Press

One summer vacation from engineering college, I worked at a factory that manufactured bearings for automobile engines. My usual job was to mill the oil groove in half shell connecting rod bearings; tedious and monotonous work that would help pay next semesters tuition. But one day the job was on a punch press — a dangerous machine. It required placing a part in the press by hand, letting the press hit it with a few tons of pressure, then removing it — 250 pieces an hour.

Because of the danger to the operator's hands, a safety device provided a "manacle" on each wrist with thin steel cables that pulled your hands back a safe distance when the ram of the press came down. The whole apparatus required a big framework of pipes above and around the operator with pulleys, etc to make it all work. The pipes were held together by screws so the thing could be adjusted for different size presses. An operator totally harnessed to the machine!

I was settling in to the rhythm of the job when George Hooper, a neighbor, came by. I had no idea that he worked full time in this shop. He ignored my greeting and just stood there watching me work. Finally he said, "You are not pulling your hands back!"

"I don't have to, the machine does it for me", I explained.

Screwing his gaze right into my eyeballs, he said, "Did you ever know of a machine that worked 100 percent of the time?"

As soon as I said, "I see what you mean", he sprang on his way as though he had been suddenly released. Oddly enough, in the neighborhood, I never thought that George had much brains, but he was giving good advice for a press operator — pull your hands back yourself — don't depend on the safety apparatus to do it for you.

The press and I 'did' one part after another, the monotony having been eased by George's unexpected passing by.

Then, only about twenty minutes later, the entire contraption of pipes, pulleys and cables came tumbling down around me. The screws holding it together had worked loose. I could have been killed just by the weight of it, but was lucky that the heavy parts missed me.

Was I ever lucky! I had been pulling my hands back myself as George had so recently advised in his indirect manner. I still have all the fingers, thanks to George. This safety apparatus was one machine that should have worked 100 percent of the time, but did not. Strange — I didn't see George again for several years. Coincidence?

As you ponder the principles outlined in these essays, you will see that there is often more to 'Coincidences' in every-day life than what we usually think of as 'just coincidence'. You will become aware that we all make mental inputs of all sorts into the world of the spirit. The more intense inputs (that usually contain emotion or strong desire) can bring about events in the physical world that we might call coincidences. It is similar to prayer except that we usually do not realize that we are doing it. This phenomenon is one of the great, but subtle, secrets of the Ancient Wisdom. It has been discovered and lost and discovered anew at various times. And so, many books have been written on one aspect or another of the subject without connecting it to the Ancient Wisdom or to prayer. Look back at the essay "The Wisdom — A Place to Begin".

Halos and Things

What does a head halo really look like?

The actors in modern-day church plays typically use an embroidery hoop wrapped in gold foil suspended over the actor's head with coat-hanger wire or some such. It is a cute prop to show who the holy characters are, and easy to make with materials at hand. In movies, a similar, but more sophisticated, ring image is sometimes portrayed floating over the actor's head.

The great religious art of the middle ages and renaissance shows a variety of representations for the halo around the particular figures that are considered to be the most holy.

For example, some artists show a light-colored disc, frequently gold or yellow, behind the person's head. Others have shown spikes of light radiating from the head of Jesus. Take a look at treasured religious paintings. The originals may be in famous museums around the world, but many fine reproductions are in books.

What do the halos in the paintings mean?

A couple of explanations keep showing up. They may have some validity, but they are pretty superficial. Let's look at them anyway.

People connected with art usually say that the halos are merely an artistic device to indicate who are the sacred individuals in a group. Or if just a single individual, that this person is being depicted as a holy one.

But those people who have studied the history of religious symbolisms have a vastly different idea. They point out that Constantine was emperor of the Roman Empire from 306 until his death in 337 AD. The official religion of Rome had been sun worship, but Christianity was growing and the pagans and Christians were in constant contention. Seeing that Christianity was on the rise, Constantine decided to go with it by making it the official religion, supposedly even becoming a Christian himself. But by a stroke of genius, he also melded the pagan symbols, rituals and dates into the evolving Christian tradition, perhaps satisfying enough people of each faction to make peace. So that:

Egyptian sun disks became the halos of the Christian saints.

Interesting as these two ideas (the device of the artist mentioned above and the Egyptian sun disk above) may be at first glance, they really just concern the limitations of two-dimensional art and also the limited understanding of the artists and the explainers. For example, the religious art of Eastern religions also shows head halos similar to those depicted in the religious art of Christianity.

A real head halo is different.   I know — because I saw one!

It happened like this: "Shadybrook House"[1] was a non-denominational "retreat house" and holistic spiritual study center in Kirtland Hills, Ohio, about six miles from where I lived. It was run by the "Laymen's Movement" organization which is based at "Wainwright House", a similar facility in Rye, NY. I had already attended an evening lecture and a couple of day-time meetings and became acquainted with Donald Boyce, the director. Mutual friends had told him that I had been engaged in serious spiritual studies with other groups.

During that summer, a highly-regarded speaker was coming to lead a week-end retreat. All available spaces had been booked up long in advance, but Don asked if I would be interested in attending if there were last minute cancellations. I agreed to come even at short notice.

Sure enough — about 4 PM Friday afternoon Don said that there was a cancellation and that the program would start at 7 PM.

I gathered some stuff and got there about 6:30. No one else had arrived yet. Finally I found the old caretaker who had long served the house, even back when it was owned by the Baldwin family. He said I could put my stuff in the dormitory on the top floor; that's where the visiting polo teams used to stay in the old days.

After settling in, I came downstairs to the main room and saw a lone woman with white hair standing in the middle of the room. I paused about three steps from the bottom.

I had been told that the floor lamps all had three-way bulbs and it was the policy to leave them on the low setting to save the cost of electricity until a group had gathered. And so at this time, the room was dimly lighted.

But this woman's head and hair were glowing, surrounded with a ball of light.

I was familiar with the photographic technique of shining a bright spot light, called a "kick light", on a person's hair from behind to create a halo effect for a photograph. So I quickly glanced around the room to locate such a spot light. But there was none.

I suddenly realized that I was witnessing a real head halo of the kind that had long been described in sacred literature!

It was a spherical ball of hazy whitish light, glowing of its own energy. It was perhaps 12 inches in diameter with edges tapering off in intensity another inch or two all around.

After about ten astounding seconds, I suddenly realized that I should not be staring at the woman and so I went down the last few steps and introduced myself. The halo quickly disappeared on the way as I broke my concentration of looking at it.

---

1. "Shadybrook House" was the original name of the private mansion of the Baldwin family. It was acquired by the Holden Arboretum and leased to the Laymen's Movement. Later it was occupied by the Lake County (Ohio) Historical Society.

It was the first time that I had experienced any significant spiritual event on my own. In contrast, when Myrus, the mind reader, read my mind (related in Section 1) that was something that **he** did and I was just the subject. This experience was different. This time I was doing it.

The lady was Ruth Gardner.

Over a period of time, I became very well acquainted with Mrs. Gardner, a highly spiritual person. Her husband Eugene Gardner was a retired mechanical engineer, a graduate of Case School of Applied Science, my own engineering college. He had been Vice President of Sales at Warner and Swasey Co. a well known machine tool builder in Cleveland, Ohio.

I felt very privileged by the incident.

Some time later, it dawned on me that there certainly must be other people like Ruth Gardner who live on a high spiritual level. And that head halos must be observed by others that have a moment of heightened spiritual awareness like I did that evening. And there may be others who can "bring up" their awareness of such things **at their will** to see what most of us never see — are never even aware of. And that these things can happen even in this day and age, not just in ages past!

The halo itself is a manifestation of etheric energy radiating from the individual. Being "close to the spirit" the person is able to access this energy, which appears to permeate the universe. And then it exudes from their head, at what is called the "seventh chakra" in the teaching of yoga. [2]

But how can the observer see a halo that is just energy? As I said, it takes an ability of "heightened spiritual awareness". In my only experience (to date) of seeing a halo, this augmented level of awareness was temporary, was unexpected and lasted only a few seconds. Without further spiritual progress, it would be a one-time, unique event. A "singularity" — as similar events have occasionally been for others. But one purpose of religious teaching is to increase one's level of spiritual awareness — to learn how to see these things — and do things.

The week-end provided many more spiritual insights.

The leader of the week-end retreat program was Tom Powers. He was truly a remarkable man, low-key, humble, but spiritually strong. Both he and Boyce had formerly worked at BBDO advertising firm in New York City. Powers had struggled for years with alcohol. Then, when close to death, had a miraculous religious recovery. For some years after, he operated a farm in upstate New York for other recovering alcoholics.

Saturday was a day of getting acquainted with others, "spiritual consolidation" and building of spiritual intensity. During his Sunday afternoon lecture, Tom Powers, with his incredible spiritual insight, directed some astounding high-level emergency advice straight at me, hardly missing a

2. A yoga master could undoubtedly see head halos any time he chose. Any further explanation of the higher forms of yoga teaching is beyond the scope of this essay.

133

beat in his lecture. He said, "Do not let the 'Kundalini' rise".[3] This meant that spiritual energy was rising up my spine. He knew that I was not prepared for the rest of this powerful experience. In complete amazement at his revelation, I instantly blocked it by directing my attention to it and willing it to stop. It made me realize what rare high-level abilities Powers possessed.

Sunday afternoon, the week-end retreat was coming to a close. But not for me! My spiritual intensity had increased. And as I sat with the group in the main room looking toward Powers and Boyce, I could see the aura around each of their bodies. I had read about this phenomenon but had never dreamed that I would ever experience it. Engineers don't do that kind of stuff!

I could feel that "sparks were jumping from my eyes". And I could see that whatever actually was emanating from my eyes, it was distracting to Powers as he tried to lecture and to Boyce. So I kept my face behind the person in front of me a good bit of the time. But each time that "I came out to look" I could again see their auras. Perhaps the Kundalini energy was rising again un-noticed.

The week-end retreat concluded.

I made no mention of the experience to the leaders because I was sure they knew more about what happened than I did. I made no mention to other people because I was sure they would not understand, but would be happy to misinterpret whatever I might say.

The literature on the subject of auras mentions two "well-known" types:

> A "first-level" aura that surrounds a person's physical body with a more-or-less colorless — but visible — energy field, like heat waves. It extends out two or three inches and surrounds the entire physical body. When I say visible, it is not visible to everybody.

> It is part of what the mystics call "the real you" as opposed to the physical body that most people take to be "the person". This is what I was observing.

And I would say that it is "obviously" a form of vibrant energy. Although I encountered many forms of energy in my engineering studies, they never mentioned anything like this. Still, there is a considerable literature on the subject of auras. But it is difficult to explain etheric matters in the English language that has few words dedicated to this subject despite a rich vocabulary, for example, in ceremonial religious concepts. As a result, explanations in print seem to mix in what appears to be fantasy. And different sources differ widely in the kind of fantasy that they mix in. As with all etheric phenomena, personal experience is the only proof that satisfies.

A "more expansive" aura (which I have not yet seen) extends in colorful streaks much farther out from the physical body, according to those people who are able to see them. The colors purportedly differ with the individual's spiritual and physical well-being and supposedly can be used to diagnose health conditions.

3. From "Kundalini Yoga", a branch of yoga, which will not be addressed in further detail here.

Over the years, I never pursued this subject any further, but instead studied the Holy Bible, other religions and other "schools of Christianity".

The head halo that I observed momentarily around Mrs. Gardner's head is supposed to indicate a high state of spiritual well-being, a level achieved by a very small percentage of the human race. These people are in direct divine connection, to some degree at least, with the spiritual energy that permeates the Universe. And the energy flows outward, the person being a spiritual beacon, so to speak, to the rest of us. In our Western materialistic culture it is called etheric energy while in Hinduism and in yoga, it is called prana, in China it is called qi, and in Japan it is called reiki (pronounced ray-kee). You can see that there is universal recognition of it.

The Bible describes the most extreme event of this energy phenomenon. Please look up in the New Testament the incident of the "Transfiguration of Jesus". It is described in Matthew 17:1-2+ also in Mark 9:2-3+ and Luke 9:28-29+. The "face of Jesus did shine as the sun." And his clothing is depicted as glowing so brilliantly that Peter, James and John are baffled. It is actually an emanation of etheric energy in the highest possible degree. A head halo could be said to be the lowest visible level of this manifestation. Both are energy, although Jesus may be the only one who has ever displayed the extreme level of energy of the transfiguration. There is good reason for that. It is said by the spiritual adepts that only the purest soul could possibly stand such intensity.

This occurrence in the Bible is, of course, described as a miracle. And would be considered even more astounding if seen by anyone today.

The great religions of the world teach how to access some degree of this energy in order to heal others, etc. Yet they hide it in symbolisms — parables Jesus called them — so that those people living on a cruder level may not profane it. The Bible hides it in plain sight so that only those who have "eyes to see and ears to hear" can become aware of it.

In order for a person to do this safely for himself or herself – without danger to others or to society, it has been found that certain human traits must be tightly contained, a personal condition accomplished after much instruction given by "one who knows".

For example, the individual must eliminate the negative and destructive thought patterns common to most of us— hardest of all — must even "purify the essence of his Soul". Jesus called it "becoming the new man".

These things are best done with the help of a "spiritual master" who can guide a student as to the proper path, the necessary disciplines. One who can watch over and protect him if the student "gets into spiritual waters over his head."

Alas! These spiritual masters are few and not easily accessible to most of us.

Distressing Incident — Extraordinary Experience

Some years ago, a most unusual incident took only a few minutes of my life — but I will remember it until I die!

I hesitate to write about it even now because people love to misunderstand — to misinterpret anything that is a little outside of their own direct experience.

I did relate this story once to a group of "spiritual seekers" who I thought would understand. But instead, they concluded that I had imagined it — or worse.

After attending church for some 30 years, I was then seriously studying "higher spiritual teachings" for about four years, saturating my enthusiasm by working with two different groups. Looking back, I think I was, at that time, about at the peak of my spiritual "sensitivity".

Our family lived in Kirtland, about 30 miles east of Cleveland, Ohio. It is a very pleasant place to live three seasons of the year, but the snow can be deep in the winter and most winter days are dreary from heavy clouds caused by nearby Lake Erie.

One fine day I was on the far west side of Cleveland on business, finished up about 10 PM and stopped at a restaurant for dinner before the long drive home (before freeways). It was one of a famous chain of quality restaurants; had a nice dining room and a counter with several stools.

Being the only one at the stools at that late hour, I ordered a meal with coffee first — and while reading the newspaper, suddenly realized that I had allowed the coffee to cool.

The counter man was nowhere around to warm it, so I gulped down about half of the cupful. The cup was cool — but the coffee was scalding my mouth and throat! How could that be?

I shouted out, "WHAT'S THE MATTER WITH THIS COFFEE — IT'S POISON!

The counter man came running out and asked me if I wanted another cup.

"OF COURSE NOT — IT'S POISON", I shouted at the top of my voice. By now, I was off the stool and out in the center of the room clutching my throat in pain.

"OH MY GOD!", screamed the manager at the cash register with "tears of fear and anguish" in her voice as she suddenly realized what had happened. She rushed out to the kitchen and there was much shouting. Although I didn't know what was wrong, I surmised that it was something serious from the sound and it concerned me.

I immediately turned inward for help. I felt in great need of some kind of immediate help. You may call it asking God for help. Or think of it whatever way you care to

I just intently **thought "HELP!"**

Instantly a calm voice from within said,

> *"As soon as you asked, I gave you the antidote."*

"WHAT?", I screamed inwardly to myself.

Again this calmest imaginable voice from within said,

> *"You drank a strong caustic. I flooded your stomach with acid.*
>
> *Had you panicked, I could not have done so.*
>
> *Now go and get some lemonade to cool your throat."*

Having studied chemistry in high school and college, I of course recognized that stomach acid would neutralize a caustic. And I realized that panic or a stress reaction would stop the stomach action just as it would stop digestion. In a panic situation, there could be no soothing flow of stomach acid — soothing and also saving my insides.

Without thinking, I followed the instruction of "the voice" and went to the ice cream cooler, lifted the first lid and there was a pitcher. I drank from it, spilling it all over my face and down the front of my clothes. It was lemonade!

The cool lemonade, another (mild) acid, felt good in my mouth and throat. And then I began to wonder: how did I know where to find the lemonade that "the voice" had recommended "to cool my throat"?   But I didn't have long to wonder.

The manager came out from the kitchen, trying desperately to appear calm — asked how I was. When she realized that I was still standing — not writhing in pain on the floor, foaming at the mouth or some such, she began to handle the situation rationally.

Of course, I could not tell her that I had already received help from within. I said that the lemonade helped, and she apparently in the stress of the moment did not ask how I got it.

I didn't tell her because I didn't know myself how I found it, except by some imagined "higher level" spiritual direction.

I said that I was OK although how would I have really known, although by that time I did have a strange peaceful feeling that "I was in good hands".

She explained that the counter man — a new employee — had mistakenly served me a cup of the caustic solution from the coffee urn that was being cleaned. Unfortunately it had taken on the color of coffee, and looked like coffee. (But it surely did not taste like coffee I might have pointed out.)

The manager insisted that I go to a local hospital for treatment, called ahead, then gave me a package of the caustic powder to show the doctor to suggest a treatment. I noticed that lye was the main ingredient, with some other ingredients that looked pretty ferocious too.

Although I did not feel it necessary to go to a hospital, she insisted and rightly so from the legal liability standpoint.

At the hospital, an East Indian intern, just roused from sleep, couldn't understand why I would "take poison". He gave me syrup of ipecac to induce vomiting. I didn't know at the time, but that is an absolute no-no for a corrosive poison because it will burn again on the way up, can get into the nose, sinus, even eat into the brain — ugh.

When there was no effect from the ipecac — undoubtedly because my stomach was so full of lemonade — he gave me another dose. Again, no effect. So he got out the stomach pumping apparatus. I took one look at it and said, "No thanks!"

On the drive home to Kirtland, about an hour later, the ipecac did finally take effect. It had been a miserable evening and I went to bed hungry. I waited for after-effects for several days, concerned more about the misguided treatment at the hospital than from the "coffee", but nothing seemed to appear. And that was that.

About "the voice" —

In one of my other essays, the one titled "Man Overboard", I mention another life-threatening situation where I turned inward for help. In that essay, I describe "the help" that I received as a "knowingness" of what to do. And I made a point that it was not a "voice" actually telling me anything.

However, in this situation with the poisonous coffee, it was clearly a voice. The words themselves were probably generated in my sub-conscious mind. But how the stomach-acid antidote from inside my own stomach took place in an automatic manner after I "asked" for help in the most general term possible — and how I then found the lemonade — must remain somewhat of a mystery. Except that I got the result that I asked for — the result that I desperately needed.

It reminded me of the passage Mark 16:17 and 18 in the King James Bible. [1]

> "And these signs shall follow them that believe; In my name shall they cast out devils; they shall speak with new tongues; They shall take up serpents; and if they drink any deadly thing, it shall not hurt them; they shall lay hands on the sick, and they shall recover."

Perhaps this experience was meant to attest to my level of spiritual progress or to confirm that there is help from within. And to "somehow" encourage my spiritual studies.

Distressing as this poison coffee incident was at the time, this extraordinary experience did clearly show me that there is much more to life — much more to being a human being — than they teach us in school. It not only demonstrated, but it proved to me beyond all doubt some of the things written in the Bible and in these essays. And I have been seriously studying spiritual matters and the Bible ever since.

After many years, this has been the only time to date that I have ever heard an actual "voice" although the "knowingness" level of help has occurred many times.

In spiritual studies, it may not be wise to think in terms of limitations. But some dire situations might seem at first glance to be so overwhelming that it would be hopeless to even ask for help. I would still ask "internally" for help anyway. I would expect to receive what might be called "first aid" even though a complete resolution would have to be provided by others.

.

1. As mentioned previously, Bible scholars point out that these two verses are not found in the earliest manuscripts, and so may have been added later by a copy scribe. But since they are traditional in the King James Version and some earlier translations, I quote them here, They do match my poison coffee experience. This discrepancy was also pointed out in the essay "Bible Interpretation - Belief and Faith".

Table of Contents

Section 3 - The Higher Consciousness

Science and Religion — Is There A Conflict Between Them?

Let's analyze it.

Science is concerned with the **physical world**.

Religion and the Bible are concerned with the **world of the spirit** — man and his relation to God.

Both seek to explain, to provide answers, each in it's own field.

These two different outlooks on the world do intersect legitimately at one point, however, and that point is mankind. Together these two great authorities should bring an increased perspective on what we humans are — the "human condition". They should do that — but the problem that we are addressing in this essay starts with a **criss-cross in thinking** by both sides. Then people choose a side; dig in their heels of ego instead of digging in with their brains.

The two-fold "problem" as I see it is simply this:

Religious people 'feel' for some reason that their literal interpretation of the Old Testament of the Bible should explain the physical world — which really is the **proper realm of science**. And scientists 'think' that their methodology that is so successful in figuring out the physical world should also be applied to religion, a field in which **their methods do not belong**. The simple solution that would clarify most all of the argument would be to **un**-criss-cross this limited thinking of both sides. And let each side get back to their proper field of endeavor.

Now how could that be done? Well —

- Religious people could study a little bit of science. Study the stuff that is in text-books, well proven, as opposed to news accounts of the latest cutting-edge work of un-proven science. Appreciate the past hard work that has brought us such a comfortable and safe life today.

- Scientists could at least read about the experiential **realities** of religion even though they might not believe any of it to be true, because their methodology does not confirm it. They could also try to understand the beliefs by which many live their daily lives.

Even a little taste of the opposite category should give some appreciation of the "other side" of this immense compilation of human knowledge that includes both physical and etheric facts.

As an engineer, I studied many aspects of science, some for use in my profession and some, such as astronomy, for my own interest. Later I began to study the underlying basis of religion. I say the basis, because I am not interested in the almost infinite variety of practices of the many different religions. Rather I have pursued the path toward the higher teachings of religion.

Out of all of that, I have come to conclusions which I would like to state here rather than at the end of the essay. Hopefully then, you will have something on which to pin the details of my discussion. Those same details that are usually given by others in the arguments about the (apparent) conflict between science and religion.

My Conclusion

To good people everywhere:

> Proven science has never been found to conflict with true religion.

And to people who are serious about religion:

> You do not have to disprove science in order to validate the Bible.

The **message** of the Bible is True! [1]

So it is some scientists and many religionists who create a pseudo argument due to an incomplete understanding on the part of each. But when a person looks at the whole picture rather than just his own perspective, it might become more apparent that the arguments are spurious.

Much of the conflict begins with the first line of the King James Bible — "In the beginning, God created the heaven and the earth." And as everyone knows, it (supposedly) took only six days. This is in the Old Testament, the Jewish part of the Bible, even though this creation story is said to have come from ancient Persia, and could even pre-date all Jewish writing.

As mentioned in the earlier essay "One Little Word" in Section 2, I point out that great Jewish theologians like Moses Maimonides (1135 AD - 1204 AD) say that **their** Torah (which is the same as the first five books of the Bible) is **not to be interpreted literally**. It is **poetry** of the ancient Middle Eastern people, but contains deep spiritual lessons. A literal interpretation can completely miss the meaning. And oddly enough, Yoga masters of India have said the same thing when reading these identical scriptures. Yet, Christians invariably read it literally, being unaware of these admonitions. And the **argument with science begins on that basis**. You may want to glance back at the essay "One Little Word" to refresh your mind about such literal interpretation.

We can say with all our hearts that God created heaven and earth. But then, what is God? How can just a word explain creation? It requires, of course, further definition, and there is plenty of that. There seems to be two basic concepts. One is the theological concept with endless variations that you can hear in church, none of which really explain creation if you honestly look hard.

Some of the explanations boil down to this: "God created heaven and earth. What then is God?" If you say, "God is a creative force or God has a creative power", this, of course, is circular logic. So this idea is a belief, and there is nothing wrong with a belief as long as you realize that it is a belief and not a solid fact. But many people do love to argue on nothing more solid than that.

---

1. But you have to interpret scripture correctly, and this is not easy to do, or to be taken lightly! See this same idea back on page 114.

The other concept of God is from those few "great ones" who claim to have directly experienced God. They are the ones that we should listen to — and from what I can tell, they have more important things to teach us than the creation of the heavens and the earth. Jesus was one such, and there are others. I try to listen to them and to follow their teaching! They teach about man and God and don't really concern themselves about our origins out of the distant past.

On the other hand, scientists have various theories in many areas and these theories don't just come out of thin air as some people seem to think. They are all based on things that are **presently known** and then **extended out** into what is not yet firmly established or even vaguely understood. As more data is gathered, theories might be seen as more true or less true — maybe eventually proven to be true, or false. At least tens of thousands of scientific facts have been proven, maybe even hundreds of thousands. However, much stuff is still being worked on and progress is being made, but some searches have taken centuries; others may yet take centuries.

At the present time, scientists envision the **"big bang"** as the creation of the Universe without bothering to wonder how "things" were before that violent event.[2] Since some non-scientific people with whom I have chatted were convinced that the big bang idea was created out of thin air just to "offset" the biblical story of creation, may I give a quick outline here as to how this theory came about. It has taken an immense amount of tedious night-time work by astronomers.

Before WW One, there was a telescope 60 inch in diameter on Mount Wilson in California and shortly after the war, a 100 inch telescope was built. It was a monster for that time and many important discoveries were made with it. Harlow Shapley, a brilliant astronomer, discovered the center of our galaxy; developed the method used to determine the distance to the far out stars and galaxies. Edwin Hubble, (the orbiting telescope is named after him) made the incredible discovery that there are billions of galaxies **outside** of our own galaxy. Shapley had believed that all of the Universe was contained within our galaxy. So it was suddenly realized that the size of the Universe was many, many times greater than previously believed.

With astronomers working on many projects, it was noticed that spectrographs of stars showed "a red shift of the Fraunhofer lines" (if you care to look that up). One explanation for that is the Doppler effect (if you care to look that up) which is used in the familiar police radar. It meant that stars in every direction appeared to be moving away from us at great speed. The Universe appeared to be expanding. In 1929, Hubble determined that the farther away a galaxy is from us, the faster it is receding, as if from an explosion.

Eventually, by "thinking backwards", astronomers reasoned that the stars of the Universe might have started from one spot some 13.82 billion years ago. Around 1950, there was much disagreement about this theory and British astronomer Fred Hoyle ridiculed the idea as a "big bang". The epithet stuck, and it has been called that ever since. Hoyle later admit-

2. British astrophysicist Stephen Hawking "proves" mathematically that time did not exist before the big-bang. So there could be no pre-existing God to set off the big-bang or begin "creation". **His** idea.

ted that he had errors in his calculations, maybe 'big bang' could be right after all. Since then there have been several correlating discoveries that appear to confirm the theory — but it is still a theory. Research continues, with ever more marvelous instruments.

Then science says that sub-atomic particles, such as electrons and protons, have an attraction to each other and they combine to form elements, the simplest being hydrogen with one proton and one electron (plus a neutron). Various conditions in the stars caused the formation of heavier elements. Lighter ones remain gases and the heavier ones have a propensity to clump together to form crystalline structures. The Bible calls these "the dust of the earth" and they do become the earth in all of the inanimate forms of rock and soil. Additional details of this process fill many books and have taken centuries to accumulate, but for this discussion need not be added here.

Religious writers point out that science hasn't explained exactly why there are these "attractions and propensities" that cause matter to evolve. Also "where did gravity come from?" and "who" made up the "laws of nature"? The form of the question (such as who) begs a certain type of answer that only religious belief seems capable of answering. And the questions seem endless.

It's true that science explains more "what than why". But "Good Grief" as Charlie Brown [3] would say — at this time in the history of science, in the history of the human race, all questions have not been answered — yet. Neither in science nor in religion! And some questions never will be answered beyond theory and speculation.

The deeper you look into the subject of creation, the more you realize that neither science nor religion has a complete model that explains with soul-satisfying details. The smart person accepts this imperfect state of affairs, drops the arguments and gets on with his or her studies, with life.

Some will feel science and the physical world more to their liking, and some hopefully, by their nature, will delve deeply into the true meanings of the world of the spirit. Especially blessed are those who can do some of each; they will have the broadest understanding. (And the deepest satisfaction with life I am tempted to say, although I have no data to support such a belief, other than my own personal joy.)

Another argument between science and religion worth discussing is this:

What is a human being?

Most people believe that they are a body. (A sadly limiting concept). And some have the idea that we are the highest of the animals, meaning that we have a mind and are the smartest. But most will agree that we do have an animal-like body. In recent years, even our DNA has been found to be very similar to that of some of the animals most like us. Only a few percent of difference.

Now that scientists are studying animals, we see that some of them are pretty darn smart too, like birds that not only fly, but can navigate the globe better than the airlines could just a few decades

3. Charley Brown is a little kid in the famous comic strip "Peanuts" created by the late Charles Schultz.

ago. And porpoises and whales do things that boggle the mind of man. And almost every species of animal is good at finding food. Even so, the dumbest man is smarter than the smartest animal.

Looking First at the Body.

In the science of biology, the theory of evolution teaches that mankind evolved from simpler life forms by a gradual or a step-by-step process. Much archeological evidence seems to support at least some aspects of that idea, although there are many gaps. In any case, it is well proven that mankind has walked the earth for a very long time, and has had many primitive civilizations.

Unfortunately, church people and clergy got all upset and jumped all over that theory as being fallacious because it seemed to negate the existence of man's soul and his connection to God. Not so, of course! The **theory of evolution**, whether valid or not, **is only about man's body**. And any theory of the origin of man's body has little or nothing to do with the reality of his divine soul. Still in the late 1800's, there was a concerted effort by Thomas Henry Huxley (1825 - 1895) and other atheists to make a religion of evolution theory itself; some say, an attempt to even replace Christianity. It caused quite a fuss at the time and for some time after.

About the Soul

Religious people are taught and many do believe that they are more than the body — they say that they have a soul, even though they may be a little vague as to what that actually means. In any case, in the religious sense, a person is considered to be a combination of a body and a soul.

Notwithstanding the above common teaching, there is a more precise understanding of what we human beings are. It is a higher religious perspective given to us by the great prophets. It teaches that **we are the soul of spirit** and that we **reside** temporarily in a physical body. Man is more than just a body with a smart mind! Much more! Seeing one's self from this higher perspective of **being** the soul is not only more accurate — it gives one the basis to gain greater spiritual understanding. Other essays will address this in more depth.

The Old Testament goes on to say, "And so God created man in his own image, in the image of God He created him ....." Genesis 1:27.

'Good Grief' again. Here we are discussing two of the biggest colossal arguments between science and religion, creation and evolution, and we're still only on the first page of the Bible. The fact that evolution theory did not jibe with the above Bible verse started the argument that is still going on today — an argument with a lot more heat than light.

The Bible teaches that man is created in the image of God. And since God is spirit, the kind of 'creation man' that God created must also be spirit. In other words, the Bible is talking about man's soul. That certainly must be the case because it is preposterous to think of God as having the body of a human. With all due respect to the incredible artistic talent of Michelangelo, his famous painting on the ceiling of the Sistine Chapel of "God giving the spark of life to Adam" is not good theology. The portrayal of God as a bearded old man lolling among angels has caused great confusion to many who take religious things literally. As I mentioned earlier, I have known people who became atheists because of this particular imagery. They had this anthropomorphic concept of God in the back of their mind from childhood and could not reconcile it with their view of the world. Unfortunately, atheism made more sense to them at that point in their lives.

The Age of the Earth

Anglican Archbishop Ussher in Ireland in the 17thCentury calculated the age of the earth by adding the ages of characters in the Old Testament Book of Genesis along with other historical records.[4] He reckoned that the earth was created in 4004 BC. It seemed like a good idea at the time and was well accepted. Others followed with similar calculations coming close to his.

On the other hand in modern times, several branches of science have worked independently using different methodologies to determine the age of the earth. Their figures all converge toward 4.5 billion years as the approximate age.

As pointed out at the beginning of this essay, the **physical world** is the field of science. But sad to say, there are some religious people today who feel that they must follow Bishop Ussher's Bible-based figure of a 6000 year old earth just because it is biblical. Criss-cross thinking!

Putting it Together

Out of all this, I have stated my own conclusions back on the second page, and I am sure that each reader will have his or her own particular conclusion, some differing remarkably from others.

I sense that the method of the creation of the earth and the heavens will never be known for sure, not by science or by religion. So why argue about it? I can look at photos of distant objects taken with the Hubble telescope with awe at the immensity and beauty of it all and "let it go at that". And I can appreciate the tremendous distances to the objects in the Universe because in college we had to repeat the type of calculations that astronomers use to determine these distances. And it is good to realize that the calculations, clever as they are, are not very precise.

How we got here on earth is not as important as **what we are and what we are becoming**, here and now. We should realize the mystic nature of what man really is — that the important part of us is the soul of spirit rather than the body that we live inside of, although the miraculous body is certainly a great convenience and in many ways an enjoyment.

Science never purported to explain the soul. And religion should teach that the man made in the "image of God" in the Book of Genesis is not the human body, but the soul.

If people only realized these things, would there be any rancor between the findings of science and the teaching of religion? My own conclusion is that, with knowledge, there is little to argue about. And there is so much more in religion, in the teaching of Jesus especially, for our benefit.

4. From Wikipedia.

Imaging in Prayer

A sailor's prayer: [1]

> "God — if there is a God
> Save my soul — if I have a soul"

This doubtful but hopeful prayer probably came into use as a last resort in the old sailing ship days when the wind was howling, the seas were mountainous and survival questionable.

It undoubtedly got some considerable use by soldiers as well, as in situations when they were pinned down with bullets whizzing by on all sides. I have had occasion to use it myself.

This simple prayer sure came to my mind one dark and stormy night during WW II when my ship, the heavy cruiser U.S.S. Quincy, was caught in a ferocious typhoon along with many other navy ships. It was June 2, 1945 east of Okinawa, and we were preparing for an assault on the Japanese home islands. I was on watch in the after engine room, 4 am to 8 am, in charge of two 30,000 horsepower steam turbine engines. We were running slow speed due to the pounding from heavy seas. The inclinometer (or clinometer as they call it in the navy) showed that the ship was rolling as much as 49 degrees, estimated since the scale only went to 45 degrees. If a crew member lost his grip during the roll, he could be dashed into the machinery and killed. So Chief Petty Officer Smith got some heavy rope, lashed the two throttle men to their sturdy bronze throttle wheels, then tied the rope to various points for emergency handholds.

The frightening part of this was the knowledge that only five and a half months earlier, the entire Task Force 38, which Quincy had now joined, had gone through the eye of a previous typhoon near Luzon in the Phillippines. Three destroyers rolled over and sank, 790 lives were lost and 100 aircraft lost or damaged. Other ships badly damaged. After the war, we got to see it dramatized in "The Caine Mutiny" movie. Would this typhoon devastate us in the same way — or worse?

Finally my watch ended. Breakfast and sleep were obviously impossible so I got to a higher deck where I could look out a porthole and see our sister ship U.S.S. Pittsburgh (built to the same design as ours) sailing on a parallel course about 1/4 mile away. Sometimes, it would disappear completely in a trough while we were on a crest. Later, I calculated from the vertical dimensions of the ship that the waves were at least 50 feet high if Pittsburgh had been heeled over in the trough, and the wave would have been even larger had the ship been upright while hidden in the trough. They were BIG waves, biggest that I had ever seen or ever want to see again.

---

1. An old Portugese proverb says, "If you want to learn to pray, go to sea." They were pioneer 'navigators' in the Atlantic Ocean in the early 1400's. Old sailing ship crews needed lots of prayer.

But Quincy was a staunch ship, 17,000 tons and 673 ½ feet long. It was the latest design and I had seen how careful the shipyard workers were the last few weeks of its construction. So I had absolute confidence in our staunch ship and our skilled captain.

My confidence vanished abruptly as Pittsburgh disappeared from view and word was passed that the ship had broken in two from the pounding of the mountainous and confused seas. We were told to stay in the middle of our ship (the bigger part) as all hands had done on Pittsburgh when they heard the agonizing cracking and ripping of steel as their ship reluctantly gave up to the cruel sea. We heard later that there was no loss of life.

As I said above, I thought of the simple sailor's prayer repeatedly as I hoped that Quincy would survive the next wave, and then prayed that we would survive the one after that. The wind howled at 120 knots (138 mph) which is as high as the anemometer could read. Suddenly the rain stopped. The wind vanished. We were in the eye of the typhoon. But the waves were still just as high. Looking out into this temporary "calm", I could see across the eye and there was the vertical wall of solid rain that we would soon plunge back into and then fight the winds and waves on the other side of the cyclonic storm. I wish I had been more observant of the nature of the eye, because I don't ever want to go back for another look. I did see that our ship flexed vertically about 6 to 8 inches under the stress of the waves, a matter of great interest to me as an engineer. (Confirmed some decades later for me by a large naval architecture firm that the ship could bend that much.)

With some damage, Quincy and other ships survived. Whether out prayers helped or not only God knows. But it's pretty obvious that the main purpose for this type of prayer is to calm the fears of the pray-er, rather than to change the outcome. Why should we expect that our trivial concerns should affect something as powerful as a typhoon? Or the fate of the ships engulfed in it? A more effective type of prayer for different purpose will be addressed below. Much as I loved the sea and being on the water, this was one of those life experiences that I could have done without.

The wording of the Sailor's Prayer at the beginning of this essay is defective, of course, because there is no "if" in God. God is! But the sailor's concentration and strong intention for survival would certainly be working in a positive manner for him.

The Navy has a longer official prayer called the "Navy Hymn" [2] and it is sung to a lovely, solemn melody. I love it. You have probably heard it. The first verse, of 4, goes like this:

> Eternal Father, strong to save
> Whose arm doth bind the restless wave
> Who bid'st the mighty Ocean deep
> Its own appointed limits keep;
> Oh hear us when we cry to thee,
> For those in peril on the sea.

2. The poem was written in 1860 in England by Rev. William Whiting (1825-1878) who had survived a ferocious storm in the Mediterranean. A year later, Rev. John B. Dykes (1823-1876) wrote the music. It was used by the Royal Navy, and in 1879 began to be used by the U.S. Navy. It is now called the 'Navy Hymn' in the U.S. FromWikipedia.

The nice thing about this prayer is that it can be used ahead of time. It was sung on the Titanic at the Sunday church service before the disaster. I wonder if those who sang it were some of the ones who were rescued.

An immense amount has been written about prayer, the things to be prayed about, the words to be used. The Lord's prayer of Jesus [3] is considered to be the ideal. He instructed us to pray in private for our own sakes rather than in the street for the approval of others as was common in his day.

But there is more to effective prayer than just words......... For a long time, people have used two approaches to be in touch with the deity, or their concept of God, whatever form that might be.

Prayer - which is an active form of addressing God with words, concentrated mind thoughts or images, often in hopes of some result in the physical world. When a result is being prayed for, it is called "votive" prayer. It usually follows the desires of the person's ego self and thus is concerned with "the world".

Meditation - which is a passive form of silently, but intently waiting for God to come close, "to speak" or to make his (its) presence known in some way. The idea is to experience the presence of what we call 'the God within us'. The practice of meditation brings the "world of the spirit" closer to the person doing it, and it can have life-changing benefits, can help bring the state of "living in God's Grace".

In our Western culture, many religious people have a disdain for meditation, saying that "it is too Eastern" and that somehow we should avoid it to be "true to our own religion". And so they may combine some aspects of meditation with regular prayer and call it all prayer without distinction.

But meditation is very important for the soul seeker and it is best learned from someone who truly understands it, who perhaps teaches classes. It is a necessary balance to the active form of prayer. There are books on the subject which might help. Due to the difficulty of conveying the technique, it will not be covered in detail in this essay.

The type of prayer that people pray depends on their existing level of spiritual consciousness. It could not be otherwise.

The best type of all round, day-to-day prayer, I am told, (and I believe and do) is to pray to have one's spiritual consciousness "unfold" or open up to higher levels. This is truly a prayer for salvation, although that might not be immediately apparent according to some theological frameworks. Blessed is the person who actually realizes and prays in this manner. Please look up how Jesus described this in Matthew 6:31-33 KJV.

3. Matthew 6:9-13 and Luke 11:2-4.

The few "great ones", who claim to have experienced God directly, say that they pray only thanks and gratitude to God, often for hours at a time. They say that there is nothing else to "pray for" in the sense that most people "see" prayer. These few live life differently, of course. They truly live in God's grace. They don't plan their lives; they let their lives unfold as God wills it. They "take no thought for the morrow" just as Jesus recommended that we take no thought for the morrow.[4]

Most of us are not anywhere near that exalted level yet. We're still living in this (physical) world, facing the daily problems of life. So we might pray for the sick, for sustenance, for protection, that our children will do well in life, and for any of the multiplicity of human needs and desires.

Here is something that is never thought of as prayer.

It is our general background thoughts. The sort of things that we think about daily, year after year. In the Book of Proverbs 23:7 [5] it says "as a man thinketh In his heart, so is he." The heart, of course, we call the 'sub-conscious mind' in modern terminology.

In the original context, this saying was a warning about evil men, but it is valid for good as well, actually for everyone. Our thoughts determine the type of person that we become, an observation made over 2500 years ago, still true today. Thoughts "set" our character.

More than that, the person who thinks strongly in this manner actually tends to bring the events of his or her life into being, that is, the type of things that occur in life. It is an 'unconscious low-level form of prayer', and may be almost continuous. This is well recognized but is a great revelation to most people. It can be very painful to accept if the individual feels that his or her life has gone badly. It is always easier for them to blame others or "circumstances" or bad luck.

The bright side is that we can change our lives by changing our thoughts. This idea is in all the gospels of the world in one form or another. Because it is not easy to do, and most of us need much help, there are study groups that go into the details of accomplishing this life-changing idea. It may take quite some time and effort to do; easier for some than for others. But contrast this idea of a fairly continuous, every day, low-level of formative thought with the minimal effect of a short prayer in church once a week, especially for the person who is not even paying attention to that. The everyday thoughts will win out and manifest in one's life. Experience shows that they do!

The principle involved here is an unconscious cause and a resulting effect. The **cause** is originated in the world of the spirit whether the person is aware of it or not, and then whatever is caused is **manifested** accordingly in the physical world. It normally 'shows up' in the physical world because most people look for the result in the physical world.

4. Matthew 6:34
5. The Book of Proverbs is thought to have been written sometime between 1020 to 500 BC. From the 'Bible Time-Line', "Christian Science Journal", 1993.

Let Us Pray, Then

God is everywhere and not just in church. Nevertheless some people still pray to a God in the sky where God was believed to be in antiquity. And some people pray to the "living Jesus" because it is easier to envision a person and to focus thoughts on Him than trying to imagine an "Infinite God of Spirit". And some who don't feel worthy to pray to Jesus, or God, might pray to a saint.

But since God is everywhere, a person serious about prayer can pray anytime or anyplace. And so you would think that a prayer to ask God for what we need should be easy. Experience shows that it is not. When done in the ordinary manner, most people find that prayer is usually not directly answered. It appears that God is not listening or that there may be no God — a not unreasonable conclusion based just on an individual's experience.

Still, Tennyson wrote: [6]

> "Speak to Him thou for He hears, and Spirit with Spirit can meet –
> Closer is He than breathing, and nearer than hands and feet."

We are one of the spirits mentioned here and God is the other. And if God is so close, why can't our words get through? Let's take a look. [7]

Back in the earlier essay on 'Wisdom – A place To Begin', some principles were presented concerning the use of concentrated directed thought to implant concepts into our own subconscious minds. Let's take another look at that idea from the standpoint of prayer, because they are directly related. Effective prayer is done the same way, but is just directed **through** our subconscious mind to the God underneath, to the God that Jesus said is within us.

A quick review from that essay

Schools that teach on this subject, say that a person can deliberately use his conscious mind to influence the sub-conscious part of his mind to achieve some benefit. This can be done by holding a strong image in thought of some desired condition, especially things concerning one's own personal health. The sub-conscious, which normally automatically controls a vast array of internal body functions, can also be enervated to selectively step up some of these, such as the immune system, to improve one's health. Or to overcome a diseased condition, even renew one's health.

This part of our mind asks no questions, but just dutifully does what we say if we say aright. And it has power to manifest in the physical world if we don't doubt.

6. Alfred Lord Tennyson 1809 - 1892. Poet Laureate of England 1850-1892. Above quotation is from "The Higher Pantheism" from the "Holy Grail and Other Poems". Strahan 1870. From several Internet sites.

7. There will be a third look and explanation in the essay "The Essence of the Teaching of Jesus". Please be assured that three "looks" at this magnificent subject are not too many.

In general, this has been known since ancient times in one form or another, but has often been clouded with religious beliefs, mysterious rituals — all of which are unnecessary to make it effective. The mystery and the rituals were to give the holder of the secrets a "cloak" to hide the secrets for themselves.

The basic ideas are taught today by various non-religious groups in the manner of "metaphysics". But there is more —much more! The metaphysics level can be used as a stepping stone to something far greater — real prayer. The difference is that working on one's own **sub-conscious** mind is great as far as it goes, but **prayer** goes a giant step farther.

The two, however, are not as separate in technique as they might seem to be in this short description. You learn the subtle difference by your own experience.

After some proficiency is developed in:

<blockquote>
concentrating on a desired image
directing this attention toward your sub-conscious mind —
</blockquote>

you can direct this attention "through your sub-conscious mind" to God, or to the "spirit" or to whatever concept of deity that you hold. This is possible, as you now know from my earlier essays, or from your own church teaching, **because God or the spirit is within you**. See Luke 17:21 KJV.

Normally we might have great difficulty "getting our message through" since the sub-conscious part of our minds is "filled with a thick layer of stuff". In the earlier essay, I called it a glob of stuff. Jesus didn't call it garbage, maybe that's a modern term. He called it **anger, worry, greed, criticism** of others and all sorts of useless concerns. A basic list is the **"Seven Deadly Sins"** [8] and all of the variations that come from those. He recommended that we "lighten up" on all of these things. This is a big chunk of the every-day teachings of Christianity, and a good place to start.

The sad part is that churches seldom say what great immediate [9] benefit we can have if we make the attempt to "cleanse" our conscious and sub-conscious parts of our minds. The benefit is that we can actually "become closer to God", or the "spirit" or whatever concept of deity that you hold. I have never heard this mentioned in any church, but admit that I may not have been there the day that it was preached. The point is that churches don't make it really, abundantly clear that this is the reason — the benefit — to cleanse our minds. The benefit is now!

Jesus told what type of things to pray for and what not to bother about. And that says it all!

---

8. Pride, Envy, Wrath, Sloth, Greed, Gluttony, Lust, all of which can lead to many other things.

9. In this context, 'immediate' means in this lifetime, hopefully near future, **not** just after you die.

It has been discovered that a **strong image of intention is far more powerful than a prayer of words**. This may be the reason why some people have remarkable benefit from prayer while others get no results. I would not want to argue with theologians or clerics about this. And I would not say to discard books of written prayers. I am just stating what has been discovered by those who have done it. Some are brash enough to say that **"God likes pictures more than words"**. Try it yourself and see for yourself. I leave it to you to interpret the idea as you wish and as your experience shows.

Some Basic Principles

These principles explain why imaging frequently works when it is properly done and usually fails when it is not. To get our intention through to God, the following factors are involved:

- Concentration of the mind on the image, that is, "sharpness" to the absolute exclusion of any diluting thoughts or doubts. The flame of "votive candles" has long been used to help concentration. The possibility of completion must seem logical to you or you will automatically introduce a feeling of doubt. Doubt ends it before you start!

- Intensity of the image in the mind, using emotional energy "to make it alive".

- Time that the image is held; A sharp short 'burst' seems to be better than trying to hold the image for a time. Most people would waver after many seconds, although that would be a good start.

- Repetition, occasionally only one time in enough, but usually several times may be needed, especially in the beginning. Many people think of prayer as a one-time thing and if it is not answered, "it is God's will". Usually not so — rather it is because the prayer is not adequate, or there is a mental block in the person's mind that must be recognized and overcome.

These four factors are inter-related. For example, if the intensity is great, as it might naturally be in a crisis situation, the time needed might be only an instant with no need for repetition. Many such instances have been reported in crisis situations, and some people believe that this is the only way that the process can work. Not true — but their experience has been limited to this type of situation. These stories are told in popular news articles.

And a master yogi, having great mind power, also would not need repetition. One "intention" would suffice. That is one reason why yoga training requires great mental discipline — so that the student yogi can learn to consciously control his thoughts at all times. Otherwise he might "activate an image" that he does not want once he begins to be adept at the imaging process.

Practical Aspects

In my own efforts, I think of the intensity and repetition aspects of imaging (since they are inter-related) using the following analogy: Perhaps you will recall this analogy from the Third Essay on Wisdom, but it is worth repeating here. The context there was the idea that a person is a creator in the world of the spirit to change his or her life in the physical world. "Imaging" here concerns prayer, a similar but larger context.

> Consider a large spike to be driven into a heavy timber. One or two accurate blows with a heavy sledge would drive in the spike. Or a larger number of blows with a medium-size hammer would also drive in the spike. But a little hammer would have no effect even with an infinite number of blows because the force of each blow would not exceed the "threshold of friction" between the spike and the wood.

The hammer blows being likened, of course, to the degree of intensity of the concentrated "prayer-image inputs" that the mind makes. And the threshold of friction being like the "layer of glop" or the veil that the image might have to go through, or the feeling of unworthiness, or the mental blocks. Few people will ever get rid of all the glop, but we can punch a hole through it with effort as described. But a prayer of words with only the force of the little hammer (in the above illustration) will go nowhere!

It is well to keep in mind that Jesus pointed out that "we cannot add one cubit (about 18 inches) to our stature by taking thought". So this should direct our attention to those things that can be changed — things that our minds would consider to be reasonably possible. Otherwise doubt takes over.

If it were easy to activate the sub-conscious mind or to have answered prayer by just ordinary thinking with our conscious mind, our every passing thought would set it off, probably much to our sorrow. It is well that God or nature has made it the way it is. There seems to be a veil between the two parts (or aspects or functions) of the mind, the conscious part and the sub-conscious part and God. But the human is actually a creative being! And with effort can become more in touch with God and become a greater creator. Scriptures of authentic religions say so.

The proper use of these principles, whether used knowingly or unknowingly, puts the potent power of imaging at our command; while inadequate use of the principles brings poor or no results. It is a skill that can be learned, although it seems to occasionally happen spontaneously with some people. People who live enthusiastically with a high energy level may use it without thinking. And the things that happen as a result then gives them more enthusiasm.

The sub-conscious mind and God respond to intense images, but not to words. This is "a great secret" in that it is necessary to the process, but does not seem to be recognized. As a result, many people tend to think in terms of words — not realizing the power of mind pictures. However, these "word-oriented" people might find the use of words helpful in building an image in their mind.

These same mental principles apply:

When a person superstitiously uses a charm or an amulet such as a crystal. Sometimes these objects, like the crystal, might help a person to concentrate, but inevitably lead to disappointment when it becomes apparent that there is no magic power in the object itself. It is sad that people put faith in the imagined power of an object, and then **overlook the real power** that is in their own mind coupled with their relationship to God. As mentioned above, the sub-conscious power of the human mind has been taught in many contexts for centuries. But used deliberately and understood by few.

However, I have not found it easy to do these things myself. Some remarkable things have happened to me, and to others, in crisis situations. And at other times has brought startling results. But it may on occasion take some time for the expected result to come about.

The ultimate goal is to be able to access my/your "imaging faculties" at will as needed, not just in a crisis. I have known spiritual "masters" who can do these things. It can be done but is not easy for most, and it is impossible if you decide that it won't work for you.

The graph on the following page can illustrate how intensity of the image input is related to the number of times the image might have to be "sent" to God. The more intensity, the less repetition.

Or you may choose to think of the inverse: How many times it will take in relation to the degree of intensity that you can muster. Living with high physical and mental energy certainly helps.

The graph is just an illustration of the idea, of course, and the correlation between the intensity of input and the number of times that might be needed is very indefinite, depending largely on how "close" you are to your subconscious, or how close you actually are to "the Father" as Jesus described the process. The important point is that it is necessary that the input be greater than a certain threshold which in itself is very indefinite.

It is best to learn prayer on a simple thing in a non-crisis situation. But if you are in a crisis, hit it hard as you can. If it doesn't bring immediate results, try again at a later time. And again. These things that Jesus and the ancients taught are bigger and harder than most people realize. You can make it work and may already be doing it successfully.

A final thought:

There are people who can make a simple prayer to God and have it answered to their satisfaction. They are blessed! And they do not need the insights presented in this essay. All of the thoughts in this essay are for people like me — and maybe for you.

Graph to Illustrate the Principle That:

a. More concentrated, sharper, energetic thought-inputs to the subconscious mind will more likely produce a physical effect, as in healing or other intention.

b. Inputs of lesser intensity will require repetition.

c. Inputs below a certain intensity will produce no effect at all. Shown here as a threshold of intensity, below which thoughts, even repeated many times, don't budge any-thing in the physical world. The level of this threshold can be lowered as the subconscious mind is cleared of "trash".

This graph is merely to convey a principle, the levels of which vary greatly among individuals and can change with time and effort.

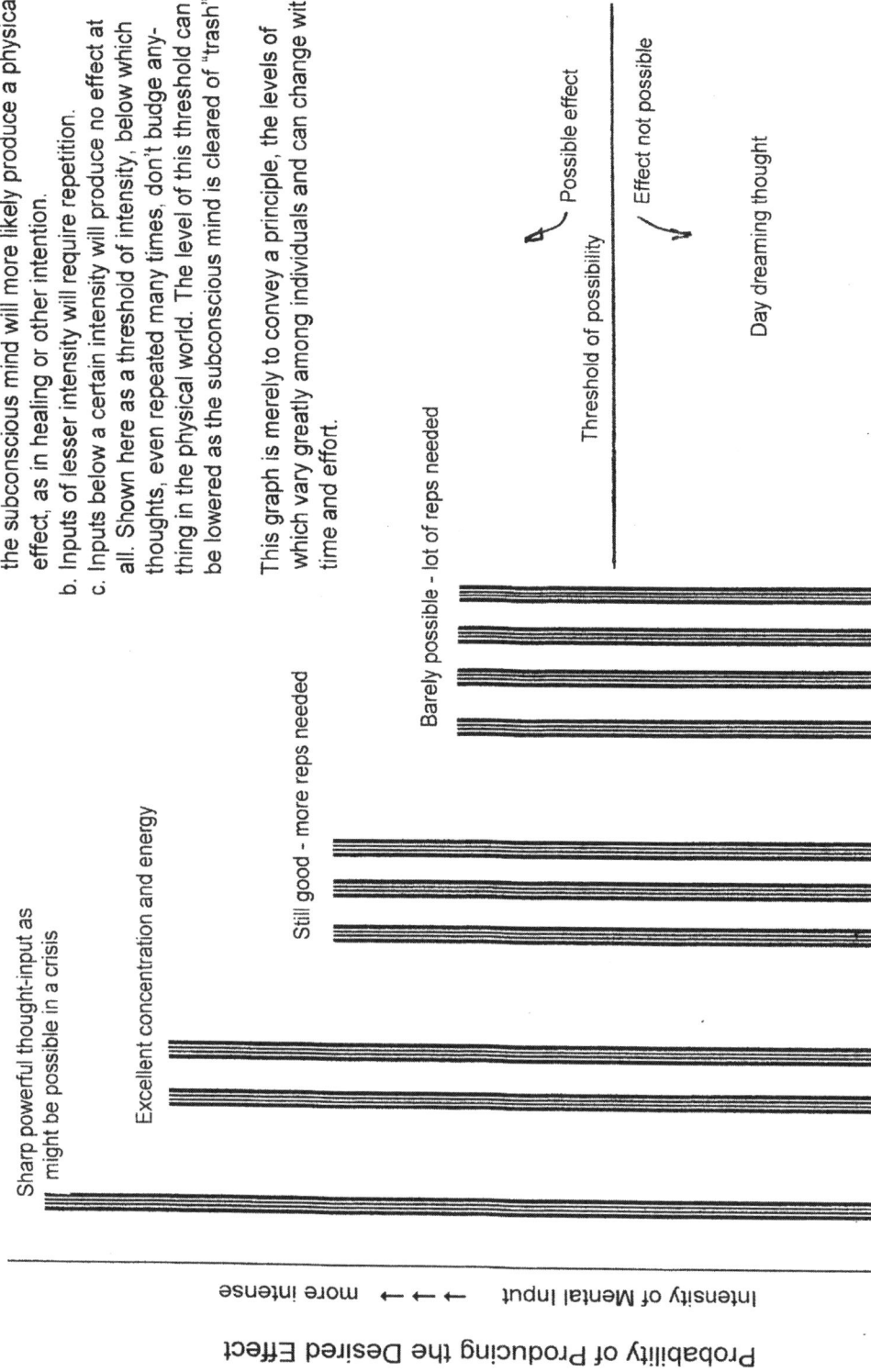

Sharp powerful thought-input as might be possible in a crisis

Excellent concentration and energy

Still good - more reps needed

Barely possible - lot of reps needed

Threshold of possibility

Possible effect

Effect not possible

Day dreaming thought

Intensity of Mental Input → → → more intense

Probability of Producing the Desired Effect

The number of repetitions of a mental input to produce a physical effect must be increased if power and concentration are at a lower level

Pray In Jesus' Name?

When I was in second grade of elementary school, the year was long ago, the teacher would often start the day with a short prayer. At that time there was no political fuss about it, probably because nobody was concerned about it, if the authorities even knew about it. My brother and I had already been attending Sunday School at a neighborhood church for about three years, so a prayer was nothing new to me.

One day the teacher finished the prayer and then went on at some length to explain that you had to end the prayer by saying, "we ask this in Jesus' name." She pointed out that the prayer would be invalid otherwise. And she implied in a mysterious manner to our fearful little minds that if we slipped up, the prayer might even be misdirected to some evil entity, the details of which she didn't dare to explain because of our innocence.

None of this made much impression on me, actually I could not have cared less!

However, after school, one of my classmates approached me with a serious question. Eventually this boy and I went all through school together. Then we both studied engineering at Case School of Applied Science (which later became part of Case Western Reserve University).

His name was Emanuel Citron — and he was Jewish.

What the teacher had said about Jesus made little impression on me but it had deeply troubled "Manny" all day long. And he asked me if I thought it was necessary to pray in Jesus' name.

As close as I can remember, this was the first time that Manny had ever spoken to me and I was puzzled why he thought I would have any knowledge or understanding on the subject. I guess he figured that I, being a gentile, might know things that a Jew would not.

I simply said, "I don't know."

I have thought of this incident many times over the years. I hope that Manny has found a suitable answer to his question. But didn't God ever answer prayers of the ancient Jews? Even the prayers of the great prophets of the Old Testament who came before Jesus? Obviously God did.

As the decades have gone by, every time the political question arises about prayer in the public schools, this incident again comes to mind. The differences in religious beliefs can have crushing consequences to religiously sensitive people of minority religions if these people are coerced by civil authority. The idea that "the majority rules" fortunately is tempered by the U.S. Constitution.

After years of study, I could now answer young Manny's question like this:

In the poetic language of the Middle East that Jesus used:

"Do this in my name" means to "do it as I have taught you."

I have heard these expressions "do it in my name" or "go in my name" used by Middle Easterners in similar contexts but other than religion. These people were of a generation brought up in the early part of the 20th Century while these ancient colloquial expressions were still part of every-day speech, that is, before the modernizing effect of television, the interaction of WW I and WW II and emigration to other countries. According to the way that they were accustomed to speak —

If you pray the way that Jesus taught, you are doing it "in his name".

That is what is important — to pray as Jesus taught us to pray — not whether you tack the phrase onto the end of a prayer. Over a long period of years, my observations of the effectiveness of prayers in church indicates that tacking the phrase on the end of a prayer is not much more than a tradition, a tradition founded on a literal interpretation of scripture. However, if you want to add the phrase to the end of a prayer, it probably couldn't hurt as long as you pray in the way that Jesus taught during the body of the prayer.

The ancient Jewish prophets, as described in the Old Testament, were undoubtedly praying in the same proper way that Jesus taught centuries later. Effective prayers to God were probably said long before Jesus. But He was speaking against the practice, common in his day as it still is now, of "praying before men" so that all may see that the person appears to be devout. He pointed out that "they get their reward" (from the esteem of others) superficial as that reward may be compared to a devout prayer done in private. See Matthew 6:5 - 8

So Jesus taught us to "turn inward" in prayer.

Why? Because:

> Behold! The Kingdom of God is within you.   Luke 17: 21
>
> God is in me and I am in God.   1 John 4:15
>
> Ye are the Temple of God and the Spirit of God dwelleth in you.   I Corinthians 3:16

Jesus said that the God that we pray to is within us. But there are still those people who look up to the sky when they pray; think of God in the sky when they pray. Wrong direction!

What is a better way to pray?

> The essence of a prayer is the intention — not the words.
>
> A really effective prayer is strongly concentrated intention — not words

A prayer must be reasonable and logical or your doubt is already telling it not to work! Example: If I pray to win the lottery, the extremely poor odds of winning makes this illogical to me.

161

The phrase "If it be God's will" at the end of a prayer nullifies the prayer. You obviously don't mean what you just prayed. This is always a cop out. Commonly used with a voice of resignation to conclude some church prayers, you can tell over a period of time that it kills results if you keep track of what has been prayed for. While this may be acceptable in a church setting because of tradition, it is best not to do it in private prayers.

Although the above statements are the essence of prayer, there are details useful in the practice of prayer that are beyond the scope of this essay. Look back in the essay on "Wisdom — A Place to Begin" and the essay Imaging in Prayer". There are "secrets" there in how to do it if you want results. Think of those suggestions in both essays as prayer. That's what it is!

I hope that you can sort out what is real from that which is just tradition, just "folk religion" or just theological nit-picking.

I hope that you use the knowledge!

Each person must find his or her own spiritual path and follow it. And it's not so easy in our materialistic culture. I wish that I had realized the above things at an earlier age.

The Essence

of the

Teaching of Jesus

✝

From the Gospels

The Essence

of the

Teaching of Jesus

✝

The Essence of the Teaching of Jesus

Jesus was a mystic and He was sent to teach mysticism to the world.

Dictionary definition of mysticism: The practice or belief that a person can obtain unity or identity with the Deity or the ultimate reality.

Whatever else a church or an individual might want to add to the life of Jesus, this is the basic. Without this central understanding, any and all interpretation of Jesus can go astray.

For me, it is easiest to understand the teaching in detail if it is viewed in two aspects:

> The new morality that He taught,   and
>
> Seeking the kingdom of God

In the four Gospels, bits and pieces of these two aspects are interspersed. But as you read, if you think in terms of these two aspects, it helps to separate and clarify the teaching.

The New Morality of Jesus

Jesus reiterated some of the Ten Commandments that God gave through Moses. (Matthew 19:18), implying, of course, that all of them are important. These "rules for living" are so basic that they would be good in any culture at any time period. And the Jews that He was teaching already accepted them, and probably followed them to a greater extent than we do today.

Jesus gave the "Golden Rule", a glorious concept, in Matthew 7:12 and again in Luke 6:31. Even though a similar thought had previously been taught in a negative sense (Don't do unto others....), He put it into the positive, active form to be a milestone of great significance in human relations that will stand forever.

Jesus added the unheard-of idea that "we should love one another", more than just family and close friends, Matthew 22:39 and again in John 16:12. "Anyone could do that", He said, and He expected better. Matthew 5:46 and again in Luke 6:32.

And He added that we were to love even our enemies! Matthew 5:43, 44 and Luke 6:27 & 6:35. What a strange teaching — even to many Christians today. Jesus was viewing human attitudes from a very lofty perspective and taught that a person would have to evolve his personal life to this higher, more exalted level in order to make progress in his own spiritual life.

As you read through the Gospels, other bits of His new morality will be apparent, especially in the Sermon on the Mount (Matthew Chapter 5 through Chapter 7).

Purpose of the New Morality

It has long been recognized that this new morality will, if followed to some extent at least, lead to a better life on earth for the individual. Our churches teach this, of course. And it has also been seen as the basis for a better, more productive society if significant numbers of people try to follow it. Our churches teach that also. Sad to say, much of our daily "news" is about people who have grossly disobeyed secular laws that have been derived from this Biblical moral teaching.

> But the great purpose that Jesus saw is that His New Morality is an absolute prerequisite for a person to aspire to the lofty goal of the kingdom of God! And for that He added new layers of morality. A person was not even to think in his own mind about immoral thoughts. Whew! Matthew 5:26+.

More about this later.

Once an individual does aspire to the kingdom of God (and few of us really do, as you will see as we go along), the **New Morality then takes on a noble purpose for that person** and becomes easier to live by. Perhaps I should say "only somewhat easier" because even St. Paul had difficulties, see Romans 7:15,19. Without that goal, however, the lofty rules seem to be endlessly antagonistic to our "normal" human desires and wants, because.....

The spiritual purpose of the morality teaching is to overcome and get control of the animal nature that is inherent in our being from the fact that our soul lives in a body that has deep-rooted animal characteristics, such as anger, greed and lust. And a further purpose is to overcome and get control of those characteristics that we think of as naturally human, such as envy and vanity.

More about this later.

The Kingdom of God

Down through history, the great sages have taught that there is a physical "reality" and there is a spiritual "reality". They might also say that this is just a way for beginners to look at the world, and learn about these two aspects. That eventually a total reality will become clear, that is, a spiritual reality is right here intermixed with the physical reality. They are actually one.

In the meantime, we are all familiar with the physical reality; we live in it, spend most of our time coping with it, even trying to enjoy some aspect of it.

Fewer people, but there are some, have an acquaintance with the spiritual reality. But the Bible is filled with accounts of the spiritual level being made known to people on the physical level. That, of course, is one reason why the Bible is viewed with such reverence. And many such accounts are also in church literature, sometimes even in "Readers Digest".

Jesus, the greatest sage of all, came to teach about the world of the spirit, and He does so in the four Gospels. He pointed out that He was not trying to get His message across to everyone, at least not in the beginning, because many people "were waxed gross". However if even a relatively small percentage of people understood what he was talking about, it could change the world. And it has!

As I have mentioned previously, He used the term "kingdom" in the same sense that we use the word today for the "animal, mineral and vegetable kingdoms". The main theme of this essay is a hasty outline of His teaching about the kingdom of God. And we will look at it by means of the direct words of Jesus in the four Gospels

I have often speculated that Jesus might have deliberately chosen the word "kingdom of God", instead of some other term, (such as the 'domain of God') to deliberately bring about His confrontation with the Roman authorities. This would have been a necessary step in bringing about the trial and the events that followed — His glorious destiny! Perhaps you have other thoughts about this.

In the spiritual sense, the term "kingdom" can also be used to denote that the individual becomes "king" over the "subjects" in his own inner life, the subjects being all of those urges mentioned above that separate us from God. In the higher states, this can also include control over his own life energy and other subtle aspects of life that few people ever consider in our materialistic culture.

When teaching about the kingdom of heaven / kingdom of God, Jesus speaks in the present tense. He teaches about something that is HERE AND NOW; just as beneficial for people today as for the people back then.

His **kingdom** is not just a reward after you die. Rather, it is a **higher level of consciousness** to be experienced now while still in the body, all for God's purpose. It is about "this" life. Jesus does also speak about life after death, but the two aspects of His teaching should be understood as separate. Much Christian teaching fails to make this distinction and creates confusion. A person may be led to study the Bible with the wrong basic assumption, not realizing that "entrance to the kingdom" can be in this life — is meant to be in this life — all for the glory of God.

The quotations from the New Testament on the following pages should make this idea clear. And then you prove it to yourself as you wish.

The Story Begins Here   Matthew 3:1-3

> "In those days came John the Baptist, preaching in the wilderness of Judea. And saying, Repent ye: for the kingdom of heaven is at hand."

169

For this is He that was spoken of by the prophet Esaias, saying,

The voice of one crying in the wilderness,
Prepare ye the way of the Lord, make his paths straight."

John the Baptist appears on the scene as "advance man" for Jesus. He announces that the kingdom of heaven is at hand, but doesn't give details in this account. He leaves that to Jesus.

When Matthew records this event, he uses the term "kingdom of the heavens", (plural in the original Greek) rather than the term "kingdom of God" used by the other Gospel writers. This is explained by the fact that Matthew, like many Jews of that era, still did not say the name of God because he was so much in awe of the deity. In Bible study, a well-accepted conclusion is that the Kingdom of God is the same as the Kingdom of heaven in most meanings in the New Testament.

To see for yourself, compare Matthew 13:31 with Luke 13:19. In these two parallel passages about the parable of the mustard seed, Luke uses the term kingdom of God while Matthew calls it the kingdom of heaven. There are other such parallel passages.

Continuing the story: Matthew 21:23

"And when he was come into the temple,
the chief priests and the elders of the people
came unto him as he was teaching, and said,
By what authority doest thou these things?
And who gave thee this authority".

Jesus taught in the temple, but was probably speaking over the heads of most of his listeners. His doctrine was different from what had been taught for centuries. He was the newcomer.

The chief priests not only didn't understand his new teaching, but they felt threatened that He was weakening their authority.

So during his three year ministry, the priests were constantly in contention with Jesus, just as today you will find some churches that teach against the higher aspects of the doctrine of Jesus.

In the above situation, Jesus answered the question of the priests with a trick question of his own. I'll let you look up the details. Matthew 21:24-27. Jesus didn't discuss the source of his authority here. But in many later statements, He attributed everything to his connection with God.

To really establish his authority, Jesus began to perform his well-known miracles. The New Testament lists about 45. Some were deliberately done to demonstrate his relationship with the Father. Changing water to wine at the wedding in Cana was his first. (John 2:1-10). And this did impress his disciples (John 2:11) as well as the servant at the wedding who knew where the wine came from. Many other miracles were performed by request or as a situation indicated the need.

Many Christians today do not actually believe the authenticity of these miracles. They imagine "logical" ways in which some of the miracles might have taken place while ignoring the ones that they cannot explain. The miracles are real! Jesus came to teach that a person, when united with God, can actually do such things. Few people really believe that today, even clergy! I do — Didn't I prove it in a small way when I healed myself after drinking poisoned coffee? [1] And I have proved to myself that the miracles were real by duplicating some that I have not described in this book. However modern technology has overshadowed the need for some of the miracles, but we should not overlook the incredible benefit of the teaching in other aspects of our lives.

Let's follow the story as it unfolds in scripture —

Jesus begins His ministry with the same admonition as John the Baptist.   Matthew 4:17

> "From that time Jesus began to preach, and to say,
> Repent: for the kingdom of heaven is at hand."

✝

And in Matthew 10:7, Jesus instructs his disciples, saying,

> "And as ye go, preach, saying,
> the kingdom of heaven is at hand."

✝

Mark 1:15 reports the same saying of Jesus in slightly different words.

> "And saying, The time is fulfilled,
> and the kingdom of God is at hand:
> repent ye, and believe the gospel."

1. See the essay "Very Distressing Incident" in Section 2. And I have seen things done by others that would jar many readers. Spiritual masters have done miracles in modern times. Maybe not all that Jesus did, but some astounding things.

171

In Matthew 6:33, Jesus invites people to seek the Kingdom of God.

"But seek ye first the kingdom of God,
and his righteousness; and all these
things shall be added unto you."

And the same incident is reported in Luke 12:30-31.

"For all these things do the nations of the
world seek after: and your Father knoweth
that ye have need of these things."

"But rather seek ye the kingdom of God;
and all these things shall be added unto you."

The invitation is as good today as it was back then. Jesus is talking about the world of the spirit and He explains why it is a good idea to know something about it.

In John 18:36, Jesus says that: His kingdom is not of this world.

"Jesus answered, My kingdom is not of this world
if my kingdom were of this world, then would my
servants fight, that I should not be delivered to the
Jews, but now is my kingdom not from hence."

This passage is out of sequence here, time-wise. It takes place much later in His ministry, close to the crucifixion. But it illustrates absolutely that the kingdom of God has nothing to do with a government on earth as so many believe.

And it sharpens the meaning of the quotation on the next page.......

And now in Luke 17:21, Jesus tells the Great Secret.......

"The kingdom of God is within you."

"And when he was demanded of the Pharisees,
when the kingdom of God should come,
he answered them and said, 'The kingdom
of God cometh not with observation:

Neither shall they say, Lo here! Or, lo there!
For behold, the kingdom of God is within you.' "

Jesus says that you can't see the kingdom of God — it is not an earthly kingdom in the usual sense — for indeed, it is within you!

Jesus is not implying that the entire infinite expanse of God is totally enclosed in any person. How preposterous that would be. He means that there is a contact point in the depths of each person that touches what Jesus called the 'Father'. And that is true whether we as individuals are aware of it or not. Jesus clarified this idea when He said that "He was in the Father and the Father was in him". John 14:1–11. More about that later in this essay.

This is what Jesus had been trying to get across with His parables. For example: The awareness of the kingdom of God begins in you, if you choose, like a tiny mustard seed and over a period of time it grows to glorious proportions. Trying to describe the invisible spirit world directly is always difficult. Yes. The kingdom of God may be hidden deep within you. But for most people, it is not so easy to find it. And as a result many people settle for a mere shadow of the world of the spirit by trying to contact the dead, divination, predicting the future or similar meaningless pursuits — sidetracks at best — certainly not the kingdom of God that Jesus glorifies.

We are fortunate that some down through the years, have followed the full teaching of Jesus and experienced the kingdom. And once they have had this experience they report that His teaching is true. The few such people that I have met then became teachers to tell others. Two started "religious" schools, others lectured, one wrote books. For most seekers, such people are not easy to meet, as I have pointed out in several places.

Some basic ideas in the New Testament are so important that they are repeated, sometimes in the same words and other times in a parallel meaning with different words. The critical concept of the "the kingdom of God is within you" is an example.

In First Corinthians 3:16, the above concept is described again as "the spirit of God dwelleth in you". And the individual person, himself, or herself, is called the "temple of God."

These two perspectives show that the kingdom of God is the same as the spirit of God.

> Know ye not that ye are the temple of God, and
> [that] the spirit of God dwelleth within you.

But do not expect to understand the meaning of this to its fullest depths just by reading the words, splendid though they be. One reason, perhaps, that people have a difficult time accepting this concept is that they emphasize in their mind the word "kingdom" rather than the word "God". If a person is stuck with the idea that "kingdom" means a government, that would, of course, make "kingdom of God within you" meaningless.

Most of us are not directly aware of the spirit of God within us, it is said, because:

- We are separated from God by our sense of self, the ego, or

- It is described that there is a veil hiding God from our awareness, or

- The spirit of God is below our threshold of awareness because in our culture we typically look outward instead of inward, or,

- Being human we are subject to the catch-all concept of "sin" — original sin of Adam even if we are trying not to sin ourselves in the usual understanding of that.

These are some of the ways down through history of describing the situation. It can be made to sound hopeless by the theologians, but the teaching of Jesus is all about overcoming this sense of separation of real, ordinary people from God.

Although looking inward is an important part of this process, I keep in mind that looking outward (rather than inward) is what enables us to cope in a practical way with the world that we live in — it is vital, especially in the earlier part of our lives as kids when we are "learning our way around" in the physical world.

It is expedient at this point to interrupt the flow of the story to explain a discrepancy in some of the more recent Bible translations. We will get back to the story on page 178.

In any Bible store, you can see that there has been an "explosion" of Bible translations into the English language in the last hundred years or so. The newer versions are in modern English for easier understanding and the awkward word order (to our ears) of ancient Greek has been smoothed to familiar form. Some are word-for-word, others are thought-for-thought and some are paraphrased for faster reading. There is plenty from which to choose.

Much of this interest in making new translations has come from the discovery, in recent years, of ancient manuscripts that are older than those used for the venerable King James Version.

Being older, they presumably are closer to the source and might have fewer errors introduced by the process of copying and re-copying by hand. As Christians, we wish that we could read the words spoken by Jesus (in our own language, of course) just as they were written by his disciples. Sad to say, no "original" manuscripts have ever been found and all that we have are these copies of copies. However Bible scholars say that the art of deciphering "Biblical Greek" (the language of the writings that became our New Testament) has been helped by the greater availability of secular writings of the period that now add to the general knowledge and the meanings of words of that era.[1] Fortunately, there are many early manuscripts of scripture that differ only in small details.

Unfortunately, **some of the most popular of these newer translations miss one of the most important aspects of Jesus' teaching** — the very 'essence of the teaching of Jesus' that we have been describing here. Most of us Christians never get to that level anyway, so few of us will be affected. Some might even say, "With all the other stuff who cares?" Still — a translation should not lead a sincere seeker astray. But some do!

Disclaimer

I do not expect anyone to believe what I have written here, except that it is directly out of Scripture. A spiritual seeker must explore meanings himself and confirm his beliefs by whatever means he has available. Just getting started in the right direction can be a big job in itself because there are so many people who want to teach what is not true, or is only partially true.

In my own mid-life years, as my interest yearned for "something more" in Christianity, I searched in many directions, took a couple of wrong turns. But as Truth began to eventually unfold in my understanding, I could finally discern "who knew" and who did not! I had much help.

The Bible "discrepancy" that I refer to is the New Testament verse Luke 17:21.

It is **correctly translated in the King James Version** (published 1611) and some other Bibles as:

> 20 "And when He was demanded of the Pharisees, when the kingdom of God should come, He answered them and said, The kingdom of God cometh not with observation:
> 21 Neither shall they say, lo [look] here! Or, lo there! for, behold, the **kingdom of God is within you**".

This correct "interpretation" is a known part of the Ancient Wisdom and has been proven by the many who have lived it. It is also backed up by other sayings of Jesus. Luke 17:21 is seldom, if ever, mentioned in church because it is above the level of most congregations and would serve no purpose for them. But for you, and any advanced student, it is important.

1. Anyone interested in Bible TRUTH should study "how our Bible came to us". There are many books on the subject for the lay person.

Sad to say, some Bibles give a poor translation as: "the kingdom of God is in your midst" or "the kingdom of God is among you". They might mention in a foot note that the word could also be translated as "within" but then give a bad explanation that "it was "unlikely" that Jesus meant that the Pharisees had any semblance of God within them, which **is** exactly the point that Jesus was making. Then they leave it to the reader to choose which interpretation that they might prefer.

Another modern translation reads, "The reign of God is already in your midst" or some such. Instead of the simple but profound statement that "God is within you", this translation brings in the idea of an "authority" and may refer to the establishment of the church.

You can see why it is important that this particular verse be correctly translated. Jesus told where to look for your personal contact with God. So if an advanced student is actually "seeking the presence of God", then his/her 'study Bible' should not lead him/her astray. And if their teacher is teaching this TRUTH correctly, their study Bible should not confuse the issue or give a contrary interpretation.

The great teaching of Jesus is about the world of the spirit which He called the "kingdom of God", using the term "kingdom" as we use it today for "animal, mineral and vegetable kingdoms".

I am painfully aware that many churches teach that "the kingdom of God" is a theocratic government in the usual sense of a worldly government on earth. Some say it means a worldly government that Jesus offered the Jews and that they refused. Not so! Others say that it is a theocratic government for the "world to come" someday when Jesus returns. This is not what Jesus taught, although I would not care to argue the point with those folks who hold this as a cherished belief.

Seeking the Meaning of the Greek Words

Just skip this section if you are not interested in searching out the translation of Greek words. But if you are — included here are some of the "helps" that are available.

I personally don't know Greek, let alone Biblical Greek. Fortunately there are some who have this ability and I depend on them for accuracy. So in writing these pages, I have turned to the **original Greek writings** as they are translated directly in the

"Interlinear Greek-English New Testaments"

One of these (from the Internet) is:

"Online Greek Interlinear" http://www.scripture4all.org/OnlineInterlinear/Greek_Index.htm.

Verses of this on-line publication were studied to sharpen the meanings of the verses that I have quoted here. Another that was used as reference is:

"Interlinear Greek-English New Testament"
Jay P. Green, Sr. Editor   Third Edition 1996

that has both a literal translation and a King James Version translation. And several other Greek-English New Testaments have been published and can be useful.

Fortunately, you don't have to know anything about Greek to benefit from the use of an Interlinear Greek-English presentation. Here's why:

The direct translation of the Greek words is provided. The direct meaning of these Greek words enables one to "separate the wheat from the chaff" in one's search for truth in any New Testament version, ancient or modern. In the pages of this essay only one such critical or controversial word is involved; it's unnecessary to analyze everything in the entire four Gospels. But you might enjoy looking up some Greek yourself.

Another help for the searcher: Since Bible scholars have argued about the meaning of words for a long time, James Strong in the late 1800's numbered each of the Greek words in the New Testament. That way, particular words could be singled out for discussion. Strong also published the "Exhaustive Concordance of the Bible" in 1890 wherein every word of the Bible is referenced to its location(s), an incredible accomplishment that is of great benefit to students of the Bible.

In the verse Luke 17:21 described above, I pointed out that the correct translation of the last line is "the kingdom of God is within you" rather than "among you" or "in your midst". Looking up this last line in an Interlinear Greek-English New Testament, you will see:

"Ho basileia ho theos entos su eimi"   (The Greek)

"The kingdom of the God inside of you is"   (The direct translation)

Then leaving the "Interlinear" and looking in Strong's Concordance: The number of the Greek word "entos" (pronounced en´- tos) is 1787 if you care to look it up. It is translated as "within" or "inside". Not "among"! The same Greek word is used in Matthew 23:36 to mean "clean the inside of the cup" not the "among" of the cup.

The individuals, or committees, who make serious translations are obviously "word people". In the ideal situation, they would also be experts in the subject being translated. That way, the nuances of words with several meanings could be selected according to best meaning without ambiguity. In something as complicated as Scripture, this ideal may not always be met, which is why there are still important differences in translations.

Another unusual factor causing differences between old and recent Bible translations is this:

When the King James Version and earlier versions were made, the translators were fluent in Classical Greek. But they didn't realize that the handwritten manuscripts were written in Koine´ Greek, the international language of commerce. It was similar to regular Greek but more limited. Words may have had difference connotations. It is said that the KJV translators thought that it was a special sacred form of the language just for scripture. Modern translators have a much better understanding derived from surviving business records of that era. Oddly enough, this has not helped to clarify the verse of interest, Luke 17:21. The old is correct— the new is not!

Now with this discrepancy in Bible translations explained, we can get back to the story.

It might appear to some people today that Jesus was "running a free clinic" to heal lots of people for their own sakes.

But He said that he did the miraculous healings and other miracles to glorify God. And then at the Last Supper, He explained (in John 14:12) to his disciples how He was able to do these things. To do miraculous things that were impossible for others to even comprehend, let alone try to duplicate.

> Verily, verily, I say unto you, He that believeth on me,
> the works that I do shall he do also; and greater [works]
> than these shall he do; because I go unto my Father.

"Going unto the Father" sounds simple, but just exactly how do you do it? The simple answer is that all of the teaching of Jesus is directed toward learning just that, and it is obviously not easy. But some dedicated people have done it down through the centuries. A teacher helps.

Yoga masters, especially in India, have been reported to do things impossible for those with only ordinary knowledge, even to the level of the miracles of Jesus. But as far as I know, none has ever claimed to return from the dead as Jesus did, a unique event in history. (Some Yoga masters in India have been reported to appear after death to some of their disciples.)

Jesus told his disciples that **they** could do even greater "works" than He had demonstrated. Remember that the disciples at this point had already had three years of instruction by Jesus and had done some healing of the sick. So perhaps the statement "works greater than these" was a reasonable expectation for them to achieve sometime in the future.

If you meet someone, hopefully an authentic spiritual teacher, who can demonstrate works-of-the-spirit even to some small degree, then you will believe that people today are able to carry out the teachings of Jesus. And when you can do a little yourself, then you not only will believe; you will know for a fact that these teachings are true. Aspiring Christians today should not think only of the superlative level of miracles that were performed by Jesus. There can be small miracles also for a person trying to lead a spiritual life, and they can be useful, and enlightening.

178

From time to time, Jesus expressed his exasperation with the disciples because they were slow to catch on to his teaching. The things that were so simple and obvious to him were not so easy for simple fishermen. And He knew that his remaining time with them was growing short.

And then the hyperbole!

I suspect that Matthew 17:20 may be an exaggeration just for emphasis.

> And Jesus said unto them,
> Because of your unbelief:
> for verily I say unto you,
> if ye have faith as a grain of
> mustard seed, ye shall say
> unto this mountain, Remove
> hence to yonder place;
> and it shall remove; and nothing
> shall be impossible unto you.

Although I have seen modern earth-moving equipment do this very feat, but in a physical way.

> For us, it is not important to learn how to
> perform miracles, as such. Rather — it is
> important to learn how to "go unto the Father".

Then, in John 14:10, more puzzling instruction.

> "I am in the Father and the Father is in me"
> Believest thou not that I am in the Father, and the
> Father in me? The words that I speak unto you
> I speak not of myself: but the Father that dwelleth in me,
> He doeth the works."

And in John 14:11, Jesus repeats the same thought for emphasis.

> "Believe me that I [am] in the Father, and the
> Father in me: or else believe me for the very
> work's sake."

Jesus expresses clearly in a few words that God must be everywhere. And being everywhere, God passes through Jesus as spirit. And so, as Jesus says, He is immersed in the infinity of God. And since God is everywhere, we also, you and I, are immersed in the infinity of God that is spirit, and this spirit passes through us just as Jesus said it passed through him.

A modern analogy given by Rev. E. L. Crump (see essay on "Rev") might help to explain:

> A hand-held transistor radio is immersed in radio waves, is it not, wherever you might want to carry it. Radio waves are everywhere. The radio waves penetrate the radio so that we can truly say that the radio waves are in the radio and the radio is in the "sea of radio waves" wherever the radio might be.
>
> Equally important to consider is this; in the radio there is a finite point (the antenna) where there is a **working connection** between the physical device and the ethereal, invisible "substance" of the waves.

Such a tangible metaphor for this profound concept was not available to earlier generations, of course. And for this teaching, I have never seen any metaphor that was expressed in the idiom of a simpler time. Apparently none was ever available, and so this particular teaching of Jesus seems to have lain dormant.

Jesus pointed out that there is just such a **working connection** between a **person** and the **God within** in Matthew 6:22 KJV and again in Luke 11:34 KJV.

> The light of the body is the eye: if therefore thine eye be single, thy whole body shall be full of light.

A simple interpretation of this verse is that we should concentrate "single-mindedly" on the important teachings of the Master. But there is more.

Jesus explains how to pray in Matthew 6:6 and gives the example of his famous "Lord's Prayer". He then calls attention in Matthew 6:19 to those aspects of physical life that are important in the life of the spirit. And the "single eye" is a reminder to pay attention to these very things.

But people who practice the life of the spirit sometimes call this "single eye" of Matthew 6:22 their "third eye" or just the third eye. And it has a profound meaning.

The mystical teaching of the third eye:

> The third eye is an imaginary point in your "mind's eye" that is between the eyebrows, behind the bridge of the nose. This is the point of the working connection on which to concentrate one's thought during prayer or meditation. Like the antenna on the transistor radio.

More could be said about the single eye, but not in this limited essay. Many of the modern translations of the New Testament miss this teaching altogether. Because they do not understand the deep meaning of passages that "sound funny", the translators try to make it sound logical to the ordinary reader. They render Matthew 6:22 in ridiculous ways, like:

"If you have good eyesight, your whole body will be full of light".

While this sentence may be literally true, it makes little sense in a book that is about the world of the spirit told in great depth.

A good idea is to read some (or all) of the Bible passages in this essay in several different translations. You will begin to see which ones are most clearly the real words of Jesus and which are merely a smooth rendition of the thoughts of men.

At the present time, a computer web site at "www.biblegateway.com" makes Bible verses available in many translations for your comparison. Or a big city library may have several translations of the Bible and New Testament available to spread out on a table for comparison.

As you have read on previous pages, Jesus advised people to seek the kingdom of God, the centerpiece of his mission on earth.

And after teaching in various places for perhaps two years or more, He was addressing a crowd along with his disciples. Perhaps He saw that some of the people were making spiritual progress and so, in Mark 9:1,

> And He said unto them: Verily I say unto you, that there be some of them that stand here, which shall not taste of death, till they have seen the kingdom of God come with power.

some would actually experience the kingdom of God before they died..

And the same message in Luke 9:27

> But I tell you of a truth,
> there be some standing here,
> which shall not taste of death,
> till they see the kingdom of God.

In a similar manner, some people today might experience the kingdom of God while still on earth in their human body. And for almost 2000 years, some few people have done just that.

The account of this happening as related in Matthew 16:28 is worded somewhat differently. Jesus says, "There be some standing here which shall not taste of death till they see the Son of man coming in his kingdom. And from this, some Bible scholars believe that Jesus is predicting that only six (or eight) days later He will be taking John, James and Peter up on a mountain to pray.

181

While there, (as described in Matthew 17:1-2) these disciples witnessed the "transfiguration" of Jesus as He was glowing with the energy of the immanent God.   I leave it to you to decide which interpretation seems most likely: a) the unique transfiguration of Jesus, or b) the possibility that some (maybe even you) will experience the kingdom of God themselves directly before "they taste of death".

Jesus is aware that crucifixion is drawing near, so with all caution aside.......
Jesus drops the block buster!

I and my Father are one.

John 10:30

And the result

Then the Jews took up
stones again to stone him.

John 10:31

With their lack of understanding of the higher knowledge that Jesus was teaching, the Jews completely misunderstood what Jesus meant. They jumped to the conclusion that He was claiming to be God, a claim that He was not actually making.

And Christians themselves have misunderstood this statement of Jesus for almost two millennia. Jesus meant that at that point in time, He was in complete union with God the Father. All of the veils that other people had — all of the barriers between Jesus the human rabbi and the Father had been erased. He was connected! He did not mean that He was identical to God as the Jews thought — and as some Christian churches maintain from their own misinterpretation of John 10:30 as it is written in the King James Version and many other translations.

To understand this better let's look back at an earlier time, in Matthew 3:16, right after Jesus was baptized by John the Baptist, "the heavens were opened unto him, and He saw the Spirit of God descending like a dove, and lighting on him." From this episode it can be seen that He is **"one with the Father"** from the **very beginning** of his ministry. And it is confirmed at his transfiguration in Matthew 17:2 + and in Mark 9:2 +. It would be helpful to read these passages before going on. Once you realize that these events can be real, you will see how incredible they are.

In the higher forms of Yoga, it is taught that the **goal** of the individual aspirant is to achieve **union with God**. The literal meaning of Yoga being **"yoke"**, **yoked to God** — not becoming God as some detractors of Yoga claim. Superficial impressions can give wrong conclusions. And in the Yoga teaching, this goal of union with God, when realized, is called "salvation". Interesting?

Since you might not have a Bible immediately handy, I will insert the above-mentioned passages about the transfiguration here:

Matthew 17:1-2 KJV
And after six days, Jesus taketh Peter, James and John his brother and bringeth them into a high mountain apart. 2 And He was transfigured before them: and his face did shine as the sun, and his raiment was white as the light.

And in Mark 9:2-3
And after six days, Jesus taketh with him Peter, and James, and John, and leadeth them up into a high mountain apart by themselves: and He was transfigured before them. And his raiment became shining, exceeding white as snow; so as no fuller on earth can white them.

This account of the transfiguration of Jesus is described, but it is not explained in the Bible. However it is known now to be a manifestation of energy. Energy drawn to Jesus from the imminent, infinite God and flowing through his <u>spiritual</u> self outwardly through his <u>physical</u> self. The three disciples are able to see the energy as visible light only because they are in a high state of spiritual consciousness from being in the presence of their master, the greatest spiritual master.

Such an intensity of energy flow (of the transfiguration) would destroy other individuals unless they had "purified their inner nature" to the degree that Jesus had. As an analogy, it is likened to a strong beam of laser light shining through extremely pure glass. The glass doesn't even get warm, because it allows the energy to flow through unimpeded. But a dark glass, like sun glasses, would absorb much of the laser energy (because of its darkness) and would shatter.

Except for this account in the New Testament, I have never heard of anyone ever witnessing an event like the transfiguration. Fortunately, we are all familiar with a "lower voltage" manifestation of etheric energy in connection with the glowing head halos which are depicted in religious art work, and which many people have actually seen (as I have) around the heads of contemporary "holy people". (See the essay on "Halos and Things" back in Section 2.)

Here is a secret. The transfiguration of Jesus, perhaps unique in history, is an ultimate degree of flow of God energy, (etheric energy) whereas the glowing head halo is a much lower level. There is a similar flow, or burst, or pulse of God energy when "miracles" are performed. **That is how they are performed**. Or as Jesus described it, "the Father doeth the works."

This gives an inkling of a part of the "higher religious teaching" of Jesus. A teaching that says that we, even as humans, are actually (potentially powerful) souls of spirit residing in physical bodies. True today whether we are aware of it or not. Or want to believe it or not. Also true today even though we may have been taught something different, by church or by culture. But it requires us to develop a higher spiritual consciousness — just as an opera singer must develop her voice way beyond normal, and an athlete must develop his body and skill well beyond normal.

Jesus had publically claimed that 'He and the Father are one', and that infuriated the Jews. His destiny was now progressing rapidly toward the crucifixion. So at the Last Supper, Jesus candidly and clearly tells the disciples many things (John Ch.14, 15 and 16) that He wants them to know so they can carry on his designated work on earth (after He has ascended). And now without the multitudes listening, He doesn't need to hide the higher teaching in parables, a teaching that is only handed down orally.

Then by himself, Jesus prays that the disciples, whom He has loved, taught, and watched over, may become "one with the Father" as He and the Father are one.

Theologians call this *"The Divine Prayer"* and its meaning does have a sublime beauty.

It is lengthy, but will be presented here. John 17: 4 thru 11.

> I have glorified thee on earth: I have
> finished the work thou gavest me to do.
>
> And now, O Father, glorify thou me with
> thine own self with the glory that I with
> thee before the world was.
>
> I have manifested thy name unto the men
> which thou gavest me out of the world:
> thine they were, and thou gavest them me
> and they have kept thy word.
>
> Now they have known that all things
> whatsoever thou hast given me are of thee.
>
> For I have given unto them the words which thou
> gavest me; and they received [them], and have
> known surely that I came out from thee, and they
> have believed that thou didst send me.
>
> I pray for them: I pray not for the world, but for them
> which thou hast given me; for they are thine.
>
> And all mine are thine, and thine are mine;
> I am glorified in them.
> And now I am no more in the world,
> but these are in the world, and I come to thee.
> Holy Father, keep through thine own name
> those whom thou hast given me,
> **that they may be one, as we [are]**

184

"The "Divine Prayer" continues with an **astounding conclusion**:
John 17: 20 thru 23

Neither pray I for these alone,
but for them also which shall
believe on me through their word.

that they may all be one; as thou Father,
art in me, and I in thee, that they may
also be one in us: that the world may
believe that thou hast sent me.

And the glory which thou gavest me
I have given them; *that they may be one,*
even as we are one:

I in them, and thou in me,
that they may be made perfect in one;
and that the world may know that
Thou hast sent me, and hast loved them,
as thou hast loved me.

Take another look at the verse John 17:20 right above. It concerns us directly.

Jesus prays further that even the people who believe in him [3] by hearing the word indirectly through the ministry of the disciples **may become one with the Father and one with Jesus**.

The disciples wrote these sayings down that they heard directly from Jesus, so that we may study them and believe in Jesus.

And Jesus said that we could become one with the Father as He and the Father were one so that we can know that God loves us just as God loved Jesus.

This Divine Prayer, of course, now includes people today and even you and me. Because now the word is written for all.

Next page —

3. The phrase "believing in him" means that a person believes the teaching of Jesus and follows it.

Oneness with the Father is the highest goal that a person can attain

Theologians call it the "Mystic Union"

The four gospels teach how to achieve it

This is the Teaching of Jesus of Nazareth

✝

WLH

Conclusion

A person living on this exalted level has a **connection with** and an **expanded love for all of mankind** that is often explained as "the infinite love of God" flowing unimpeded through him. I have experienced this, to some degree at least, from my teacher and it can be overwhelming. Jesus experienced it directly from God and He wept. I and many others also have wept just feeling some degree of this overpowering love. (Jesus may have also wept for all of humanity.)

Let's review the main points of this essay because they are so very important. The reason that they are important is on the next page. Whatever way you may think of Jesus, God or man, this is the teaching of a *spiritual master*, undoubtedly the greatest one who ever lived.

Jesus said to seek God. He called it the "kingdom of God", using the term kingdom as we use it today for the Animal, Mineral and Vegetable kingdoms. It means the spiritual domain or realm where God may be found.

He said that God is within you. (Luke 17:21) Not in church or some faraway place. The point at which an individual touches God, the point at which God can be realized, is within each individual. And this is true whether he or she knows it or not, believes it or not.

The details of how to do this are pretty vague. Jesus spoke in parables so that only those who had some spiritual understanding could fathom the <u>very advanced lessons</u> that He was giving. (In the earlier essay titled "The Greatest Secret — Greatest Revelation", it is like the 'paradox'.) He said that most of the population had "waxed gross", that is, were not worthy to receive his high teaching. On the other hand, He said that He was speaking "straight out" to his disciples. It has been argued for centuries whether this 'inner teaching' was included in the Gospels or was kept as an oral teaching. Be that as it may, teachers 'who know' have handed down the knowledge orally to small groups of neophytes ever since.

Jesus performed miracles and said that we could do the same. He explained that "He went unto the Father and that the Father did the works." He was really vague about how to "go unto the Father" and, as a consequence, very few people today are able to do this. The four that I have had the privilege of knowing were all teachers of this higher wisdom. So I know it is being done today.

Jesus prayed that you and I might become "One with the Father as He and the Father were One". (John, entire Chapter 17) We would then have the power and the knowledge to potentially live and act on this high level. Incredible!

In order to do the above, it is necessary to "become a new man", (or woman). Now we come to the nitty-gritty. The 'new man' would have to overcome the <u>animal traits</u> of the body in which we live. And then would have to overcome <u>human characteristics</u> that are common to everyone and seem to be accepted as OK by most. But they are not acceptable for the new man. An 'evolution' to the new man is necessary to prevent the person from doing damage to himself and others with the tremendous power that would be available — that becomes available — from the 'Father', depending, of course, on how intimate and complete is the rapport.

The teaching of Jesus in the four Gospels, Matthew, Mark, Luke and John is the 'mother lode' of spiritual knowledge — seeking God and possibly becoming "one with the Father". This is true salvation and Jesus called it our birthright.

> Once a prospector has found the mother lode
> he can stop panning for gold in the river.

It was pointed out on the previous page that it is important for a seeker to truly understand the main teaching of Jesus. He taught many things, **but it is not generally recognized that they all lead to his main message.** In the light of this, the reasons that a clear understanding of the main points of his teaching are so important are these:

Many church theologies are derived from the **secondary aspects of this great teaching**. They are simple to accept on faith and may be satisfying to those who have not heard the full extent of the teaching. However, these limited theologies can hide the fact that there is more to Christianity, and so they can be a spiritual dead-end to those who might want to go deeper into the spiritual life.

Once the main teaching is seen in its full depth, you can make more accurate interpretations of New Testament scripture by using a new method. You set aside the present method used by scholars of comparing one passage with another passage in hopes that together they might define a meaning. Instead, you compare any particular passage against the main teaching that is known by the great ones and is described on the previous page. If your interpretation meshes with that, it is likely to be the most accurate.

I don't spend much time studying the Old Testament. That was the Covenant of the ancient Jews. Instead, I concentrate on the "New Dispensation", the New Covenant given by Jesus, written down by the disciples and carried out by St. Paul. That is what the first Christians did! And that is what I have been doing for many years.

> "Ask and it shall be given you;
>
> Seek and ye shall find.
>
> Knock and it shall be opened unto you."
>
> Matthew 7:7

It is not the purpose of these pages to tell you how to do all of these things. Much has been left out. There are books, there are teachers, few as they may be. This is just a map of one path that can be taken, if you choose to do so.

Fact Or Belief — A New Idea to Many

In the previous essay, the doctrine that is presented has been proven to be true by those who have lived it. It is not a matter of interpretation. Those relatively few people down through the centuries who have followed the full teaching of Jesus to the very end are the very ones who have proven it beyond any shadow of a doubt.[1] And many of them have testified to this.

> But now in the following pages, we come to the words
> of Jesus that are not as provable, as will be seen.

Which brings us to an important principle of thinking which is seldom taught. I have found it to be useful in many areas of daily living, but especially useful in my spiritual studies. It was first mentioned in the essay "Sorting Knowledge — Especially One's Own" that is back in Section Two. The same idea is expanded here in connection with some important religious questions.

Review: We as individuals possess many bits of knowledge, some of which are fact and some of which are "just" beliefs. And we should be aware of the difference. Many people make no distinction in their thinking, and this can cause them much confusion. Beliefs, treasured though they may be, obviously do not have the weight of facts.

U.S. Senator Daniel Patrick Moynihan [2] said it well, "You are entitled to your own opinion, but you are not entitled to your own facts."

As outlined in the "Sorting Knowledge" essay, in my own thinking I "catalog" bits of data in my mind into the following three categories: But only for important things, of course, because our minds do contain a lot of data. [3]

- Fact = those things that I know to be true.

- Belief (or theories) = ideas that I presently believe as being useful for the time being.

- Fantasy = things that I know are not really true but may or may not have a purpose.

My personal rules for deciding "what is what" were given and need not be repeated here. You, of course, would make your own "set points" to bracket these distinctions to whatever level of stringency that you choose. As a practical matter, I find that I am more strict in some subjects than in others in making these distinctions. And I don't think about this all the time, only when a clarification would be beneficial.

1. I have mentioned "those relatively few people" in many places, such is my gratitude to them.

2. Politician, ambassador, sociologist, b 1927 d 2003   Wikipedia

3. This idea of separation of mental data into these three categories is a teaching of Dr. Thurman Fleet, b 1895 d 1983   Chiropractor, writer. Founder of the "Concept Therapy Institute", San Antonio, TX.

In your spiritual life, as well as your intellectual life, you can make these distinctions as you go along in your studies. It is a useful method in working toward intellectual truth in areas of unfamiliar intellectual territory and especially in spiritual subjects which cannot be observed in the ordinary sense.

It was pointed out that the information we get from reading a book would be considered hearsay in a court of law, and would not be allowed as testimony. It would actually be a belief. And while we might not doubt really well-proven material, it still would not be of our own direct knowledge.

In the light of the above, the things that we read in the Bible are beliefs.[3]

Few Bible readers would care to see it this way. But even though the Bible itself might be true without error, **we still make our own interpretation** (or accept someone's interpretation that pleases us.) And every Bible reader finds that as we progress in spiritual understanding, our personal interpretation of scripture evolves to higher levels of belief. And then some of these beliefs may become our own facts as we prove them one by one by our actual experience.

Some of these things that we read (as **beliefs**) we can prove to be **fact.** But there are some Bible beliefs which **are not provable**, as we shall see, and should be held as beliefs (if you care to) — cherished beliefs perhaps, but beliefs nonetheless.

Two of these categories are:

The Second Coming of Jesus

The Afterlife

---

3. For those who truly believe the Bible (as I do).

What About the Second Coming of Jesus ?

In many Bible verses Jesus said that he would come again. Let's look at John 14:1-3

"Let not your heart be troubled: ye believe in God, believe also in me. In my Father's house are many mansions [can also be translated as abodes]: if it were not so, I would have told you. I go to prepare a place for you. And if I go and prepare a place for you, **I will come again**, and receive you unto myself, that where I am, there you may be also."

Many more Bible quotations about "coming" are on a following page.

As I have pointed out, the doctrine that is presented in some of the previous essays has been proven to be true. Those few people down through the centuries that have followed the full teaching of Jesus to the very end are the ones who have proven it beyond any shadow of a doubt. They have written about it and taught it to others, albeit seldom in the church setting. But now we come to the words of Jesus that can be accepted only on faith.

Since they are not directly provable, a variety of interpretations attempt to explain them. There are at least three different interpretations of the phrase "I will come again".

One of them can be illustrated from the Book of Revelations 3:20 (the words of Jesus):

"Behold, I stand at the door and knock: if any man hear my voice, and open the door, I will come in to him, and will sup with him, and he with me."

This is an allegory about something that can happen in a person's spiritual consciousness. Most of the time Jesus spoke as the rabbi teaching his doctrine. But sometimes He appears to speak as "The Christ", that is, from a higher level of consciousness. Speaking thus, He means in this verse that He will **come to the prepared individual as the Christ consciousness.**[1] That, of course, is what his teaching is all about if you have followed the previous essays. So this interpretation has been proven by the people who have experienced this high level of spiritual awareness. But the experience being internal to themselves, they find it difficult to convey it to others, although their new "gifts" and a "new countenance" may make the change apparent.

Another interpretation is:

Jesus has come to individuals in apparitions or visions. This also has been reported for centuries. Some say that His presence is so real that the body of Jesus is actually there in the flesh. While these encounters may be life altering experiences for the individual, they can not be reliably conveyed to others because they are brief, fleeting, personal and usually one-time occurrences. They tend to be spontaneous and can not be "produced".

---

1. See St. Paul's statement in Galations 2:20. He gives this understanding in only 16 words in KJV. These 16 words will also be explained in detail in a later essay.

A third interpretation is the most common and has been anticipated since early times. It is that:

> Jesus is coming to earth again "in the flesh". He will set up his terrestrial kingdom and will reign as King of Kings and Lord of Lords. Frequently there is a connotation that He "will straighten things out" in the errant human race. And there will be "heaven on earth".

Since this hasn't happened yet, you might say that it is all hope and conjecture at this point, even though the time-table might be based on the combining of certain passages of Old and New Testaments. (A rather tenuous compilation of unrelated verses, or so it seems in my studies.)

The disciples did expect to see Jesus again in the flesh after his final 'Ascension'. As far as we know today, they did not. And down through the centuries there have been many predictions of a so-called "Second Coming" sometimes with very specific dates, all based on a literal interpretation of scripture. Much disappointment so far!

This No. 3 interpretation has become big business in recent years. Authors write books and make predictions as to when it might happen. TV "ministries" make predictions and then sell books. There is even a subscription service that will send daily reports of the world's earthquakes for those who want to fine-tune their own expectation of the time of the "coming". See Matthew 24:7 for the "sign" of earthquakes.

The strange thing is that when the event doesn't take place at the predicted time, the same author can write another book, update his prediction and people buy again. They actually do! And the church denomination that has had several wrong predictions over a period of a century still has members who hope that the next prediction might be right.

Church doctrines vary in their beliefs as to the order that various events will take place when it happens. And even though the different systems are based on the Bible, usually even the same passages, they give opportunity for argument.

This expectation of an actual return of Jesus in the flesh has a great appeal to religious people. Who wouldn't want to see Jesus? Even if only on TV. But since no one knows what He looked like in his last appearance, I suspect there would be many doubters. So how can we tell? The miracles that 'made Him God' in the minds of the ancients just wouldn't cut it in today's world.

There may be another reason that so many look for this "great expectation". It can **substitute** for a person having to **do the really tough work on one's self that is required by the doctrine that Jesus taught**. And if Jesus is really coming in the near future to somehow solve the antagonisms of the world for us, then why should **we** bother to do anything about it in the meantime?

This portion of the words of Jesus (that is, the second coming) must be taken on faith according to your interpretation of the Bible. When I say "your interpretation", I don't mean that you have to interpret the Bible yourself or even just the New Testament; there are a multitude of interpretations already. Most people pick one that is closest to their own wishes. I leave it to you to decide.

And then you may (as I have done at some length) study the diagrams that some churches have created that combine OT and NT verses to supposedly predict future events and the timing of their arrival. It is a worthwhile exercise to do even if you or your church has other beliefs.

Here are some more Bible verses related to this subject for you to look at in their full context: —

Matthew 24:36 KJV
(Jesus is talking to his disciples on the Mount of Olives) "But of that day and hour knoweth no man, not the angels in heaven, but my Father only. 42. Watch therefore: for ye know not what hour your Lord **doth come**."

Matthew 25:13
(Still on the Mount of Olives, Jesus says it again)
"Watch therefore, for ye know neither the day nor the hour wherein the Son of man **cometh**."

Matthew 25:31 +
(Still on the Mount of Olives)
"When the Son of man **shall come** in his glory, and all the holy angels with him, then shall he sit upon the thrown of his glory: (continued — for you to look up).

Matthew 10:23
(Jesus gives instructions as He sends out his disciples to teach and minister)
"But when they persecute you in this city, flee ye into another: for verily I say unto you, Ye shall not have gone over the cities of Israel, till the **Son of man be come**."

Matthew 16:26-28
"For what is a man profited, if he shall gain the whole world, and lose his own soul? Or what shall a man give in exchange for his soul? 27 For the **Son of man shall come** in the glory of his Father with his angels; and then He shall reward every man according to his works. 28 Verily I say unto you, There be some standing here, which shall not taste of death, till they see the **Son of man coming** in his kingdom [spirit kingdom - WLH].

Matthew 24;14 +
(Jesus is talking to his disciples on the Mount of Olives)
"And this gospel of the kingdom shall be preached in all the world for a witness unto all nations; and then the end shall come. 21 For then shall be great tribulation ..... 27 For as the lightning cometh out of the east, and shineth even unto the west; so shall also the **coming of the Son of man** be. 29 Immediately after the tribulation of those days....... 30 And then shall appear the sign of the Son of man in heaven: and then shall all the tribes of the earth mourn, and they shall see the **Son of man coming** in the clouds of heaven with power and great glory. 34 Verily I say unto you, **This generation shall not pass, till all these things be fulfilled**." [This last line is frequently ignored by those who are looking for a modern-day 'coming' - WLH]

Matthew 26:64   (At His trial by the high priest)
"Nevertheless I say unto you, Hereafter shall ye see the Son of man sitting on the right hand of power, and **coming** in the clouds of heaven."

Luke 12:40   (Jesus is teaching the multitude)
"Be ye ready therefore also: for the **Son of man cometh** at an hour when ye think not."

Luke 22:27 +   (Jesus talking)
"And then shall they see the **Son of man coming** in a cloud with power and great glory. 32 Verily I say unto you, This generation shall not pass away, till all be fulfilled."

Luke 22:18 (At the Last Supper) Jesus said,
"For I say unto you, I will not drink of the fruit of the vine, until the **kingdom of God shall come**."

John 14:28 (Jesus talking to his disciples at the Last Supper)
"Ye have heard how I said unto you, I go away and **come again unto you**. If ye loved me, ye would rejoice because I said, I go unto the Father: my Father is greater than I.

Matthew 6:33 +

"But seek ye first the kingdom of God, and his righteousness; and all these things [the things that the gentiles seek] shall be added unto you. 34 Take therefore no thought for the morrow: for the morrow shall take thought for the things of itself. Sufficient unto the day is the evil [the problems of living] thereof. [insert by WLH].

Notice that people had anxiety about the future back then even as today. And Jesus recommended his "problem-solving" doctrine in preference to the normal habit of worrying about the future.

Next: The Afterlife

We All Wonder About the Afterlife

Jesus came to earth to teach his doctrine of the Mystic Union described in the essay on "The Essence of the Teaching of Jesus"

Most of the teaching of Jesus concerns a person's spiritual life while here on earth — in the "here and now". And as I have pointed out in several essays, the people who have lived this teaching have proved it beyond any shadow of a doubt. But his sayings concerning life after the death of the body are not so easily proved if they can be proved at all.

So we can think about the afterlife as **belief** rather than provable **fact.**

Still there is much evidence to consider! Let's look.

a. People who have had "near-death experiences" feel that they have entered paradise for a quick glimpse. Remarkable as their experience is to them, it could just be the outskirts of paradise that they are touching on. Still, they all say that after returning from the near-death, they have completely lost their fear of death. Remarkable! And fear of death is almost universal.

b. Lots of people claim that they remember bits and snatches of one or more **previous** lives while in a body here on earth. This would imply that if there were past lives in bodies, there might be future lives in bodies here on earth. The idea of reincarnation. That is, an immortal soul living in a succession of bodies. This belief, of course, is held by millions of Hindus, Buddhists and others with lots of variations. And also by many Christians that I know!

c. There are individuals today who believe that they are recently reincarnated and that they can find evidence of the life that they remember leaving. Books have been written about the searches that have been made for this recent past life. One such book, easy to read, that is believable is "Soul Survivor" by Bruce and Andrea Leininger and Ken Gross, 2010.

d. *There is a most remarkable teaching of which few people have ever heard!* It concerns this doctrine of the Mystic Union in connection with the afterlife. I believe it is true, but have not experienced it myself and may never in this lifetime. It is this:

> The great sages say that if you follow the teaching of Jesus all the way, you will understand life to a depth that most people can't even imagine. And that if you understand life to this depth, you will also understand life after the death of your body even while you live, here and now.

Few of us could ever do that. But if an occasional 'great one' has done that, we should at least listen to his words. So we can take the words of Jesus, and others, interpret them the best we can and accept it on faith (as a belief). From these great ones is where we get the teaching of an afterlife in the first place.

There has been so much written about the afterlife by Bible scholars, theologians and clergy, it seems that little more could be said. I leave it to you to select the church teaching on the subject that makes the most sense to you. However, this is an area that cannot be easily proven, even though it has been described by these advanced spiritual masters and so we can accept it on faith if we are believers.

Jesus repeatedly said that anyone who followed his teaching would never die. But a Bible student must be careful in studying this subject because Jesus sometimes is referring to spiritual life and spiritual death and other times He is referring to physical life and death. We must discern.

Here are some Bible verses concerning life after death for your further study.

John 11:25 + (Jesus is talking to Mary and Martha just before He resurrects Lazarus)
Jesus said unto her, "I am the resurrection, and the life; he that believeth in me, though he were dead, yet shall he live; 26 And whosoever liveth and believeth in me shall never die. Believeth thou this?"

John 6:47 + Jesus talking,
"Verily, verily, I say unto you, He that believeth on me hath everlasting life. 48 I am the bread of life. 51 I am the living bread which came down from heaven: if any man eat of this bread, he shall live forever: and the bread that I will give is my flesh, which I will give for the life of the world." ["the bread" is his teaching. WLH]

John 5:24 (Jesus speaking at the pool of Bethesda)
"Verily, verily, I say unto you, He that heareth my word, and believeth on him (God) that sent me, hath everlasting life, and shall not come into condemnation, but is passed from death unto life."

John 3:13 (Jesus is talking to Nicodemus)
"And no man hath ascended up to heaven, but he that came down from heaven, even the Son of man which is in heaven.

Luke 18:28 +Then Peter said, "Lo, we have left all, and followed thee."
29 And He (Jesus) said unto them, "Verily I say unto you, There is no man who hath left house, or parents, or brethren, or children, for the kingdom of God's sake, who shall not receive manifold more in this present time, and in the world to come life everlasting."

John 14:2 + (You saw this verse earlier under 'Second Coming', valid here also)
Jesus speaking at the Last Supper, "In my Father's house are many mansions [abodes]: if it were not so, I would have told you. I go to prepare a place for you 3 And if I go and prepare a place for you, **I will come again**, and receive you unto myself, that where I am, there ye may be also."

John 5:28 + Marvel not at this: for the hour is coming, in which all that are in the graves shall hear his voice, 29 And shall come forth; they that have done good, unto the resurrection of life; and they that have done evil, unto the resurrection of damnation.

John 6:40
Jesus talking to the Jews, "And this is the will of him that sent me, that everyone which seeth the Son, and believeth on him, may have everlasting life: and I will raise him up at the last day."

John 8:51 Jesus talking to the Jews,
"Verily, verily, I say unto you, If a man keep my saying, he shall never see death."

One of the simplest and clear cut things that Jesus said about the afterlife is in Matthew 22:30. The Sadducees had given Jesus a long, involved question about marriage "in the resurrection" involving a widow that had several husbands on earth. Whose wife would she be in the afterlife? Jesus answered and said unto them, "Ye do err, not knowing the scriptures, nor the power of God. 30 For in the resurrection, they neither marry, nor are given in marriage, but are the angels of God in heaven."

John 14:23 Jesus talking to his disciples at the Last Supper, "If a man love me, he will keep my words: and my Father will love him, and make our abode with him."

Christians have long been taught that we will be judged some day on our behavior in this life. Many of the serious church people that I have known imagine that the Ten Commandments pretty well covers what they must live up to. While that may be the BIG BASICS, Jesus said there is more.

In Matthew 25:31 to 45
Jesus on the Mount of Olives, gives a description of the last judgement to his disciples. I'll let you read it yourself and will quote only verse 40 (Jesus talking) "Verily I say unto you, Inasmuch as ye have done it (given a drink of water) unto one of the least of these my brethren, ye have done it unto me." (More about this in the later essay "The One Life".)

The lesson: — Treat everyone as you would treat Jesus. (To the degree that you can. But living in the every-day world, we must use judgement or people will think that we are crazy.)

And in Matthew 25:46, Jesus tells the result. Most, but not all, Bible versions are worded just as drastically as the King James Version. In the KJV it says, "And these (the evil ones) shall go away into everlasting punishment: but the righteous into life eternal."

It is a very high level of Christianity that may be beyond our ability to practice in a competitive world. Theologians say that this verse has been used for centuries by preachers to bludgeon their church members to "walk the straight and narrow". But now, some researchers say that the word "everlasting" is mistranslated from the Greek.[1] The Greek word means a 'time period', but it cannot be 'everlasting'. This is an arca to study if this verse bothers you.

And the most heartening saying of Jesus concerning the hereafter, Luke 23:43 KJV.
When Jesus was on the cross, there was a repentant criminal on a cross alongside."And he said unto Jesus, 'Lord remember me when thou comest into thy kingdom'. And Jesus said unto him,

'Verily I say unto thee, Today shalt thou be with me in paradise.'"

There is also a mention in Revelation 2:7 "To him who overcomes will I give to eat of the tree of life, which is in the midst of the paradise of God."

1. According to Tony Nungesser and Gary Amirault at http://www.tentmaker.org.

A Deeper Look

Jesus came on earth to teach a process for spiritual enlightenment. It is a process of evolution of a person's soul to higher levels of spiritual consciousness.

These few words, when understood in depth, outline a life's work for the person who is serious about his spiritual well being.

You read this simple, but somewhat enigmatic, statement earlier in Section One where it was written without comment. Now let's take a deeper look at the idea of "spiritual process".

Jesus gave all of the details for carrying out this process by the individual (even you and me). Although he never actually called it a process (perhaps the word was not in the Aramaic language at that time) Jesus described it as a process in the parable of the mustard seed. He taught that when the concept of the kingdom of God entered a person's mind, it might start out as small as a mustard seed. However, with spiritual growth from following His teaching, it could increase to magnificent proportions.

This parable is told in three of the Gospels with an interesting "twist". Matthew, ever the devout Jew, believed that the name of God was too sacred to be uttered by mortals. So, in Mt.13:31, he referred to the "kingdom of heaven" [1] starting small like the mustard seed. Whereas Mark 4:31 and Luke 13:19 use the term "kingdom of God" in the same context. So the terms "kingdom of heaven" and "kingdom of God" refer to the same spiritual concept.

Then I noticed that St. Paul described the important steps of the entire process in only 16 words words:

> "I am crucified with Christ: nevertheless
> I live; yet not I, but Christ liveth in me."
> Galations 2:20 KJV

1. In the original Greek, the term is "kingdom of the heavens" — plural.

St. Paul's brutal phrase "I am crucified with Christ" does not refer to his body, of course. Rather, it is his realization that his ego, his sense of self, his false sense of separateness from God has been crushed — or at least subjugated and under his control. He may well be including the negative aspects of his animal nature and shortcomings of his human nature.

Nevertheless his body lived on — but not his old carnal mind — rather with a new mind.

The thing described in this verse is considered to be a very advanced level of spiritual understanding. So if the following explanation of it sounds "new" and strange, it is because it is not taught in most churches.

Paul is describing (in this case himself) the triumph of the individual in total humility over "original sin". Original sin being that which separates a person from God, the animal nature of the body and the foibles of human nature, the things that are to be overcome.

Now when Paul says "I am crucified",

> He is referring to his "ego self" — the sense of his individuality.
> He has purposely subjugated his ego — the strongest basic human
> aspect that separates us from a direct experience of God.

Still his body and mind lived on — but not his powerful identity of separate self. He has replaced these aspects of humanhood by letting "Christ live within him".

The phrase "Christ liveth in me" was called, for some centuries, the "Christos spirit". Then in the 20th Century, it began to be called the "Christ consciousness".

This made me realize that Paul was not only a great builder of churches, as we all have heard, but that he also followed the teaching of Jesus to a very high degree. This was never brought out in any church that I attended. Undoubtedly because no one understood the entire process.

The above is a bare-bones explanation. There is a substantial literature that gives details in a variety of idioms.

To me, this is a most incredible verse — only 16 words in the King James Version.[2] That there can be so much meaning in so few words is a strong suggestion — even a warning — that other parts of the Bible may have equally powerful enigmatic meanings in a cryptic phrase or two. So that a literal reading and a literal interpretation may well miss the deep meaning, the only real meaning.

---

2. The wording in the King James Version is more concise than many other translations.

In the higher forms of Yoga, there is an odd saying with a similar idea to Paul's.

> Before you may stand in the presence of the Masters,
> your feet must be washed in the blood of the heart.

The heart being your subconscious mind, this conveys the idea that much must be wrenched loose from your old self, probably as painful as St. Paul implied with his "crucified with Christ" figure of speech. Only then would a spiritual aspirant be ready for the highest teaching on the level of the Spiritual Masters and to become equal to them in spiritual abilities.

In recent times, more people than in times past are actually seeking this divine level of human experience — or at least aspire to some degree of it. Over the years, I have met many people who were working on this spiritual process in their own lives. Yet none ever figured it out from Paul's terse mystic statement without help from "someone who knew".

Note that there is the idea of an evolutionary growth of spiritual consciousness — starting small, maybe even insipid. But then growing into a being that is greater, and perhaps making continuous progress toward God until death.

The personal evolution is from the starting level of the "simple sinner", no doubt unaware of his lowly spiritual state, toward the experience of being closer to God, eventually perhaps growing to the level of "Oneness With the Father".

This is in contrast to the method of some of the great Christian preachers of a century or two ago. They talked about "instantaneous conversion" of a non-believer to Christianity. And even today, there is a belief in some church denominations that a person must "make a decision" at some particular point in time, that he can then point to as being the instant that "he was saved". And the common interpretation of that is "I am now in the fold and all I have to do is keep my nose clean by avoiding a long list of sins." The same for girls and women, except that they may have a shorter list of sins to watch out for — shorter and lighter — than the boys and men. (Just my thought.)

All of these ideas are a good beginning, of course, but are only a beginning of spiritual growth.

In Christianity, as in other religions, there must have always been an oral teaching by "those who knew" who could explain the symbolisms of the written scripture. There are those few even today. You might find one teaching a high-level study group.

Divinity of Jesus

Some people say that Jesus is Divine,
Others say that He was human,
And there are those who say that
He is both human and Divine

This argument is resolved to some extent once you realize that all humans are basically divine. Just ask any "God-realized" sage or prophet — if you can find one in our materialistic culture. I have.

The divinity of humans doesn't imply that all people must act like angels. In fact, many don't even act as humans should. Not much question about that!

The great sages, including Jesus, taught that a person **is** a soul of spirit residing temporarily (for a life time) in a physical body. This is true whether the individual is aware of it or not, and some few are aware of it, whereas most people are not. *One of my spiritual teachers gave me the unusual experience of actually seeing my "soul of spirit".[1]* It was a life-changing event, as you can imagine, for which I am eternally grateful. Jesus apparently was aware of his divinity at an early age.

God is also considered to be SPIRIT, which is why we are said to be made in the image of God[2] since a part of us is the same spirit as the spirit of God. This is a very high level of spiritual understanding. It may be mentioned in church as words from the Bible, but it is not actually taught as being real because it is way over the level of most clergy and their church congregations. Churches must teach on the level of their people, otherwise they have no viable mission. People would get up and leave.

Early Christianity did, of course, define Jesus as God, son of the Father. As Son, He is then God in his own right. There may have been some lack of conviction about this on the part of early Christians, so the Council of Nicaea was held in 325 AD to make it very clear that Jesus was of the same substance as the Father and therefore was God in the same manner.[3]

This solemn declaration of the Council might sound clear enough at first hearing. But on second thought, it does not really clarify the situation at all, because you and I and all of humanity are also "of the same substance as the Father", according to footnote 1 below. Note that this refers to our "souls of spirit", not our bodies that are said to be made "of the dust of the earth". (What else is there?) More about this in the essay The One Life". However, I would not care to argue these points with those who might have other interpretations. There are many levels of understanding.

1. This was mentioned back on page 88. It was so unusual that I like to point it out again.
2. Genesis 1:26-7 KJV. In the higher teaching, "spirit" is also called "etheric energy".
3. From the Internet - www.dailycatholic.org/history/councils.htm.

202

There are numerous references in the New Testament, many of them familiar to any church goer, that describe Jesus as "son of God". But Jesus himself usually referred to himself as the "son of man". The following verses about 'son of man' and 'son of God' are for your interest.

Note in these quotations from the KJV New Testament, that Jesus, who is speaking from a very high level of spiritual understanding, calls himself a man. On the other hand, the people who have a lack of spiritual understanding, are frightened and awed by the demonstrations that Jesus performed and that they have witnessed. They call Jesus "Son of God."

Matthew 18:11 Jesus talking, "For the Son of man is come to save that which was lost." (Some authorities say that this verse is not in earlier manuscripts.)

Mt 24:37 Jesus talking, making a prediction, "But as the days of Noe were, so shall also the coming of the Son of man be."

Luke 19:10 Jesus talking, "For the Son of man is come to seek and to save that which was lost."

Luke 21:27 Jesus talking, "For then shall they see the Son of man coming in a cloud with power and great glory."

John 3:13 Jesus talking, "And no man hath ascended up to heaven, but he that came down from heaven, even the Son of man which is in heaven."

John 6:62 Jesus talking, "What and if ye shall see the Son of man ascend up where he was before?"

Acts 2:22 Peter speaking, "Ye men of Israel, hear these words; Jesus of Nazareth, a man approved of God among you by miracles and wonders and signs, which God did by him in the midst of you as ye yourselves also know:"

Mt 14:33 The disciples in a boat after Jesus walked on the water to them, "They that were in the boat came and worshiped him, saying, Of a truth thou art the son of God."

Mt 27:54 After Jesus died on the cross and there was an earthquake and other frightening things, the centurion said, "Truly this was the Son of God."

Mark 15:39 Another reference to the above same incident.

Luke 4:41 Jesus was healing people and 'casting out devils' and many of the devils "crying out, and saying Thou art Christ the Son of God."

John 6:69 Peter talking, "And we believe and are sure that thou art that Christ, the Son of the living God."

Acts 8:37 Philip is baptizing a eunuch, "And he [the eunuch] answered and said, I believe that Jesus Christ is the Son of God."

Acts 9:20   Paul, who has just been miraculously ushered into Christianity, "And straight-away he preached Christ in the synagogues, that He is the Son of God."

Note that Paul's letters (as above) were used in the early churches as "gospel" years before the books that are attributed to Matthew, Mark, Luke and John were written. So these latter books may have been heavily influenced by Paul's writings and his version of Christianity.

Here is a totally different thought:

Some followers of the higher teaching of Christianity that I have known say that it was a mistake for the early church to "make Jesus God". They say that this "nullifies" His great teaching. They reason like this:

The deep teaching of Jesus is that we should strive to "become one with the Father as He and the Father were one". Recall the essay "The Essence of the Teaching of Jesus" — in the "Divine Prayer" of Jesus (John Chapter 17) He prayed that you and I might become one with the Father. And He said that we could do miracles greater even than the ones that He did (if we 'went unto the Father' as He did). But if Jesus is God, how could we mere mortals possibly think of doing what He did. How could we even think of becoming one with the Father as He directed us. Or to do any kind of miracle. On the other hand, they say that if we "see" Jesus as the great teacher that He was, rather than as God, maybe we could try to follow His teaching as He expressed it. And some have.

I leave it to you to form your own beliefs or to follow the teaching of your church.

But to me, the life of Jesus on earth was so incredible that I prefer to believe that He was an advanced soul who was sent by God **as a man** to teach and **to be an example of what we are to strive to become**. This gives Him greater honor and awe in my mind than for Him to be set apart as a God above humanity, a ***concept which then contradicts and nullifies much of his teaching***.

As pointed out at the beginning of this essay, Jesus was both human and divine. But to truly understand the entire truth about this on the highest level, it helps to have the assistance of an authentic teacher.

Two

Interpretations

of a Saying

# of Jesus

Some Thoughts

Two Interpretations - Preface

There is only one spiritual reality, but many descriptions of it, each of them incomplete and imperfect.

Once you accept that, you can begin to <u>look for the reality</u> instead of arguing about the description that someone else has that may be different from your own.

This could be called "Step One in the Life of the Spirit".

God whispers, "Experience the divinity that is within you. It is your birthright." But the whisper cannot be heard unless you are quiet, least of all during an argument.

When reading the Bible, people interpret various passages according to their existing level of spiritual understanding. It could not be otherwise.

As their spiritual perspective grows, the meanings that they derive will often change, hopefully so. This is called spiritual growth. But if presented with a meaning, for example by clergy, that is too deep to be understood, they tend to let it go over their heads. It could not be otherwise.

The best interpretations of Bible verses are those which come closest to SPIRITUAL TRUTH. They should not be a matter of opinion. Because spiritual truth is fact and not just belief, not even if the belief is a cherished belief. Many of us have been taught, sad to say, that "religion is essentially belief".

This essay examines one such well-known Bible quotation of Jesus with an attempt to come closer to the spiritual truth of it, and a similar verse spoken by Peter.

Two Interpretations of a Saying of Jesus

There is no interpretation
higher than truth.

The Verse: John 14:6   King James Version

"Jesus saith unto him,

I am the way, the truth, and the life: no man cometh unto the Father, but by me".

The Setting:

At the Last Supper, Jesus is telling his disciples some of the events that will occur in their near future. In verse 4, He says, "And whither I go ye know, and the way ye know." But then Thomas objects in verse 5, "Lord, we know not whither thou goest; and how can we know the way?"

Jesus answers with verse 6 quoted above, "I am the way, the truth, and the life ...."

Literal Interpretation

Many churches interpret the Bible literally, including this verse. They say that the Bible is the word of God and it means just exactly what it says in the most simple way. So, for the meaning of this verse, they teach that a person is "saved" if he or she just believes that Jesus is the way, the truth, the life etc. as stated above. And that this salvation takes effect largely after a person dies.

Comment:

This stark, literal idea emphasizes Jesus the messenger while ignoring his message to a large degree. As Christians, we love and revere Jesus, of course. However this literal interpretation conveys the idea to the individual that belief in the messenger does it all — but since it is supposed to take effect largely after the person dies, the belief cannot be proven in any satisfactory way. So it remains just a belief. This is satisfying to many people and gives them hope for a glorious afterlife in place of a deep fear of the unknown. However, many people do not realize that there is more to true religion than just belief — that a true teaching is provable fact. So they do not realize that there is any need to study diligently on the message that Jesus taught. A message that requires work on ourselves in order to produce uplifting change in our lives. Becoming a "new man" [1] in Christ and experiencing, to some degree at least, the things that Jesus said are ours (our birthright) in the "here and now".

---

1. Ephesians 4:22-24 and Colossians 3:8-10

A More Insightful Interpretation of John 14:6

The idioms of the languages of the Middle East are considerably different from modern day English. The Middle-Eastern people that I have known that were influenced by late 19th century language usage (which probably had not changed for centuries) sometimes used the term "me" to mean "what I represent". And the term "go in my name" meant to "tell people that you know me", or similar, depending on the situation. So from this different usage of words, it is certainly possible that Jesus was referring to his teaching rather than to him-self, personally. That is: "My teaching is the way"; "No one comes to the Father but by my teaching". After all, He came to teach and we have the voluminous record of it in the four gospels.

The "I" in verse John 14:6 has also been interpreted as meaning the "God Consciousness" (or the "Christ") that was inherent in Jesus. Throughout the New Testament, Jesus referred to himself as the "Son of Man" and He was a man, but He had this higher level of God Consciousness. Such an interpretation is certainly true. "God consciousness" is the main theme of the Bible and the teaching of Jesus. And scripture urges us to aspire to achieve "God consciousness".

Thesis

The reason for presenting these broader interpretations here is that it is a known fact that for centuries some dedicated spiritual seekers have **"come to the Father"** through the teachings of Christianity, and others have come to the Father through the teachings of the higher forms of Yoga. Perhaps some have even come to the Father through other teachings as well.

Over a period of years, I have been privileged to meet four people — perhaps five — who were able to "go unto the Father" at will. People like this are extremely rare! Each of these individuals was involved in spiritual teaching on a very high level, although they did not do spectacular demonstrations in public as Jesus and the disciples did.

Two of these men came to this high spiritual state by teachings other than Christianity. Two of them apparently blended two or more different teachings. One followed the teachings of Jesus, pretty much to the exclusion of other teachings since he never mentioned any other.

When Jesus said that , "no man cometh unto the Father but by me" He was ignoring the teachings of the higher forms of Yoga which had brought "seekers" unto the Father for some hundreds of years BC. Jesus certainly must have been aware of this, but why should He bring that up at the Last Supper when his disciples were reeling from three years of intensive teaching that they understood only in part. And being told of upcoming events that puzzled them and troubled them deeply.

The teaching of Jesus may be the best "way" to spiritual attainment, especially for seekers in our western culture. But clearly it is not the only "way". (I use quotation marks on "the way" because Jesus called his teaching the way.)

May I again use a quaint expression from the Old Testament, (somewhat out of context here to be sure) to present a logical thought. "Is the Lord's arm so short [2] — " that He cannot teach Wisdom and extend salvation to more than just one little local sect on this great planet? Meaning, of course, ancient Israel. The God, creator of the Universe, that I personally believe in could do so.

If you allow the real meaning of this verse to refer to the teaching rather than just to the teacher, it correlates exactly with what is known about teachings from other sources. Actually, the various teachings are more similar than different when understood in depth. But a literal interpretation of this verse denies these known facts, and is therefore suspect.

The implication for sincere seekers is immense! Religion is more than just belief — it is provable fact. Other passages in the New Testament indicate that the teaching of Jesus is about the **spiritual** aspects of life here and now, as well as extending into the afterlife. To follow the teaching means doing work upon one's self, a process that has been proven beyond all doubt by those relatively few people down through history who have done it.[3]

Making personal progress in this process, to whatever degree, helps to bring a person closer to God, as explained in the essay "A Deeper Look" a few pages back.

Another Verse — same thought: Acts 4:12   King James Version

"Neither is there salvation in any other: for there is none other name under heaven given among men, whereby we must be saved."

The Setting:

After Peter and John healed a lame beggar at the Temple, they preached to a crowd of 5000 people. The authorities were angered and detained Peter and John until the next day. During an interrogation, Peter gave a long "defense" including the quotation above. Despite the obvious fact that Peter and John were "unlearned and ignorant men", the Sadducees "marveled" at their understanding. The point that Peter was making is that the teaching of Jesus was real, whereas the idea of spiritual salvation by following the complex Jewish law of Moses was a dead end. Jesus and the disciples had to argue this point every time they confronted the Sadducees, Pharisees and other Jews who were strictly dedicated to teachings of Moses.

2. Numbers 11:23 OT paraphrased. You read this same idea on page 89. It is a powerful thought and should cause those who believe that their church has **the** "exclusive" dispensation to look further.

3. Please see the essay "The Secret Path" back in Section Two.

My Own Conclusion

As in the example of the John 14:6 verse three pages above, Peter in this verse has no need to bring up alternate teachings from faraway countries since his point is against the false idea of salvation by carefully keeping the Jewish law of Moses, a complex of 613 or so rules for Jewish life. He is expounding to a local group, and he probably had no knowledge of other teachings anyway.

We should consider the vital importance of "the message" as well as the name of the "messenger" — the teaching as well as the teacher. Both are important. I believe in both with all my heart!

Perhaps you do too.

Why did Jesus have to be crucified?

Many people erroneously believe that the crucifixion of Jesus "happened" from the efforts of the Romans and the Jewish authorities. It might seem that way at first reading. There have been modern-day lawyers who say that Jesus did not "put up a good defense" before Pontius Pilate. And one, at least, has written a "brilliant" defense that "would have gotten Jesus off", or so he believes in retrospect.

A careful reading of scripture shows that Jesus planned his own death under the direction of "the Father" above, and He then deliberately provoked the authorities into carrying out the sentence. It was meant to be — as part of the miracle of the Resurrection. Jesus, the spiritual Master, **was in control of His own destiny on earth while consciously carrying out the will of the Father in heaven**. A Master on the exalted level of Jesus "commands" events as He chooses.

I can say this from observation of the people that I knew who had spiritual abilities akin to spiritual masters and were well on the way to becoming masters. Events did not just happen to them; they caused events, most of the events anyway. And people seldom realized that they were doing it, myself in the beginning. But then my teacher would tip me off what he was doing with little clues. His manner was never facetious, and his purpose was always to further the enlightenment of his students. Learning from such a one, I began to see the events of biblical times in a completely different light.

For example: Jesus setting the stage.

In John 2:16, Jesus said to those who sold doves, "Take these things away! Make not my Father's house a house of merchandise." Here He not only upset their traditions, but also called the Temple HIS Father's house. He infuriated the authorities. Their response could not have been anything less.

For example: Jesus setting the stage some more.

John 10:39 "Therefore they sought again to take him, but He escaped out of their hand." The Jews were accusing Jesus of blasphemy and were going to stone him to death. He infuriated the authorities. But Jesus was not ready to be apprehended yet, so He just "slipped away".

For example: Jesus setting up the details.

John 13:26, Jesus answered, "He it is to whom I shall give a sop (bread) when I have dipped it." And when He had dipped the bread, He gave it to Judas. Then Jesus said to him, "That you do, do quickly" [WLH note: Jesus, the spiritual master, would have realized that Judas had a plan to "finger him" to the authorities for money, so He is using Judas' greed to carry out this plan as a necessary step toward his destined trial, crucifixion and resurrection. Otherwise He would have blocked Judas and set up a plan of his own. A master that I knew made things happen <u>his</u> way].

211

For example: Carrying out His purpose.

John 18:10. When the priest's men came to capture Jesus in the dark of night, Simon Peter drew his sword and attempted to stop the arrest. So Jesus said to Peter, "Put up thy sword, into the sheath. Shall I not drink the cup which my Father hath given me?"

For example: Setting up conditions in advance.

Matthew 26:33. Peter answered and said to Him, "Though all men shall be offended because of thee, yet will I never be offended." Jesus said to him, "Verily, I say unto thee that this night, before the rooster crows, you will deny me three times" Apparently Jesus is giving Peter the order to stay out of jail. If Jesus had wanted Peter with him in jail, He would have given Peter the order to do that. As usually interpreted, poor Peter gets the blame for being weak when it was really the command of Jesus to stay out of jail, or so it seems to me.

For example: Deliberately giving a poor defense.

John 19:9+ Pilate said to Jesus, "Whence art thou?" (Where are you from?) But Jesus gave no answer. Then Pilate said to him, "Don't you know that I have power to crucify thee, and power to release thee?" Jesus answered, "Thou can have no power at all against Me except it were given thee from above." (Belittling the authority of the Roman judge is a poor defense.) So you see, Jesus dutifully and deliberately carried out the plan given to him by "the Father".

For centuries, theologians have been trying to fit the meaning of the death of Jesus into the particular religious beliefs of their time.

St. Paul's explanation was in the context of **his** former Jewish beliefs. He said that Jesus' death was a blood sacrifice to atone for the sins of both Jews and gentiles. The Jews had, for centuries, made blood sacrifices of animals to propitiate their angry God. They sprinkled blood of the dead animals around the altar in the temple in the belief that this purified any remnants of sin or evil. Blood was somehow a cleansing agent in their religion. One time long ago, I counted 338 references to blood in the Old Testament, King James Version, and might even have missed one or two. Blood seemed to be an important part of the ancient Jewish ritual since their every-day slaughtering of animals to eat was familiar to everyone.

Paul was talking to Jews who also had the annual ritual of sticking a list of their accumulated sins onto a scapegoat that was then driven off into the wilderness. This was meant to be a symbolic cleansing of the sins of all the members of the house. And these old Jewish customs were not easily dropped by the Jews that Paul was trying to convert. So he explained "the new" in terms that made sense to those who were stuck with the mind-set of the old.

On the basis of St. Paul's beliefs, we have in some of our Christian churches today the "Doctrine of Vicarious Atonement" whereby the death of Jesus is considered to be a blood sacrifice to atone for the sins of mankind. The word "vicarious" meaning "acting on behalf of someone else".

I have to admit that it is comforting to believe that someone else can absolve me from sin, especially "original sin" which for many of us is a rather vague concept. And since we didn't actually commit any original sin that we can remember, why are we being blamed for something we didn't do? We still must avoid present-day "sin" to the best of our ability, of course. Much of the practical teaching of most religions is about how to resist the natural human tendency to make the easier but harmful choices in everyday life. The choices that affect our relation to God as well as our health.

Jesus, however, did not cast himself primarily in this role!

Instead, He said that He came that "we might have life and that we might have it more abundantly" He meant "spiritual life" as well as temporal life. And this "more abundant life" would be the result of a person following his teaching. He didn't claim to personally take men's sins upon himself in the sense that some people believe today. Rather, He showed us the way to spiritual life.

In John 10:9 and 10, He states his purpose clearly:

> "I am the door: by me if any man enter in, he shall be saved and shall go in and out and shall find pasture. The thief cometh not, but for to steal, and to kill, and to destroy: I am come that they might have life and that they might have it more abundantly".

"Might have life and have it more abundantly" That was his reason for acquiring disciples, for teaching, and for demonstrating with miracles. I accept His word for the reason that He came to earth. And when it comes to the reason for the **crucifixion**, I prefer to take **Jesus' own words** for that also. In John 12:32 He said,

> "And I, if I be lifted up from the earth, will draw all men unto me".

He reasoned that the crucifixion and his glorious resurrection **"would draw all men unto me."** And it has done so — partly.

And, I am confident, will draw all to him (to his teaching) someday!

An interesting thing in the teaching of the higher spiritual truths in Christianity and in some other religions: a person's past becomes a "thing of the past" once he or she sets foot "on the path". The same thing is true for groups that teach the higher truths but in non-religious formats. This is a true forgiveness of past "sins".

213

The Keys
of the
Kingdom of Heaven

Some Suggestions

The Keys of the Kingdom of Heaven

"That thou art Peter, and upon this rock I will build my church; and the gates of hell shall not prevail against it. And I will give unto thee the keys of the kingdom of heaven:"   Jesus talking. Matthew 16:18-19 KJV

The "keys to the kingdom" are, of course, spiritual knowledge. And as far as I know, there never has been a list of what the keys might be. It would be foolish for "one who knows" to compile such a list lest it fall into the hands of would-be "spiritual criminals" of various sorts.

But it couldn't hurt to have some keys just to the outer gates so that a spiritual seeker could get a straight start in studying the Bible. And so I present here some suggestions that I have heard seekers discuss among themselves. Maybe they are not the highest level keys. So I call them "keys to the outer gates". It is expected that anyone using them will confirm them one way or another. Lacking confirmation, they can still be followed tentatively for confirmation at a later time.

Key No. 1
The Holy Bible is a text book to teach about the world of the spirit. The lessons in the Old Testament are repeated in the New Testament in the teaching of Jesus in a much clearer way. That is where to look. But some modern Bible translations mislead on the "higher teaching". So it is necessary to have an authentic teacher who knows. If you can find one in the flesh, that would be best. But a good teacher can also come through writings (or audio or some such). And sometimes a teacher can take you part way and then you find another. Some writings can take you only part way and then you look for another author.

Key No. 2
"The kingdom of God is within you!" Luke 17:21 KJV. Jesus said so! And He said that you should not look anywhere else. Others have found this to be true. The "kingdom of God / the kingdom of heaven" is the realm of the spirit. It is not some mythical government on earth that is expected to "come" sometime, maybe soon — the computed time of the coming being based totally on conjecture. Sad to say, some churches are waiting for "this something" conjured from a false interpretation. And so the people hope, but do little or nothing to develop themselves spiritually. The worst part is that they try to convince others of their myth in order to bolster their own shaky belief.

Key No. 3
You are a 'soul of spirit' residing in a physical body. Realizing this gives you a perspective to make spiritual progress that other people do not have. You are divine as well as human. This idea could make a beginner get "puffed up", but you are not a beginner if you have read this far. So keep this knowledge to yourself, except where it is appropriate to share.

Studying the higher teaching results in a benefit in this lifetime while in your physical body, not just after you die. This gives a more immediate incentive and satisfaction "to do the work".

217

Key No. 4

It is necessary to overcome the animal nature that we all possess. Most people live mostly by that nature and see nothing wrong in doing so. But the animal nature, being so immediate and so demanding, does overshadow the spiritual side of man. And it is the source of the emotions of greed, vanity, anger and lust. In the "Revelation of St. John the Divine", as you know, Jesus is speaking through John's vision. And eight times Jesus points out the great benefits of "overcoming" the "beast that is within us". Please study this in the Bible translation of your choice at Revelation 2:7 and 2:11 and 2:17 and 2:26 and 3:5 and 3:12 and 3:21 and 21:7. Typically, it is described as "purifying" one's self, and it is taught in church.

Key No. 5

A person is not "saved" just by "believing on Jesus" as some churches teach. This is a good beginning, of course. But a person should not stop there, thinking that there is nothing more and that he or she has accomplished all that could be done. And it is cruel to teach anyone that "just believing" is the entire message, cutting short their desire to continue toward their birthright. So many of our TV ministries and so much of the efforts of churches is to **encourage people to get started** on the ground floor, so to speak. The message is simplified with that in mind. After a good start, one must look for some "advanced presentation" in order to go further.

Key No. 6

"**Be still** and know that I am God." Psalm 46:10 in the Old Testament.

This confirms what I said about meditation in the essay "Imaging in Prayer". Meditation is a practice that is completely compatible with Christianity. The idea is to **experience the presence of what is called "The God within you"**. It is best learned from someone who understands it. In our busy Western culture, it is not easy for most people to be still for any reason. Brought up with music always in the background, with TV going continuously even though no one is actually listening or watching. And with electronic games lurking even in our pocket to fill every waiting minute. Not easy to just be still with our thoughts. But after a person learns the rudiments, it is surprising how many little bits of idle time can be used for meditation. And it brings a depth of satisfaction that "entertainment" can not provide. Meditation is the method by which a person can experience God. But it might take a long time for some to learn, longer for others, like myself.

Key No. 7

God's GRACE is at hand. Love God.

"Behold, I stand at the door and knock: if any man hear my voice and open the door, I will come in to him, and will sup with him, and he with me.

Revelation 3:20

218

That which appears to be a "particle of God" or the "spirit of God" that is within each of us wants to be recognized; **it is truly the most important part of our being**. It apparently waits for us to handle our concerns in the physical world, so the knock described above is subtle and is heard, if at all, only when we are in the deepest silence. But the knock is persistent and waits for us to open the door. It is sometimes compared to the glory of the stars as seen in the dark sky that are also there all day long, but not visible in the brightness of the day. In this case, we are the ones causing the obliterating "brightness" by our lack of silence.

Finding what "the door" actually means is not easy. The "door" is within us, and once we have located it, we can open it when we feel ready to do so. Even so, for most of us, opening the door can be daunting because of the unknown. When I mentioned this to a teacher, I was advised to pray for courage – couldn't hurt. Keep in mind that this is an allegory, and that we must find in ourselves what the knock and the door actually allude to.

In the beginning, and along the way, it can be useful for a seeker to pray to make spiritual progress. There is no better prayer. Then help and direction are sent "from above".

God blesses the seeker.

The
One Life

A Glimpse of a Profound
Spiritual Truth

The One Life

We are not humans having spiritual experiences –
we are spiritual beings having human experiences!

Wayne Dyer

A person is a soul of spirit
residing in a physical body. WLH

Can you consider a high level of spiritual truth even though you may never fully understand it just from reading an essay such as this?

Many people are more comfortable with conventional church teaching and there is nothing wrong with that. So if an unfamiliar religious idea upsets you – or if the thought that there may be a higher level of spiritual understanding troubles you, please do not read further.

Jesus said many things in the four Gospels that clearly show that he taught from a very high spiritual perspective. His teaching was vastly more than just a guide to morality as some seem to think. Yet I have never heard mention of the following concept in any of the Christian church doctrines – either written or conveyed orally – that I have encountered. In the Bible, it is alluded to, but not explained directly. It apparently is a secret teaching – one that is handed down from a person who knows to one who seeks such knowledge.

I am one who has not experienced all of these things first hand — only some.

But I have been taught by one who certainly knows!

In what is termed the "Olivet Discourse" [1] in theological circles, Jesus is teaching his disciples a long series of lessons while they rest on the "Mount of Olives". Theologians have analyzed this record in the New Testament at great length and have arrived at considerable differences in interpretation. And the argument about the various meanings goes on even to this day.

Although the teaching in the Olivet Discourse that is argued about is in three of the Gospels, only the version in Matthew has an odd little story that is of interest in this essay. Not being con-troversial, it is normally ignored even though it contains the kernel of an amazing spiritual truth. It is Jesus' final lesson starting at Matthew 25:35 and continuing to the end of the chapter. Although Jesus is referring directly to his disciples, He puts the lesson into story form.

It starts out:

> "For I was hungered, and ye gave me meat: I was thirsty and ye gave me drink: I was a stranger and ye took me in: naked and ye clothed me: I was sick and ye visited me: I was in prison and ye came unto me.

---

1. The Olivet discourse is in Matthew 24:1-46, again in Mark 13:1-37 and again in Luke 21:5-3.

Then they asked (I paraphrased a little here. You will read it yourself, of course)

> "Lord, when saw we thee hungered, and fed thee? Or thirsty and gave thee drink? When saw we thee a stranger and took thee in? Or naked and clothed thee?
>
> And the king [meaning Jesus in the story] answered and said unto them, Verily inasmuch as ye have done it unto one of the least of these my brethren, ye have done it unto me. KJV

Then the story is repeated in a negative aspect for emphasis, like many of the stories in the New Testament.

I have heard this read in church and you may have also. Various levels of interpretation have been rendered. Be that as it may, the level of spiritual truth in this essay is higher than any interpretation that I have heard in church.

I have postponed writing this essay for over 40 years because, as a single essay, it could not stand alone, would not be read alone and very few people would care to read it anyway. I do understand it intellectually, more deeply each passing year, but have not experienced it directly in its total grandeur as some say they have.

However, sometimes an analogy can help us to "feel" that we "sort of" understand something that is difficult to visualize directly. But remember that all analogies are imperfect.

The concept:

> *The great spiritual teachers throughout history have taught their*
> *students that there is only one life and that this "Life" is God.*

How do they know that?

They claim that they have had the direct experience of it, and it changes their view of everything of course. Sages and prophets have had a full awareness of God's presence and that is what sets them apart. In different parts of the world and in different eras, they experience this same spiritual truth — a truth to them — even though it may not be to the rest of us.

What these great sages are saying is that people — like you and me — are not just individual physical bodies sustained by food, air and water.

Rather we are souls of spirit living in these physical bodies even though most of us — indeed most of humanity — are too busy living in the physical world to recognize our true spiritual nature.

And these sages teach that these souls of spirit are really just little bits of God. Even though the energy of our body may be generated by carbon-oxygen chemical reactions, the actual life that is within us exists by the unrecognized divinity within us, holding us up from within, so to speak. And so we are said to be "expressing a tiny portion of God as the individuals that we are". (Keep in mind that this understanding is about the soul, not the body.)

224

How could this possibly be?

When I first heard of this profound concept, an analogy came to mind that has caused me to ponder, — rather than dismiss out of hand — this teaching for these several decades.

The analogy:

> During World War Two, I served on the heavy cruiser U.S.S. Quincy. After battles at Normandy, Cherbourg and in the Mediterranean, and taking President Roosevelt to the Yalta conference, we sailed to the Central Pacific theater of war.
>
> For some weeks our ship sailed alone back and forth along the Equator. We were just standing by while an armada was being formed for the assault on the strategic Japanese-held island of Okinawa.

(Just as an aside, to me down in the sweltering hot engine room, sailing along in the hot weather of the equator was as close to hell as I ever want to get. The air temperature was higher than a human body can tolerate for more than a few minutes. My station at the phone was between two 30,000 horse power steam turbine engines that radiated heat like the sun. The only means of survival were the two ventilators that blew a ferocious blast of air from topside. The crew of 5 and I huddled under them, venturing out only for a minute or two to check the machinery.)

> In the western Pacific ocean, there are thousands of islands, large and small. Some of them had Japanese "ship watchers" whose job was to radio to Tokyo the movement of our ships. Needless to say, our captain was careful not to sail close enough to any of these islands to be spotted.
>
> In our isolation, it sometimes seemed like we must have dropped off the edge of the earth. One day, I plaintively asked my friend, the Assistant Navigator, how far it was to land.
>
> He said, "about four miles".
>
> I looked around the horizon in anticipation and saw nothing but water.
>
> "What direction", I asked.
>
> "Straight down", he answered, pointing in that direction.

He had given a different perspective — true enough — even though it was not what I wanted to hear. I was thinking, of course, of the mariner's chart of the islands — land that we could walk on. He had pointed out that we were never really very far from 'land' — Mother Earth.

A chart shows the islands as being separate, as they certainly are from the perspective of the mariner. But from the perspective of the geologist, the islands are mere bumps on the surface of the earth that happen to be high enough to poke above the surface of the ocean. The islands are all connected — actually much more connected than separated.

In the latter part of the Twentieth Century, the ocean floors have been nicely mapped using sonar. Valleys, crevices and thousands of bumps can be seen. And in the Western Pacific especially, thousand of these bumps are high enough to poke above the surface and appear to us as islands.

> While the oceans might seem incredibly deep to us, the average depth of the oceans compared to the size of the earth is like the thin coating of frost that you might get on a large orange when taken from the refrigerator. (Four miles average ocean depth compared to a radius of 4000 miles of the earth — one to a thousand.) Considering the size of the earth, the height of a bump needed to stick above the surface of the ocean is practically no bump at all, despite its importance to the people who want to live on it.

Hopefully my analogy conveys the idea that we are separate individuals as bodies and minds only on the physical plane of reference (above the surface of the ocean in the analogy). But on a spiritual frame of reference we are not separate at all. We, as souls of spirit, are like little bumps on the vastness of God.

"So what?", you might ask. "Should that make me feel any different?"

The great teachers logically point out that we should treat each other as we would like be treated — the Golden Rule [2] — because, in the spiritual perspective, we are all "ONE LIFE". The same for the Ten Commandments [3] and other aspects of the great teachings.

And then the above story of Jesus that puzzled the disciples (Matthew 25:35) about food, drink, being a stranger, clothing, sickness and prison begins to make some sense. Otherwise how could doing something to one person be the same as doing it to another? Jesus saw it clearly! But sad to say, not many others have, which is why the world has always been in such chaos. And even today, the average person has no need or desire to understand this profound TRUTH. Most people are still just trying to survive as their physical bodies, some trying to get an unfair advantage over others. Jesus taught, on the other hand, that we should serve others in some manner. And most good people do serve — by doing their everyday job, by being parents, by lending a helping hand if an occasion warrants. Or by just "holding a place" in the community as a decent citizen.

To the sages, because of their lofty perspective, these great spiritual truths are apparent, and they have written and taught them for centuries. They see it as the final step in the evolution of mankind and when a sufficient number of people reach that level, world peace will finally be assured.

For most of us though, it is a struggle to see beyond our individual perspective of separateness. Fortunately, some few have. And the four such people — maybe five — that I have had the privilege of meeting all became teachers of what Jesus called TRUTH, once they reached even the fringes of that exalted level.

2. Matthew 7:12 KJV "Therefore all things whatsoever ye would that men should do unto you, do ye even so to them." (The Golden Rule). Luke 6:31 is similar. Similar references are in the Old Testament.
3. Exodus 20 + The Ten Commandments.

The very few who have reached this incredible level of human existence are truly *spiritual masters*. They have learned the ultimate truth — *that there is no separation between their soul and God*. They have fulfilled the admonition to "Know Thyself" [4] and gone beyond. They can enjoy freedom from the illusion of ego-centered selfhood. [5] And these great ones say that the sight that they can actually realize is also true for us, whether we know it or not, whether we believe it or not. *So if our spirit selves are not separated from God, then they are not separated from each other.* [6] A fantastic revelation by itself, even if we just hold it as a belief.

This is the level from which Jesus was teaching. As we realize that fact today, it can throw brilliant light on some passages of his lessons that might presently be poorly interpreted from a lower plane of understanding.

If a person experiences the "One Life" directly, or even if he just believes in the concept, it is certain that he will follow the familiar time-worn teachings (of the Golden Rule and The Ten Commandments) realizing that God is what underlies, supports and constitutes all life.

Because I believe this, it has profoundly affected the way I view life. The details of what has changed in my outlook and demeanor would fill a book.

This is just a quick sketch of the teaching of the "One Life", and I realize how inadequate it is to try to describe it in mere words. It is a concept that few have even heard of — true nonetheless the sages tell us. And someday you may begin to ponder this idea, then you can search the advanced writings of the spiritual masters.

It does become easier to grasp as spiritual consciousness grows, and you may even experience it directly yourself and then understand it beyond all doubt.

4. Remember the essay "Know Thyself" in Part 1?

5. I realize how ridiculous this last statement must sound to the person living on the average level of spiritual consciousness. It is a very advanced level of human existence realized by only a few, mainly because very few people search for it in Western Culture. Skip this idea for now, if you like.

6. On the last page of the "Myrus" essay on mind reading in Part 1, it was pointed out — "the great sages say that if a person can delve deeply into his or her own soul, then they can be in touch with other souls...." That is a brief, simpler, partial understanding of what is presented above.

Wrap Up

Final Thoughts About Science and Religion

Scientific investigation in the Twentieth Century brought results in many fields. In my estimation, the two greatest advancements from the philosophical and religious standpoint are these:

- Astronomers found that the Universe is incredibly larger than anyone had dreamed and that stars are continually being formed anew and eventually die. The Universe — apparently expanding in size — is never finished. Not in six days — not ever!

- Physicists discovered and proved that the **material** of the Universe is composed of **energy** in one form or another. And they have already implemented this understanding in some useful ways, for example, atomic power plants.

We can hope that this grand understanding of science will be enlarged and developed in the coming centuries for the good of mankind in a manner similar to electricity — perhaps in astounding ways that we cannot even imagine today.

For some thousands of years, the great **mystics**, whether you call them rishis, prophets, God-realized sages or yoga masters, supposedly have had this same understanding that energy underlies the visible world. Because their discovery comes from an experience of looking within themselves, it is not explainable in depth to others. During high levels of spiritual consciousness, they view the world as a form of etheric energy [1] which they see as light. Everything sparkles, dances with vibratory energy, even inanimate things like rocks. They have learned how to manipulate what they have discovered in some small, but astounding ways. At least they can demonstrate that to people; and the people call the demonstrations miracles. I do too. Then religions get built on the teaching of these great ones, but soon go off in shallower directions closer to the immediate needs of people. The deep teaching is often forgotten or kept secret by a few.

Would it accomplish more if the mystics collaborated with the scientists? Probably not. The scientist is born with or develops a logical thinking mind. That doesn't mean that scientists don't also get inspirational insights. They do. The mystics, on the other hand, tell how they get their deep understandings and abilities, but few want to follow them because of the difficulty. And it is **very different** from the approach of the scientist, as you have seen from some of these essays. So far, the incredible understanding of the mystics about energy does not seem to have had direct benefit to people in the physical world that science has had on this same finding of underlying energy.

So — science, in the specialty of physics, has duplicated in understanding the deepest aspects of religion known only to a few mystics since ancient times.

---

1. Recall the essay on "Halos and Things".

228

Furthermore, scientists make measurements which extends the usefulness of all that they discover. Even so, there is much that cannot be measured and that is still the province of religion and that includes much of life. It remains only for a "congruence of understanding" between science and religion for this Twentieth Century parallel discovery to be recognized. The terminology is an obstacle, of course, being vastly different between science and religion. For example, $E = mc^2$ Maybe also some egos, because each group considers its findings to be separate and unique.

This understanding of both science and deep spirituality (arrived at separately) about underlying energy is the most incredible thing that has happened in my lifetime. It would take more than one book to explain it in detail and it is still only partially understood. I hope that someday all involved parties will see what I see —

that perhaps both science and religion now have the "ultimate understanding" of physical matter. All is energy, says science. All is God, say the sages.

I am speaking in broad generalities, of course. Science still has great discrepancies in the mathematical description of the atom and much to decipher about the Universe. And the sages can tell us <u>about</u> it, but they can't actually communicate their deep experiences to us.

Final Thoughts From the Teaching of Jesus

As I said in the beginning of the book, there is a lot of meat in these essays. Too much to assimilate in a short time. You can't read this like a novel — better to take it in small doses. But studying it over a period of time can be worth your while. Adopt the parts that seem to speak to you.

These essays are about the Ancient Wisdom which is also the teaching of Jesus in the four Gospels. Jesus pointed out that "the least in the Kingdom of God were greater than the greatest who were not in the kingdom." He indicated that there are degrees of spiritual awareness and degrees of spiritual accomplishment, and that even a little is better than none. But the ultimate that is possible by a dedicated person is mind-boggling.

He taught that:

- The "world of the spirit" is real — the eternal truth. It concerns our true selves — our divine selves. Words are used to describe the reality, but the words are not the reality. Yet many Christian churches present the words as reality and many Christians accept the words as reality. The churches get away with this deception because they "cast"

229

the reality into the afterlife — as being only in the afterlife. So proof of anything is difficult — until we hopefully get there "someday".

- The spiritual reality is actually here and now and the words are meant to teach that. The only change needed is to cast the interpretation of the teaching into the present — as being valid here and now, as well as in the afterlife. Some understanding of the world of the spirit would then add a worthwhile dimension to life here and now. It addresses the ultimate meaning of life.

- Jesus selected ordinary people to be his disciples to learn from him and then to teach others. They have done so.

- If ordinary people could learn it back then, ordinary people can learn and achieve it now — and have.

This is the "real" teaching of Jesus of Nazareth as interpreted by those who have found it to be true. And I have learned some of it from them. And in these essays, I am conveying some of it to you. For many people, it is worth just knowing that this knowledge exists. And for many, it is worth learning and living every aspect of it.

The underlying truths and the teaching are often called our birthright [2] and the person who has achieved even part of it is truly saved. There is more, of course, but these are the basics.

God blesses all who seek.

2. Books of the Old Testament use the term 'birthright' in mundane family ways, but St. Paul uses it in Hebrews 12:16 with the same meaning as I use the term above.

About The Author

Bill was born an engineer. Even in kindergarten, puzzled out why two blocks could be made to stay up over a doorway of a building of blocks. Learned in college that it is called two opposing force couples.

Built boats as a boy, loved sailing on Lake Erie. Navy officer in WW II, engineer on a combat ship. After the war, became automotive engineer on big trucks; later invented road building machinery, manufactured it. Invented and marketed other things.

At age 37, began lifelong study of the "higher teaching" of religion which proved to be "The Ancient Wisdom". Despite a personality narrowly shaped by science and technology, was able to directly experience aspects of the 'world of the spirit' which became the basis of the book.

Used with permission © Lifetouch Inc.

Acknowledgments

Photos

Photo page 101 by author
Photo page 103 by John E. Atkinson

Computer Assistance
John E. Atkinson

Spiritual Teachers

Rev. Edward L. Crump, who started it all.
Dr. Thurman Fleet, Rev's teacher and mine.
Katherine Calhoun who taught with Rev.
V.G. Kulkarni, Hindu Brahmin Priest.
Donald Boyce, Director, Retreat Center.
Tom Powers, Powerful retreat leader.
And many, many others along the way

First Readers

Arline Stephenson
Marsha Jane Hamilton
Donna Liszewski
W. E .Hamilton

32007256R10136

Made in the USA
San Bernardino, CA
25 March 2016